A RAKE AND HIS TIMES

The Effigies of the Most Noble George
Duke, Marquess, & Earle of Buckingham, Earle of
Coventry, Viscount Vil- lers, Baron of Whaddon
& Knight of y^e most No- ble order of the Garter &c

SOLI COGITULA

FIDE COGITULA CRUX

R. White sculp.

George Villiers, 2nd Duke of Buckingham

A RAKE AND HIS TIMES

GEORGE VILLIERS
2ND DUKE OF BUCKINGHAM

JOHN HAROLD WILSON

FARRAR, STRAUS AND YOUNG

NEW YORK

To Brenda and Robin

Acknowledgments

I am indebted to the John Simon Guggenheim Memorial Foundation for the funds which enabled me to do the research for this study in the libraries of England and France. I am indebted also to the Right Honorable the Earl of Jersey for permission to use the materials in Buckingham's Commonplace Book, now in his possession. I am grateful to William Charvat, Richard D. Altick, and Louise Walker Wilson for reading the manuscript with patience and understanding.

CONTENTS

I

THE HERO
1628–1665

To SEE LONDON in the Sixteen-Sixties, take a pair of oars at Wapping Old Stairs below the Tower on a midsummer morning when the tide is making up river. From the Cockney watermen who crowd about you crying, "Hoars, gentlemen, will you have any hoars?" choose a sturdy fellow, bargain with him for a shilling, and embark in his wherry. On the breast of the rising green flood you should make the trip to Westminster in an hour or less.

Below London Bridge the river will be crowded with shipping—seagoing merchantmen with bluff bows, high sterns, and towering white sails swelled by the westering breeze; coasters and hoys beating up with cargoes of hay, greenstuffs, firewood, and Newcastle coals; slow barges, swift scullers, and rowboats of every size and kind; for the Thames is the main highway of London. Don't be surprised if every boatman within earshot salutes you with a volley of coarse chaff. That is the custom of the river, and your own boatman will reply with equal vigor and perhaps superior obscenity.

While "rogue" and "whore" echo thinly in your ears, turn your eyes to the right bank of the river, where the houses of the city begin their march toward the green northern hills. First come the gray walls and turrets of the Tower—fort, arsenal, and prison—with a sloop of war tied up near the Traitor's Gate under the black muzzles of a dozen forty-pounders. The river bank upstream beyond the Tower is lined with pile-mounted wharves and warehouses, close-packed wooden structures, gray and brown under the morning sun. Behind them rises a mass of red-tiled roofs and a forest of church spires under a pall of low-hanging smoke.

Here is London Bridge, a street of houses flung across the wide river on nineteen stone piers, with one small drawbridge to give the coasters access to the upper reaches of the stream. The force of the tide pouring through the arches makes this a perilous passage for a wherry. Unless you are willing to be "soundly washed," disembark below the bridge and rejoin your boat above it, at the Old Swan. The upper river, too, is crowded with shipping, and in the eddies near shore an occasional file of swans bobs along in line-of-battle formation. Now you are opposite the heart of the City—old London, within its walls. The waterfront buildings are higher and more tightly packed together; the church spires bristle in ragged disarray; and the white mass and square tower of old St. Paul's rise up ahead near the western walls.

There is little to attract your eyes to the left bank. Southwark has few houses and fewer churches. The famous old theatres—the Rose, Hope, Swan, and Globe—have long been gone, and only the Bear Garden still stands on the bankside, a place of bloody combats and low resort.

At Puddle Dock the river begins a wide sweeping curve to the left, and the character of the right bank changes. You have come now to the homes of the wealthy, mansions of brick and stone set back from the river toward the Strand, with formal gardens fronting on the waterside. Each house has its river stairs and watergate. After Whitefriars Stairs (with a pretty little garden and park) you come to Essex House, Arundel House, Somerset House (owned by the Queen Mother, Henrietta Maria), Bedford House, Durham House, York House (property of the Duke of Buckingham), Whitehall Palace—a scramble of roofs and walls rising from tide level—Derby House, Manchester House, and at last Westminster Stairs.

Disembark here, fee your weary waterman, and add a penny for beer and his blessing. Now you must climb the stairs and exercise your cramped limbs. Here you are in bustling New Palace Yard. Stop a moment, if you like, to pop your head into Westminster Hall, a vast, vaulted enclosure, where law courts and lawyers compete with the clamor of hucksters, sempstresses, and vendors of books, toys, and gloves. If you value your purse, don't linger; and if you value your stomach, avoid the three adjacent taverns, "Heaven," "Hell," and "Purgatory."

Leaving for another day the tour of Westminster Abbey and rambling old Westminster Palace where Parliament meets, walk on out to King Street and turn to the right, down river, picking your way through the clattering traffic of coaches and drays. A few hundred yards along the narrow, shop-lined street brings you to the King Street Gate, a Gothic tower spanning the roadway. Beyond it, to your right, is the Privy Garden, hidden from view by a high brick wall. Over the wall you can see the gables and chimneys of Whitehall Palace. There lives King Charles II with his queen, Catherine of Braganza, and a host of officials, servants, and pensionaries. The buildings on your left—the Tennis Court and the Cock Pit—are within the purlieus of the palace. Through passageways between them you will get brief glimpses of the trees in St. James's Park.

Another hundred yards brings you to the Holbein Gate, a massive, turreted structure of tessellated brick which joins Whitehall proper with the buildings on the left-hand side of the street. Pass on under the archway into a cobble-paved street so wide that the great ceremonial coaches have room to turn around after discharging passengers at the Court Gate. There on your left is the Guard House, where the Horse Guards are quartered. On your right is the Banqueting Hall, a splendid sample of the art of Inigo Jones. It was from a window in this building that Charles I stepped onto the scaffold where the block and ax awaited him.

Shed a tear for the Royal Martyr and walk on toward Charing Cross, past Scotland Yard on your right, until you come to Wallingford House on your left. Here George Villiers, second Duke of Buckingham, was born on January 30, 1628, and here he lives now with his wife, Mary, and a buzzing swarm of servants.

Stop a bit. All this bustle of footmen and pages at the front door must mean something. There comes a six-horse coach, looking like a giant acorn swung on leather straps

THE HERO

between four great wheels. A very gaudy acorn it is, to be
sure, highly varnished and decorated with gilt lions and
peacocks. The coachman sits on a little seat mounted above
the front axle, and four running footmen trot along behind,
holding to the straps. The coach rattles up before Wallingford House and pulls to a stop; the footmen open the door
and stand at attention.

Here comes the duke down the stairs to the street. He
is a tall, robust, fair-colored gentleman, very fine this
morning in a long cloth-of-silver coat reaching below his
knees. There are cascades of point lace at throat and wrist,
and the diamond star of the Garter blazes on his left breast.
Beneath the coat he wears a dove-colored satin vest, light-
blue silk breeches, white stockings (the left one crossed
by the blue ribbon of the Garter), and diamond-buckled
shoes. His fashionable blond periwig falls in curls to his
shoulders and half conceals his bold, handsome face, with
its dark brows, strong nose, and pencil-thin mustache.
Atop the periwig, perched like a gull on a wave, is a wide-
brimmed, plumed hat. He wears the hat everywhere, in-
doors and out, even at table, and takes it off only in the
presence of the King or when he goes to bed. (At bedtime
he takes off the periwig, too, and wears a round, embroi-
dered night-cap over his shaven poll.)

A murmuring crowd of beggars gathers from nowhere
as the duke stands there a moment putting on his long-
fringed gloves. He gives them a flashing smile and a hearty
"Good day t'ye, friends!" tosses a handful of silver, and
disappears into his coach in the scramble. The coachman
cracks his whip; the coach rumbles off with the footmen

[5]

leaping up behind; and the crowd shouts "A Buckingham!
A Buckingham! God save the Duke of Buckingham!"

Wallingford House, a fine old mansion, reverted to the
duke with all his other confiscated properties at the Restoration. He made it his residence partly for convenience—it
was just a whisper from Whitehall—and partly for econ-
omy. The simple fact is that one of the wealthiest men in
the kingdom could not afford to live in his own palace,
York House. Instead, he rented it to a succession of foreign
ambassadors, who beggared themselves to keep up the
splendor befitting the agents of kings.

During his years of exile, while Cromwell ruled the land,
Bucks lived a hand-to-mouth existence on the proceeds
from the sale of his father's pictures. Although he regained
his estates soon after Charles II landed at Dover on May
25, 1660, it was many months before he began drawing
an income. In the meantime, needing cash, he turned to the
bankers and scriveners, "who brought the gangrene of
usury into the body of his estate." It never recovered.

No matter. At that time Buckingham was the first duke
of England, after the royal family, and he was keenly con-
scious of *noblesse oblige*. In the extravagant round of dinners, balls, and receptions which followed hard upon the
glorious Restoration, he held his own at vast expense. At
the Coronation, where he carried the orb before the King,
"no subject appeared in greater splendor." It was rumored
that he had spent £30,000 on his equipage—a sum likely
enough in a day when men outdid women in jewels, feath-
ers, and finery. When he entertained at dinner, everyone
commented on the prodigality of the dishes—and ate greed-

ily. His generosity was notorious. He helped his friends, pensioned his old retainers, and gave double the sum asked by the beggar at his gates. In the early years of the Restoration he lost great sums at the gaming tables and paid with lordly indifference; then he gave up that expensive sport.

To spend money, even in excess of his income, was right and proper for a great duke; to earn money was beneath his dignity. Yet on occasion, at the insistence of his friends, or hell-bent on some scheme of his own devising, he lowered himself to do so. Usually his ventures failed, but he was interested in too many projects, he lived his life too fully and vigorously to worry about his losses. Rarely, as he hurried through the blare and din of his busy world, pursuing fame, power, or some fantastic idea, he saw the folly of his pursuit. Once he wrote wryly in his Commonplace Book, "For me to seek fame rather than riches is as if a man in hunger should buy fine clothes rather than meat." Then he was off on some new extravagance. It was said of him that "he would rather lose his friend (nay, the King!) than his jest." He would also rather lose his estate.[1]

At the time of the Restoration he was thirty-two years old and equipped with everything his world valued. He had wealth, noble birth, a right royal upbringing, a good education, and a rank so high that—unless he became a king—he could go no higher. Unfortunately, he thought himself the equal of a king. A few months after George Villiers, first Duke of Buckingham, was assassinated, Charles I took his children to rear. Mary, five years old when her father died, George, an infant of seven months, and Francis, posthumously born, were brought up at Court as if they were members of the royal family. When the young Stuarts

came along—Prince Charles in 1630; Mary, the Princess
Royal, in 1631; James, Duke of York, in 1633; Henry,
Duke of Gloucester, in 1640; and Princess Henrietta in
1644—they were already equipped with an older sister and
a pair of older brothers. In effect the Villiers children lost
their mother, too, when she married a second husband, but
the King and Queen nurtured the orphans and gave them
servants and tutors, privilege and wealth. At twelve, Mary
Villiers was espoused to a short-lived husband, Lord Her-
bert. At fourteen, she had a second husband, the Duke of
Lennox and Richmond, the King's nearest kinsman. Splendid marriages and careers were planned for George and
Francis, too, but the Civil War broke out while they were
still at Cambridge. It was hard for Buckingham to remember that he was not truly a prince.

Certainly Parliament treated with him as if he were a
prince during the Civil War. The two boys ran away from
Cambridge to join the King's forces at Oxford. But their
guardians thought them too young for war, and sent them
abroad to wander for six years through France and Italy,
where they lived like scions of royalty and became pro-
ficient in languages, literature, and love. At first Parliament confiscated the Villiers estates; then, eager for the
duke's support, it restored them. In 1648, when the Cavalier cause was already lost, the two young men came back
to England and took part in Lord Holland's abortive rebellion. Lord Francis lost his life in a skirmish near King-
ston. The duke cut his way through his enemies and escaped. Parliament offered him his estates and a pardon if he
surrendered within forty days, but he chose to join Prince
Charles in exile, and lost everything.

For the next few years the young duke followed the
fortunes of the prince who became King Charles II when
his father was beheaded on January 30, 1649. He went to
Scotland with Charles, fought gallantly beside him at the
Battle of Worcester in 1651, and, like his master, made a
romantic escape from that stricken field. Thereafter Buckingham roamed Europe, looking for something to do, now
and then spying out England in disguise or dropping in for
a visit with the exiled King at Paris, Aix, or Cologne. Under the great French general, Turenne, he studied the art
of war at the sieges of Arras and Valenciennes.

In 1657 he returned to England to woo Mary Fairfax.
Mary was no beauty, but she was the sole heiress of
Thomas, Lord Fairfax, the great Parliamentary general
who had been granted a goodly share of the duke's confiscated estate in Yorkshire. Fortune-hunting was quite
respectable in the seventeenth century, and, after all, Bucks
ventured his neck for the fortune. Cromwell, a tyrant in
spite of himself, was a most unpredictable ruler. Buckingham deserted the Court of Exiles, slipped quietly into England, and flitted about London in disguise for five or six
months before he made his proposals to the Fairfax family.
His personal charms plus his title made an irresistible combination. On September 15, 1657, the twenty-nine-year-old
duke and the nineteen-year-old heiress were married at a
church near the Fairfax home, Nun Appleton, in Yorkshire. The officiating clergyman declared that he saw God
in the duke's face, and Abraham Cowley, Buckingham's
friend and fellow collegian, penned a pretty ode for the
occasion.

Only Cromwell was unhappy, and he very soon found

an excuse for sending Bucks to the Tower. In later years the duke loved to tell the story of his days there and his narrow escape from death in September, 1658. "As soon," he said, "as Oliver Cromwell was dead, they proclaimed his son, Richard Cromwell, Protector of England, with the same solemnities that even Kings of England were proclaimed kings. I was then close prisoner in the Tower, with a couple of guards lying always in my chamber, and a sentinel at my door. I confess I was not a little delighted with the noise of the great guns, for I presently knew what it meant, and if Oliver had lived for three days longer, I had certainly been put to death."

Eventually Bucks was freed, and he took a notable part in the events which led to the overthrow of the Rump Parliament and the return of the exiled King. Then came the glorious Restoration. Now Bucks had all his estates again—and an unwanted wife, to boot. He treated her with courtesy and kindness.

"For his person," said his kinsman and agent, Brian Fairfax, in a brief *Life*, "he was the glory of the age and any Court wherever he came. Of a most graceful and charming mien and behavior, a strong, tall, and active body, all which gave a lustre to the ornaments of his mind; of an admirable wit and excellent judgement." Beside him, King Charles, with his lean figure, dark skin, and stern, deeply lined face under a black periwig, was a very ugly fellow indeed. King Louis XIV of France declared that Bucks was "almost the only English gentleman he had seen." Even his enemies admitted that "his qualities and condescensions, the pleasantness of his humor and conversation, the extravagance and sharpness of his wit, unrestrained by any modesty or religion, drew persons of all affections and inclinations to like his company." He was a wit: a man of intellectual ingenuity and sparkling conversation.[2]

A lesser man would have been content to live out a peaceful life, enjoying his possessions; a greater man, concentrating on a career, could have changed the course of history. Buckingham the versatile, "chemist, fiddler, statesman, and buffoon," sought to excel in all things. His world never saw him in the round; it saw only different aspects of his multiple personality.

The Court of Charles II, especially in the years from 1660 to 1665, saw him as a merry fellow, one gifted at mimicry, a mocker and *railleur*, unstable, irreverent, and a wencher. The Court was nearly right. One side of Buckingham's personality fitted smoothly into the artificial world of Whitehall Palace—a world of polished manners, witty speech, ungodly jests, and shocking behavior. Here were elegant courtiers, cultured and honorable gentlemen who fought duels, lied, plotted, cheated, and betrayed their friends, wives, or daughters for their own advantage. They dressed in thousands of pounds worth of silks and satins— and substituted perfumes for baths, spat on the floors, and often used the fireplaces as privies. The French Court had the same pleasant habits. The story is that in King Louis' great palace at Versailles—a thousand rooms without a bath—there was once a sign: "Il est défendu de faire pipi dans la chambre du Roi!"

At Whitehall of an evening a dozen periwigged gentlemen paid their court to the King's reigning mistress, Barbara Palmer, Countess of Castlemaine, a tall, hungry blonde, considered the most beautiful woman in England, and prob-

ably the most vicious. Nearby, the swarthy King fondled
his romping spaniels, listening with half an ear to the scold-
ings of Lord Chancellor Clarendon; a gay group sat at
cards with stacks of gold on the table before them; in one
corner an amorous gentleman made love to an open-
bosomed Maid of Honor; and at another table the great
Duke of Buckingham built card castles for the amusement
of pretty, empty-headed Frances Stuart.

Frances was one of the Queen's Maids of Honor. The
daughter of a threadbare baronet, she had ambition, beauty,
and—to everyone's surprise—virtue. Amorous King Charles
wanted her to sleep with him, but all his gifts, promises,
and caresses failed to move the frivolous beauty. Charles
moped about, grieving and despairing. Now was the time
for all good pimps to come to the aid of the King. Buckingham formed a "committee for the getting Mistress Stuart
for the King." The other members were his own wife,
Sir Henry Bennet, Secretary of State, and Mr. Edward
Montagu.

Buckingham's enemies declared that he pimped for the
King in order to get power for himself. Perhaps they were
merely envious. He may have been motivated, too, by
pique at his cousin, Lady Castlemaine, with whom he was
feuding at the moment. Anyway, pimping was fun, and
not in the least immoral—when done for a king. It was a
splendid outlet for the duke's furious energies and mani-
fold talents. Frances was pleased as a child by the little
songs he wrote and sang to her, by his witty, scandalous
stories, and above all by his droll imitations of well known
courtiers: Sir Henry Bennet, Chancellor Clarendon, and
others. He was getting along famously until he forgot his

rôle, saw Frances as a beautiful, desirable woman, and tried to act as the King's taster. He was rebuffed for the same reason the King was: both men were married, and Frances ("a cunning slut," said Pepys) wanted a wedding ring.

Buckingham gave up, and Bennet tried the serious approach. He was a tall, dignified man with a ceremonious manner, a round, plump face, and a black plaster covering a scar on his nose. He had hardly begun his windy diplomacy when Mistress Stuart remembered Buckingham's caricature and burst into wild laughter. Bennet quit in disgust, and "the whole committee broke." This was in 1663; four years later the still virginal Frances married the Duke of Richmond.[3]

To Buckingham, such grave, dignified men as Bennet were irresistible butts. Of another grandee he wrote, "God has stigmatized his gravity with the despair of a beard," and of still another that he "once in an hour plucks a gray sentence out of his beard." He had no cause to love pompous, gray-bearded Edward Hyde, Earl of Clarendon and Lord Chancellor. The two had been enemies during the years of exile and remained so after the Restoration. To Clarendon, who loved order in everything, Bucks represented all the evils of disorder, levity, and loose living. To Buckingham, Clarendon was an old fuddy-duddy and a stupid reactionary. In one of his little verse satires, Bucks compared Clarendon to a sober owl, who is by day, "God wot! but dim of sight," and so grows fat "by doing mischief in the night." All day (he wrote) the owlish Chancellor lies "in a calm ivy bush . . . on bed of cogitation." When the "ebon night" comes, it "gives the bird a pull,"

Makes him awake from his consultless trance,
And out of bush his broad face to advance.
Then, as the pensive toad (which in cold weather
Had subtly crept away, the Lord knows whither)
Revives with vernal heat, the liquid fowl
Starts up, and stares itself into an owl.

Buckingham was not content to sting his foe with satires. The proud Lord Chancellor went everywhere—even on friendly visits—with two retainers bearing before him the purse and mace which were the tokens of his office. So Bucks "did often act and mimic this great man in presence of the King, walking stately with a pair of bellows before him for the purse, and Colonel Titus carrying a fire shovel on his shoulder for the mace." The King was enraptured.[4]

But even the King was not safe from Buckingham's jibes. Seeking an object for the love that Mistress Stuart disdained, His Majesty laid siege to Winifred Wells, a fresh-colored, shapely Maid of Honor. After a token resistance, Mistress Wells surrendered, and the King took possession. Buckingham could not resist the temptation to pun on the lady's surname. He wrote in French a dainty squib in which he represented the King as appealing at a crucial moment to Progers, his confidential valet. It may be rendered roughly thus:

When the King felt the terrible depths of this well,
"Ah, Progers!" he cried, "what's happened, and how?
I sound, but can't tell;
Were I seeking the center of earth's hollow shell,
I should have been there by now!"

Such trifles were the diversions of Buckingham's idle hours. He found the lunatic fringe of the Court a constant cause of merriment. Since fools were made for the entertainment of the wise, he amused himself at their expense, without malice. Of one fop he wrote kindly, "He's much to be commended, for in this age of wickedness he only plays the fool." Sometimes, of course, his careless buffoonery must have hurt his victims. Once the foolish Lady Muskerry, who dearly loved dancing, insisted on coming to Court for one of the Queen's parties, even though she was "six or seven months advanced in pregnancy; and, to complete her misfortune, the child had fallen all on one side, so that even Euclid would have been puzzled to say what her figure was." Her friends gave her the appearance of symmetry by pinning a small cushion inside her dress so as to balance her wayward burden. While she was happily capering about in the first round of the dance, the cushion came loose from its moorings and fell to the floor. "The Duke of Buckingham, who watched her, took it up instantly, wrapped it up in his coat, and, mimicking the cries of a new-born infant, he went about inquiring for a nurse for the young Muskerry among the Maids of Honor." [5]

Buckingham's reputation as a wencher rests on rather dubious evidence. Yet, said Fairfax, "he was the only person in a vicious age and Court that was publicly censured for women; not so much out of hatred to the crime as the person. He lay under so ill a name for it that if he was shut up with a fox-hunter, a chemist, a politician, or a poet, it was said to be with a woman." Of course, in the priapic Court of Charles II he would have been looked upon as a freak if he had not kept a mistress or occasionally visited the brothels in Moorfields, Lewkenor's Lane, or Dog and

Bitch Yard. Courtiers with handsome wives usually kept them in the country—no pretty woman was safe from the predatory King—and kept their mistresses in town. Some courtiers loved their wives and lived chastely, but they were in the minority.

Mary, Duchess of Buckingham, loved her handsome husband and patiently bore with "those faults in him which she could not remedy." He was fond of her, but no more than that. Mary was virtuous and pious, plump, dark, and homely, rather vain, and fond of trifling amusements. She was hardly a woman to inspire passion. The dashing Duke of Buckingham was full-blooded, ardent, and by turns romantic and cynical. He needed a woman to worship and admire, one who could meet his ardor with equal passion.

When Princess Henrietta, the King's younger sister, came to England for a visit early in the Restoration, Buckingham promptly fell in love with her. It was a chivalric rather than a sensual love. Pretty Henrietta was no languorous, seductive beauty, but she was a princess, and in Buckingham's bewildering personality there was something left of the old courtly love tradition. He became her *preux chevalier*, adoring her to the point of idolatry. When she returned to France early in 1661, the duke accompanied her and aroused so much jealousy in the Duke of Orleans, her husband-to-be, that finally King Charles had to order him home.[6]

Buckingham confided to his Commonplace Book his views on the mercenary women who satisfied his lust. "A wench," he wrote, "is good flesh when she is fresh, but she's fish when she's stale." "Wenches are like fruits, only dear at their first coming in; their price falls a-pace after."

And again, "Her chamber is the center of all my goods;
they'll never rest till they are there." "Neither her purse
nor her — could ever be filled by anybody." Of a lustful
woman he wrote ungratefully, "Such a woman was made
to punish man, and the Devil to punish such a woman."
"Her whole morning is nothing but the preparation of herself, and her afternoon the preparation of others, for her
sins at night." "Her impudence spoiled the relish of it: it
tasted too much of the brass." [7]

These were occasional bedfellows, *pis-allers*, so to speak.
If Bucks had a semipermanent mistress during these early
years, the liaison escaped the eyes of most of the gossips.
Philiberte, Comte de Grammont, a picturesque exile from
France who lived in England for a couple of years and
returned later for several visits, remembered in his old age
some curious stories about Buckingham. As he tells it, in
Queen Catherine's train of Portuguese there was a handsome idiot who called himself Don Pedro Francisco Correo
de Silva. Flippant Buckingham translated his name as Peter
of the Wood. "He was so enraged at this that, after many
fruitless complaints and ineffectual menaces, poor Pedro
de Silva was obliged to leave England, while the happy
duke kept possession of a Portuguese nymph more hideous
than the Queen's [Portuguese] Maids of Honor, whom he
had taken from him." To Grammont all Portuguese were
hideous.

This was in the autumn of 1662. The affair—if Grammont can be believed—may have lasted about a year. At
least, we are told that at some time in the next few months
another exile, the philosopher St. Evremonde, scolded
Grammont for placing himself in ambush on the stairs and

pulling Buckingham "back by the leg when he was half-way to his mistress's chamber," and that in the autumn of 1663, when the duke made love to Mistress Stuart, "he forgot his Portuguese mistress." So says Grammont, drawing from the depths of his marvellous memory. The Portuguese nymph appears nowhere in history.[8]

Like all positive people, Buckingham had many enemies, chiefly politicians. He had also strong friends, who saw sides of his character rarely disclosed to the Court. They were a widely diversified group, each member chosen because of some special appeal to the versatile duke. Such men as George Porter, Henry Killigrew, and Sir Ellis Leighton were valued for their wit and whimsy. Porter, a quarrelsome, talkative fellow, was a Gentleman of the Bedchamber to the Queen Mother; Killigrew, a magnificent liar, was a Groom of the Bedchamber to the Duke of York; and Leighton, something of a subtle knave but "one of the best companions at a meal in the world," was Secretary of the Prize Office. The presence of Buckingham or any one of these was enough to enliven a party, and two could make it very gay. Once Lord Arlington wrote to the Duke of Ormonde, "My last told your grace I was going into the country to pass my Christmas at my Lord Crofts', and when I tell you that the Duke of Bucks and George Porter were there you will not doubt but we passed it merrily." Evenings at Wallingford House when all the jesters were together and the wine flowed freely must have been hilarious.[9]

But these men were lightweights who ate the duke's food, drank his wine, and occasionally ran his errands. His real friends were poets, philosophers, and virtuosi—men of letters and learning. Chief among them was Abraham Cowley, his old schoolmate—the most learned poet of the age, and, in the eyes of many, the greatest of all English poets. Although he was retiring by disposition, preferring rural peace to urban turmoil, Cowley was much at Wallingford House. Some time in 1663 Buckingham went to the Queen Mother's agents to buy the lease of a farm at Chertsey, up the Thames from London. The agents protested, "That is beneath your grace, to take a lease"—implying that so great a man had only to ask the King and the property would be given to him. "That is all one," said Bucks, "I desire to have the favor to buy it for my money." The "favor" was granted. When the deal was concluded, the duke gave the lease "to his dear and ingenious friend, Mr. Abraham Cowley, for whom purposely he bought it." Cowley spent his placid last years at Chertsey.[10]

Close to the poet in Buckingham's regard were Martin Clifford, his secretary (another fellow student), and Thomas Sprat, his chaplain, a young man recommended to the duke by Cowley and Clifford. Known generally as "Malicious Matt," Clifford was a little, flat-faced man "of a facetious conversation . . . learned, very critical, positive, and proud." Sprat, a clergyman of liberal leanings, was "a man of learning, wit, good nature, good manners, a graceful person, and decent behavior." The poet, the secretary, and the chaplain formed a close bond of friendship with each other as well as with Buckingham.

Revolving around this family group were the philosopher-in-exile, Charles de St. Evremonde; the old Cavalier poet, Edmund Waller; the surveyor general (and poet) Sir John Denham; the astronomer-architect, Christopher

Wren; two of the young Court wits, Sir Charles Sedley and Charles Sackville, Lord Buckhurst; and an ever widening circle of wits, scientists, bishops, politicians, and men of affairs. With such friends the duke could discuss everything under the sun from the latest Court scandal to the best method of breeding carp or improving the English language. A few years after the Restoration he joined with some choice spirits in founding a Society for the Improvement of Natural Knowledge, aimed primarily at "the polishing of the English tongue." The gloss was to be achieved by the members reciting or reading aloud their own works. Other founders were the poet John Dryden, John Evelyn (an expert on smoke and gardens), Cowley, Sprat, Clifford, and Waller. There were three or four meetings at Gray's Inn; then, because of the Dutch War of 1665, the Plague, and the Great Fire of London, "it crumbled away and came to nothing." Rather a pity.[11]

Brian Fairfax could never decide which of the duke's amusements cost him more, "his field pleasures of horses and hounds, or his domestic, his chemistry." He kept his stables well supplied with racers and hunters, and, particularly at Newmarket where the Court went every autumn for field sports, his racers were usually well up in the running. In Yorkshire, where most of his estates lay, his fox-hunting became legendary. But his great passion was chemistry.

His enemies charged that he spent a fortune seeking the Philosopher's Stone, that mythical mineral which could change base metals into silver or gold, heal wounds, cure diseases, and perfect all things in their kind. This was nonsense. Buckingham's chaplain, Sprat, writing in 1666 about the folly of alchemists who sought the Philosopher's Stone, said, "The truth is, they are downright Enthusiasts [fanatics] about it. And seeing we cast Enthusiasm out of divinity itself, we shall hardly sure be persuaded to admit it into philosophy." Bucks was no "Enthusiast"; he was far too practical-minded to believe in the chimeras of alchemists.

As the duke said himself, he "delighted and exercised himself" in distillations. At Wallingford House he had a laboratory, complete with forges, furnaces, balances, and stills; he kept always a tame chemist in pay and amused himself by distilling all kinds of volatile substances, from eggs to mercury. He was a dilettante, no doubt, but he had the true spirit of scientific curiosity.[12]

One of his chemists, Monsieur Le Cann, cost him, says Fairfax, "above £20,000." However, the money was not entirely wasted. The Republic of Venice had long maintained a monopoly of the making of fine glass simply by keeping the process a secret. Some time in 1662 Le Cann came up with a process for making flint glass equal to the best Venetian. Using Martin Clifford as his agent, Buckingham took out a patent for making mirrors, drinking glasses, coach glasses, and the like, imported Venetian workmen, and set up a factory at Lambeth, "where they made huge vases of metal as clear, ponderous, and thick as crystal; also looking-glasses far larger and better than any that came from Venice." The Venetian Ambassador was not at all pleased.[13]

It was inevitable that Buckingham, the chemist, should have been one of the earliest members of the Royal Society, that amazing collection of half-credulous, half-skeptical virtuosi that was formally organized and chartered soon after the Restoration. When he was admitted on June 5, 1661, the society requested that he "order charcoal to be distilled by his chemist." He agreed, and as a further proof of his devotion to science, "promised to bring to the society a piece of an unicorn's horn." That commodity was so rare and expensive—perhaps because a unicorn could only be captured by a pure virgin—that it was often counterfeited.

Six weeks went by. The piece of horn was solemnly presented by the duke (Heaven knows where he got it!), and just as solemnly tested. A spider, said all the old authorities, could not get out of a circle made of true powdered unicorn's horn. The savants powdered some of the horn, made a circle with it on the floor, placed a spider in the center, and watched it blithely scurry out. The trial was repeated several times with the same result. Once the weary spider even "made some stay on the powder"—panting for breath. Had the duke been cheated? Was the powder a base imitation? Was the test valid? No one could say.[14]

Buckingham's interest in natural philosophy brought him into some very queer circles. Once he went with a young Yorkshire neighbor, Sir George Savile (the future Marquis of Halifax), to the house of Mr. John Digby, whose father, Sir Kenelm, was the most famous crackpot of the century. Young Digby, as eccentric as his father, surrounded himself with astrologers, alchemists, soothsayers, and oddities of every description. At his house Bucks met "Doctor" John Heydon, a Rosicrucian who styled himself "A Servant of God and Secretary of Nature." In addition to describing his visions in feverish prose, Heydon cast horoscopes, told fortunes, prescribed medicines, and pretended skill in distillations. Buckingham made sport of the queer, intent philosopher. Like everybody in his generation, he had a lingering faith in astrology and once had his own horoscope cast, yet he could write with ironic intention, "I can't imagine how astrologers should be miserable unless the stars are angry with them for revealing their secrets." However, an episode in 1663 shook his skepticism.

In the early spring of that year, Bucks came back from Newmarket to London. While he was waiting at the Sun Tavern in Aldgate for his coach to arrive, Heydon accosted him and "told him his fortune was to die as unfortunately as his father, or at least [assassination] would be attempted." At the moment Bucks paid no attention. Something over a month afterward, the duke and his wife were having a very late supper—Bucks was a lively night owl—with only a maid attending them. About one o'clock in the morning, a servant, Abraham Goodman, obviously mad as a hatter, got out of bed and stole to the duke's chamber, sword in hand. He knocked, the maid opened the door, and Goodman rushed in, crying, "It is thou that I seek! It is thou I will have!"

The maid screamed and ran. Buckingham, who had been sitting by the fire talking to his wife, leaped up and seized a knife and napkin from the table. With these poor weapons he met the maniac's charge, fenced with him a moment, then got within his guard and took his sword. Other servants came running, secured Goodman, and carried him off to prison.

Was Heydon truly a prophet, or was he a conspirator, privy to a plot against Buckingham's life? The duke sent for Heydon, questioned him, and decided that he was too silly a fellow to be a plotter. Heydon himself claimed to be a prophet; later he bragged of eighty-one successful predictions, among them "the first precaution or prediction he gave to His Highness the Duke of Buckingham two months before the evil was practised, and his enemy Abraham Goodman lies now in the Tower for attempting the death of that noble prince." Of course, it was the duke's quick wit and courage that saved him, not Heydon's prophecy.[15]

After the Goodman episode, Heydon attached himself to the duke and clung like a cocklebur, often visited him, wrote him letters begging for money and for "receipts" for distillations, and boasted widely of his friendship with the great man. Good-natured Buckingham, who seems to have felt himself under an obligation, helped him out of trouble a couple of times: once in August, 1663, when "the Secretary of Nature" was imprisoned for writing a supposedly seditious book, and again a year later when Heydon was in prison for debt. The time was to come when Heydon would repay his patron in full measure.

From science to music was no great step, and Buckingham took it in stride. He kept in pay a quartet of musicians, "two violins, and a bass violin, and theorbo . . . the best in town," and sometimes pricked out tunes for them to play. His own skill with the violin was enough to draw from St. Evremonde (in Holland in 1669) the comment, "Should I visit England [again] it would rather be for the pleasure of conversing with my friends than of seeing the Fellows of the Royal Society, and I should prefer the Duke of Buckingham's violin to his laboratory, however curious it might be." [16]

Occasionally the talented duke turned his hand to literature, amusing himself and his friends with satires, lampoons, and erotic little songs, most of which have perished. However, one of his earliest attempts at drama survives in its original French. *Sir Politick Would-Be* (1662) is a mildly amusing comedy, markedly indebted to Jonson's *Volpone*. Bucks wrote it in collaboration with St. Evremonde and Louis Stuart, Sieur d'Aubigny, Grand Almoner to the Queen. Since St. Evremonde knew very little about the stage, and d'Aubigny was "a person of good sense, but wholly abandoned to ease and effeminacy," the chances are that Bucks did most of the work. He drew his own character in the hero of the play, *Mylord Tancred, homme d'esprit*, an English traveller who amuses himself at Venice with a parcel of English, French, and German tourists. They are just such people as Bucks might well have met during his sojourn in Italy in his youth. At the end of the play, with the fools all properly punished for their folly, Tancred remarks (as Bucks himself might have said), "It must be admitted that I have a pleasant star, to make me fall into the hands of fools and fantastics of all nations. They help pass away the time, but at the last they bore me, and, thank God, here I am rid of them." If the comedy was ever produced, the fact went unrecorded.[17]

Somewhere in the intervals between wine, women, buffoonery, hunting, horse racing, chemistry, glass-making, music, and literature, Buckingham acted as Lord Lieutenant of the West Riding of his home county, Yorkshire. This was a post of great responsibility; in effect he was the military governor of a province. In any emergency, he was expected to leap on his horse, gallop to Yorkshire (two or three days of hard riding), call out the militia if necessary, and settle the situation. Since the county was full of "fanatics,"—an impolite name for those Protestants who refused to conform to the Church of England—he was in the saddle rather often.

Because of his engaging manners and his open hospitality, Bucks was very popular with the gentry of Yorkshire. "His Lord Lieutenancy," said Brian Fairfax, "cost him more than anything could have recompensed but the universal love and esteem of the county, which he got by his courtesy and generous behavior among them." He was popular with the common folk, too, not only because of his liberality but because he held the odd notion that justice should be denied no man, rich or poor, Anglican or Quaker. As far as he dared, he defended the Nonconformists, the underdogs of that intolerant age. On a visit to York in 1661 he found a number of poor wretches imprisoned in York Castle, "confined there out of spite," and promptly set them free. In 1663 he did his best to save some misguided "fanatics" who were caught red-handed in a trivial conspiracy, and it was largely because of his efforts that only seventeen or so were hanged.[18]

It was not that Buckingham was more humane than his fellow magistrates. It was rather that, as Bishop Kennet wrote disapprovingly, he favored Nonconformists "upon no better account than a strong affection to the universal liberties of opinion and practise." One might well ask what better reason he could have.

But to the Cavalier government of Restoration England, which forbade all forms of worship other than Anglican, drove Puritan clergymen from their pulpits, and persecuted

Catholics and Nonconformists alike, a man who believed in liberty "of opinion and practise" was capable of anything, even treason. The Cavaliers' fears of Catholicism dated back to the time of Bloody Mary and the fires of Smithfield. The fears of Nonconformism resulted from the Civil War. The Nonconformists were all tainted to some degree with the evil of republicanism, and no one could forget that Cromwell's famous regiment of Ironsides had been made up chiefly of Independents. The government merely suppressed and outlawed the moderate Presbyterians, but it feared and persecuted the numerous splinter sects of Protestantism—the Baptists, Brownists, Come-Outers, Family of Love, Fifth Monarchists, Independents, Levelers, Quakers, Ranters, and their ilk. These were "enthusiasts," or "fanatics"; they insisted upon interpreting the Bible in the light of their own reason or inspiration and set their duty to God above their loyalty to the King. Buckingham, a liberal in an age of reaction, championed the Nonconformists chiefly because he believed that it was "unchristian and inhumane, and contrary to the natural right of free-born man" to persecute them. It must be admitted, however, that he had another reason which did him less credit: he needed a party to head. He was politically ambitious, eager to follow in the footsteps of his famous father and become chief minister of state.

The crusty old Cavaliers who held the chief offices of state—Clarendon, Lord Chancellor; Southampton, Lord Treasurer; and Ormonde, Lord Lieutenant of Ireland—watched Buckingham fearfully and set themselves to frustrate his ambitions. They thought him insincere and a kind of Cromwell-in-embryo. "He pretended," said Clarendon, "to have a wonderful affection and reverence for his country. He had always held intelligence with the principal persons of the leveling party, and professed to desire that liberty of conscience might be granted to all, and exercised his wit with most license against the church, the law, and the Court." [19]

The King's chief minister was quite right to be fearful; Buckingham was dangerous to the established order. He would have been even more dangerous if he had not fallen in love.

II

ENTER ANNA-MARIA
1658–1666

IN THE SUMMER OF 1658, while the blight of Puritanism still lay heavily on England, a Roman Catholic peer, Francis Talbot, eleventh Earl of Shrewsbury, went a-courting. Shrewsbury was not a particularly important person. He was a peaceable, easy-going gentleman with large estates in Worcestershire; he bore an honored name, and he had served King Charles I as captain of a troop of horse. At the end of the Civil War he had "compounded" with Cromwell's government (i.e., paid a heavy fine for the privilege of keeping his estates) and retired to the hereditary seat of the Talbots, Grafton Manor, near Bromgrove, to raise his family. He was a man of few ambitions, and had the Fates been kind, history might never have heard of him.

Shrewsbury was a widower. Although he had fathered three children upon his first wife, Anne Conyers, only one, a daughter, had survived the perils of infancy. Obviously he must marry again to get an heir to his title and estates. In 1658, Lord Shrewsbury was only thirty-five years old (five years older than the Duke of Buckingham).

His second wife must be young, of course—everyone knew that young mothers produced the healthiest babies. She must be handsome, if possible; a Catholic, to be sure, and well equipped with family, rank, and dowry. Earls did not merely marry; they contracted matrimonial alliances in the most literal sense.

At Deene, near Stamford in Northamptonshire, Shrewsbury found two likely prospects. The older of the two, Mary—daughter of Robert Brudenell by his first wife, Mary Constable—was "unhandsome and crooked," and interested him only briefly. The younger, Anna-Maria—the first of Brudenell's three children by his second wife, Anne Savage—was really beautiful: a tall, deep-bosomed wench, with light-brown hair, lush lips, and promising dark eyes. She was sixteen years old and a Catholic bred, even if her family was somewhat "liberal." Her father was heir to Thomas, Baron Brudenell of Stanton, a tough old royalist whose fidelity (plus a thousand pounds given to Charles I in a time of dire need) had earned him a still unconfirmed patent as Earl of Cardigan. The Brudenells were wealthy and well connected; for example, Anna-Maria's maternal uncle was John, Earl Rivers, chief of a powerful clan.[1]

Certainly Anna-Maria was tempting, but Shrewsbury was a cautious man. (He would have been even more cautious if he had seen the horoscope erected for her by Bernard: she was a child of Aries—"dry, hot, choleric, violent.") He hardly knew the girl, and she was really more French than English—in fact she was not legally an

English subject. Old Lord Brudenell had sent his son abroad at the outbreak of the Civil War, and Anna-Maria and her brother Francis had been born in Paris, where, except for occasional trips home, they had spent their short lives. The girl was convent-bred and well educated (her spelling was much better than that of most English ladies), and she was undeniably well mannered. Her ripe young body and dancing eyes made her immensely attractive, but her ways were, well—different. Moreover, although the Brudenells had owned large estates, much of their property had been confiscated, and more might be. Of course, if the King came back! But in the summer of 1658, hopes of a restoration were at their lowest ebb.

While Shrewsbury temporized, Anna-Maria and her mother went back to France. The hungry earl turned his attention to another prospect. Then in September came the death of Cromwell. The tenor of the times changed; there was bold talk of the King coming into his own again, and the fortunes of the Brudenells improved. Anna-Maria and her mother came back to Deene, and Shrewsbury came back to Anna-Maria.[2]

The negotiations—Anna-Maria's dowry, the amount of her jointure in case of Shrewsbury's death, and all such financial details—were handled by lawyers, of course. Probably the actual courtship, as usual in such affairs, was a mere formality: the two met in the presence of others, exchanged compliments, and gradually got acquainted. Everything in Anna-Maria's background had prepared her for just such a marriage, and in the eyes of society she was a very lucky girl. The chances are that her likes and dislikes were not even consulted. Certainly love had no place in the picture.

The two were married on January 10, 1659, at the parish Church of St. Giles in the Fields, London. No priest presided, but a justice of the peace, one Peter Bradshaw, was there to see that everything was done according to the formula for marriages prescribed by the Rump Parliament. Thus, after a few preliminaries, the earl took his bride by the hand and said, "I, Francis Talbot, do here in the presence of God the searcher of all hearts, take thee, Anna-Maria, for my wedded wife, and do also in the presence of God, and before these witnesses, promise to be unto thee a loving and faithful husband." Anna-Maria in turn repeated the formula, vowing that she would be a "loving, faithful, and obedient wife." Then Mr. Bradshaw declared the couple "to be from thenceforth man and wife," and the business was done.[3]

In the eyes of an orthodox Catholic this was hardly a marriage, but it was all that the times permitted in public. Priests were proscribed, Catholic worship was banned, and Catholics were forced to attend Protestant churches or suffer penalties as recusants. But religions have a way of thriving on persecution. Various members of certain holy orders dodged about England dressed as jingling cavaliers, riding from the country house of one Catholic lord to that of another, hiding in "priests' holes" when the sheriff's men came armed with warrants, conducting masses in secrecy, and marrying, christening, and shriving. In 1658 one William Johnson, O.S.B., was living happily "with the noble family of Talbot at Grafton, in Worcestershire." We may be sure that Francis and Anna-Maria were not long without the nuptial benediction.

While wedded bliss ran its usual course, the affairs of the nation turned upside down; republics went out of fashion like the farthingales of an earlier age, and Charles II was invited to come home and rule his turbulent people. If Anna-Maria made one in the glittering show that crowded the windows along the Strand to watch the royal entry on May 29, 1660, she stood with some difficulty. Four weeks later she gave her husband an heir and the King his first godson, a darkly handsome child, named, of course, Charles, after His Majesty.

In the following year the Talbot and Brudenell families prospered. Just before the Coronation (April 23, 1661) old Lord Brudenell was created Earl of Cardigan, and by the combined interest of the two families, the Earl of Shrewsbury became also Earl of Waterford in Ireland and was appointed to a minor post as Housekeeper of Hampton Court Palace. By ancestral right, Shrewsbury bore the second sword at the Coronation, and his nineteen-year-old countess sparkled in his glory. That summer Anna-Maria and her brother Francis were naturalized by Act of Parliament, with the King signifying his assent in the usual manner: *Soit comme il est désiré.* In those rich months the prestige of the two families rose steadily. The King had reason to value his Catholic lords; few had been more stubbornly loyal than they.[4]

Since Shrewsbury's duties brought him often to Whitehall, he and his young wife became—perforce on his part—courtiers. He was a staid man who found little pleasure in the constant round of balls, picnics, entertainments, and plays that delighted the King and his Court. In the seventeenth century many men of forty were ready for the fireside and the slippered pantaloon. But in the summer of 1662, Anna-Maria was barely twenty, in the full bloom of her beauty, eager for the joys of London, and ripe for intrigue. She became one of the most admired beauties of the Court, pursued by a pack of gay dogs who ran panting at her heels.

Although, like other beauties, she enjoyed such liberties as kisses and certain intimate caresses, she seems to have kept her chastity, acquiring, however, a mighty reputation as a flirt. Grammont, the cynical chronicler of the Cytherean Court, declared that "as no person could boast of being the only one in her favor, so no person could complain of being ill received." There were several gentlemen, he said, who wore locks of her hair made into bracelets as trophies of the hunt, and one frustrated fellow, turning to a more hopeful mistress, offered to sacrifice to her "Lady Shrewsbury's letters, pictures, and hair." Innocent offerings, truly, but in the hot-blooded world of Whitehall small favors could be fatal.[5]

As the summer wore on, Henry Jermyn, twenty-six, Master of the Horse to the Duke of York—a handsome little rogue with a large head, black brows, bold dark eyes, and a sensual mouth—became a suitor to the countess. For a time it seemed that his wealth and reputation might bring him success. His most formidable rival was an older man, Captain Thomas ("Northern Tom") Howard, a notorious duelist with a hot temper and a taste for murder. But Lady Shrewsbury kept the two nicely balanced, distributing her smiles and favors equally.

One night Howard invited her to an "entertainment"—music, wine, sweetmeats, and his own gallant attentions—at the Spring Garden, a popular resort in the east end of St. James's Park. Jermyn heard of the appointment, boldly crashed the tête-à-tête, and made himself thoroughly obnoxious by courting the countess, "railing at the entertainment, and ridiculing the music." Howard, no hand at small talk, sat silently fiddling with his sword and controlling his temper while planning revenge. When the evening was over he followed the custom of the country (and, of course, broke the law) by sending Jermyn a challenge.[6]

The challenge was accepted, seconds were appointed, but nothing happened. A few days later (August 18), Howard's temper hit its boiling-point. He donned a sword-proof leather jerkin, cut the heels off his riding boots, and strapped a heavy dueling sword to his side. With his second, Colonel Cary Dillon, similarly armed and armored, he rode to St. James's Park, dismounted, and waited outside the Tennis Court. When Jermyn and his friend Giles Rawlins (his second) came out of the court, Howard barred their way. He would fight here and now, he declared. The others protested that they had only light dress swords; they asked at least that they might exchange swords with their footmen. Howard refused and charged upon them so fiercely that neither had a chance. At the first exchange he killed Rawlins, whose bodkin bent almost double against Howard's buff. Then he engaged Jermyn (with whom Dillon had been fencing "carelessly, as if willing neither to hurt nor be hurt") and quickly skewered him thrice. "Now," said Howard, wiping his sword, "we have done justice. Let's begone." With that the two fine gentlemen mounted their horses and rode off to the nearest seaport, where they took ship for France.

The affair made a bit of a stir at Court. Since both Jermyn and Rawlins were his servants, the Duke of York was particularly annoyed. In a short time everybody knew that "the Countess of Shrewsbury was the cause, a very beautiful lady, Howard being jealous of the better fortune and purse of his rival." The gossips and scandalmongers set to work at once, and they were even more enraged when Anna-Maria went on quietly about her affairs, proudly saying nothing. Grammont commented viciously, "As for Lady Shrewsbury . . . I would take a wager she might have a man killed for her every day, and she would only hold her head the higher for it; one would suppose she imported from Rome plenary indulgences for her conduct." Although she had certainly been indiscreet, it is not easy to see how she could be blamed for Tom Howard's criminal behavior. Nevertheless, the gossips succeeded in so thoroughly blackening Lady Shrewsbury's reputation that, although she had been slated for appointment as a Lady of the Bedchamber to the new Queen, Catherine of Braganza, when the list finally appeared her name was missing.[7]

In spite of his three wounds, Jermyn recovered within a few months and returned to his philandering. In December, flown with insolence and wine, he made love to the King's mistress, Lady Castlemaine, and was promptly banished from Court by the irritated monarch. After a three months' absence, Tom Howard and his second came back to England, submitted to the law, and were formally acquitted of the charge of manslaughter. In the autumn of 1664, Howard became the third husband of Buckingham's still beautiful older sister, Mary, Dowager Duchess of Richmond. It was reported that they were "the fondest couple that can be," although the duke was "mightily troubled at the match." [8]

For the next two years or so, Anna-Maria went unmentioned in news letters, a proof of discretion if not of chastity. Part of her obscurity was accounted for by certain natural events, among them the death of her grandfather in September, 1663, the accession of her father as second Earl of Cardigan, and the birth of her second son, John, in February, 1665.

Some time during those two years, Buckingham's friend, Henry Killigrew, "having nothing better to do," said Grammont, "fell in love with Lady Shrewsbury; and as Lady Shrewsbury, by a very extraordinary chance, had no engagement at that time, their amour was soon established." Grammont was usually well informed on the mating habits of courtiers, but in this case he seems to have been deceived. His informant was Killigrew himself, a gentleman notorious at Whitehall as "Lying Killigrew." Twenty-eight years old, he had spent his life in a succession of brawls, duels, and intrigues. His wild tongue and wilder fancy made him an excellent drinking companion, but his friends always discounted his stories. As Charles, Prince Palatine, once wrote of him, "He will never leave his lying as long as his tongue can wag." Once an ignorant stranger asked Harry what relation he was to "Lying Killigrew." He replied, "Sir, that is no distinction in my family. We are all liars; my father was a liar, my uncles were liars, my brothers were liars, but I suppose you mean my cousin Will, who never spoke one word of truth."

According to Grammont, Killigrew was "amazed that he was not envied, and offended that his good fortune raised him no rivals" in Lady Shrewsbury's affections. Therefore he proceeded to brag of his supposed conquest and, especially "when he was a little elevated with the juice of the grape," to give "luxurious descriptions of Lady Shrewsbury's most secret charms and beauties, which above half the Court were as well acquainted with as himself." [9]

Deducting Grammont's obvious bias against Anna-Maria (had he been an unsuccessful wooer?), we are left with a very dubious claim. If, as seems likely, Anna-Maria had remained chaste in spite of numerous would-be seducers, Killigrew, by claiming success, would be able to crow over his fellow cockerels in the Court barnyard. One would give heavy odds that his brag was a lie. He was certainly a pathological liar (and a cad, to boot). He lied to inflate his own ego, to entertain his friends, or out of sheer malice, and by repeating his lies he came in time to believe them himself. Very likely Buckingham had him in mind when he wrote in his Commonplace Book, "He has lied so long that now it is no sin in him, for he can deceive nobody." Evidently Killigrew deceived Grammont.

Moreover, one fact which the feline Grammont fails to mention is that in 1662, by his marriage to Anne Savage, a daughter of John, Earl Rivers, Killigrew had become Anna-Maria's cousin. Such a relationship was no bar to adultery; in fact it would tend to help rather than hinder that sport. A cousin—even by marriage—had much better opportunities for intimacy than a mere friend, whose pres-

ence in a lady's bedchamber might give rise to some suspicion. On the other hand, however, a cousin, who could
come and go as one of the family, was often admitted to
bedchambers while the ladies were dressing, and had a
brotherly license to make free with them ("touzle and
tumble them," as Pepys put it) while they were still in
their smocks, half naked. There was no need for Killigrew
to lie with Anna-Maria in order to discover quite a few
of her "most secret charms."

No matter how he acquired his information, Killigrew
was free enough at dispensing it. At the Duke of Buckingham's table he described again and again the beauties of
his luscious cousin. Grammont argued that Bucks was "one
of those who could only judge from outward appearance;
and appearances, in his opinion, did not seem to promise
anything so exquisite as the extravagant praises of Killigrew
would infer." (A likely story. The chances are that he
simply refused to believe Killigrew's tale of conquest.)
However, said Grammont, since the duke's ears were continually "deafened with descriptions of Lady Shrewsbury's
merits," he decided—some time in the winter of 1665-66—
"to examine into the truth of the matter himself."

According to Grammont, then, Bucks' chief motive for
seeking Anna-Maria's better acquaintance was curiosity.
Curiosity, indeed! Bucks knew the lady, of course. He had
seen her often enough at Court, and his manor of Worthrop
in Northamptonshire was only six miles from the Cardigan
estates at Deene. In the loose décolletage fashionable at the
moment, Anna-Maria ordinarily displayed enough charms
to tempt an anchorite. Killigrew had argued, with all kinds
of circumstantial details, that the lady was a wanton. If so,

she was meat for any man, and Bucks never underestimated his own powers. His motive was lechery, of course.

Buckingham had no scruples against betraying his own wife; he had done that often enough already. "Marriage," he confided to his Commonplace Book, "is the greatest solitude, for it makes two but one and prohibits us from all others"—a prohibition obviously to be ignored. Again, "Wives we choose for our posterity"—and Her Grace of Buckingham was childless—"mistresses for ourselves." "To love but one is the monastic life of love, and may justly be suspected of sloth." "One mistress is too much, and yet twenty not enough." He might have felt some qualms at displacing his friend (if Killigrew's story turned out to be the truth), but "He that mocks a cuckold, it's a thousand to one but either he mocks himself or some of his best friends." True, Killigrew was not Anna-Maria's husband, but the principle was the same with lovers. Betrayal was the way of the world.[10]

At first, Buckingham's intrigue was no more than a flirtation. He was an experienced hunter, careful not to frighten the game. He could meet Anna-Maria in many public places: at the Banqueting Hall, where the King dined in state; in the Stone Gallery at Whitehall, where the Court gathered to gossip of an evening; at the Groom Porter's, where they all gambled; at either of the two theatres or in the Ring at Hyde Park of an afternoon; or at a ball or masquerade, where he could dance with her, hold her with lingering fingers, or whisper wickedly in her ear as she swung past in the steps of a coranto. It was not long before Killigrew learned that he had the rival he had wished for, and, inconsistently, he was furious. From that moment his friendship for Buckingham turned to bitter enmity.

Much to Buckingham's surprise, Anna-Maria did not immediately fall into his arms; in fact, she turned out to be quite difficult. Perhaps she was really as chaste as she pretended. On the other hand, it must be admitted that the duke had very few opportunities with her. War with Holland had been declared on February 22, 1665—the logical result of commercial rivalry between the two nations. All spring the Fleet was being prepared for battle, and when the Duke of York took command as Lord High Admiral late in March, every gentleman of spirit prepared to go with him as a volunteer. Buckingham, too, was infected by the martial virus, although as a Privy Councilor and a Lord Lieutenant he had no business going to sea.

He suggested first that he attend the Duke of York in his flagship. When that offer was refused, he asked the King for a ship, and was assigned to a small vessel, the *George*. Joining his ship early in April, he was full of enthusiasm, and "very noble to the seamen." But trouble developed while the Fleet still lay at anchor; York held a council of war and neglected to invite Buckingham. Angrily the duke protested that he should have been present not only because he was a Privy Councilor but also "for his quality's sake." York replied that he could do nothing without the King's orders, and Bucks promptly took horse for London. But York sent his groom, Harry Killigrew, with his version of the situation. Killigrew, seeing a chance to hurt his rival, rode posthaste and got to London six hours ahead of Buckingham. Forewarned, the King refused to get involved in the argument, and the disgruntled duke returned moodily to his ship. There had long been concealed enmity between York and Buckingham; this was another black mark on the score which some day Bucks would try to even up.

On April 21 the Fleet sailed for the coast of Holland, with all the gentleman-volunteers spoiling for a fight. Wisely the Dutch admiral kept out of the way. For nearly a month the English ships wallowed off the Dutch shoals, daring the hated "butter-boxes" to come out and fight. Then, with provisions low and beer kegs running dry, York gave up and returned to England.

Cheated of his chance for glory, constantly snubbed by the Duke of York, and thoroughly bored, Bucks hurried up to London as soon as the Fleet anchored. His impatience made him miss the great Battle of Southwold Bay on June 3, a glorious but costly victory for England. Both Fleets were shattered in a day-long engagement.[11]

Bucks made only a brief stay in London; it was no place for a gentleman. Early in the spring bubonic plague had broken out in the dock regions of the City, brought from Holland by infected ship rats. The plague spread rapidly westward, assuming epidemic proportions in May. Even in Covent Garden, less than a mile from Whitehall, watchmen were chalking red crosses and "God have mercy upon us" on door after door. A mass exodus began. The well-to-do dispersed to country houses and remote towns. The Court fled to Hampton Court Palace, then, as the plague grew worse, to Salisbury, and thence to Oxford. At Whitehall, stout old George Monck, Duke of Albemarle and Lord General of the Army, stayed alone to represent the government. By midsummer no one was left in London but the swarming poor, who died by thousands under a brassy, pitiless sky. At night their stark bodies were piled into carts, carried to the outskirts, and dumped into pits, where lime and earth covered them thinly.

But neither plague nor war could hinder love. It was probably at Hampton Court that Buckingham wrote a love poem to Anna-Maria. Dated July 20, 1665, it is probably only one of many that he wrote to the same address. Wooing by witty rhymes was a standard procedure. The seventeenth-century lover urged his coy sweetheart to be "kind"—that is, surrender her charms to him—and threatened her with one or more of several standard penalties if she refused. Invariably, he addressed her by a classical pseudonym—Phyllis and Chloris were most popular—and referred to himself as Strephon or Amintas. In the following, for Phyllis read Anna-Maria; for Delia, Mary, Duchess of Buckingham:

> *Though, Phyllis, your prevailing charms*
> *Hath forced my Delia from my arms,*
> *Think not your conquest to maintain*
> *By rigor, or unjust disdain.*
> *In vain, fair nymph, in vain you strive,*
> *For Love doth seldom Hope survive. . . .*
> *When age shall come, at whose command*
> *Those troops of beauty must disband,*
> *A rival's strength once took away,*
> *What slave's so dull as to obey?*
> *But if you'll learn a nobler way*
> *To keep this empire from decay,*
> *And there for ever fix your throne,*
> *Be kind—but kind to me alone!* [12]

Buckingham could play the game of love as skillfully as the best, and his Commonplace Book is full of remarks designed for a lady's ears. "I desire all, hope little, and dare ask nothing," he wrote in assumed humility. "It would content me if you did but dream of me, or if I could dream that you did so, but I shall never sleep enough for thinking of you to dream at all." In a more impatient mood he wrote, "If you allow me only your face and outward dress, I am no more beholding to you than you are to your looking-glass." "You are in everything a goddess, but that you will not be moved by prayers." And, ironically, "If contemplation be the manna of love, give me the flesh-pots."

Wise in the ways of women, he could turn off many a fine compliment: "Her face is so smooth that the eye slides off it—smooth as Waller's verse—smooth as the path of day that's beat in Heaven by the swift wheels of the ever-traveling sun." The pure beauty of her flesh drew a neat conceit: "That we do not see thy body quite through is not the want of whiteness but the excess." As for her bosom,

Such were the breasts at which, when earth was young,
The shining twins of fair Latona hung,
Upon such milk their growing god-heads fed,
With such a white their beams were nourishéd. [13]

Time passed and the Plague still raged in London. In October, Parliament met at Oxford; the little town was jammed with courtiers, noble lords, country gentlemen, and ladies of every description. If Bucks saw his sweetheart at Oxford, he had small chance for courtship; there was neither world enough nor time. Then came Christmas; the gentry dispersed to their estates all over England. The

Shrewsburys went to Deene, and Bucks spent the holiday season at Saxham, Suffolk, "in warm country dances." Winter and spring rolled by, and Phyllis continued unmoved by compliments or promises.[14]

This was getting to be a painfully long courtship; Buckingham, the irresistible, had met his match. "Love's like a game at chess," he once wrote, "if both be cunning gamesters, they'll never make an end." And again, "Kisses—sharp-headed kisses that wound deep—are but like sands of gold or silver found upon the ground, which are not worth much in themselves but as they promise a mine near to be digged." It was not merely that opposition whetted appetite, or, as Buckingham argued,

> *Love's flame kept in, as dangerous does become*
> *As charcoal fires closed in a narrow room—*

Far worse was the fact that, for perhaps the first time in his life, Buckingham was seriously in love. Mysterious, tantalizing, alluring, Anna-Maria had captured him so completely that he was like a besotted schoolboy. He lost his head as well as his heart.[15]

In the summer of 1666, the Dutch War flared up again. Once more the two Fleets met and wrecked each other in the terrible Battle of the Channel (June 1-5). France had joined Holland in alliance against England; the air was full of rumors of invasion. Buckingham spent the summer in Yorkshire, preparing the county against raiders from the sea. He made his headquarters at Fairfax House, a fine old mansion in Bishopshill, York, but he himself was all over the countryside, arranging for watchers and beacons on the coast, overseeing the building of a watchtower on the steeple of York Cathedral, and raising and drilling a troop of horse.

Early in July, he and his duchess were at Hull, where quite by chance they met the Earls of Cardigan and Shrewsbury, their families, and "other persons of quality." They were all sumptuously entertained by the authorities of the city and then separated—not, however, before Bucks had persuaded the Cardigan-Shrewsbury families to pay him a visit at York.[16]

They came "with a great retinue" some time later that month. Since Fairfax House was too small for such a company, Buckingham rented Lord Irvine's mansion in Minster Yard for his guests. Here he entertained them "at vast expense for a whole month." Sir John Reresby, a deputy-lieutenant of the West Riding and an officer in Buckingham's troop, recorded the events of that month with dour disapproval.

"The days," he wrote, "were spent in visits and play, and all sorts of diversions that place could afford, and the nights in dancing sometimes till day the next morning." Buckingham, now thirty-eight, was tireless as a boy, but "the two earls [Cardigan and Shrewsbury], not being men for those sports, went to bed something early." Anna-Maria was twenty-four. Twice she had performed her wifely duty, presenting her husband with two fine boys; now she was ready for a fling. The mild summer nights were ideal for love. Buckingham, ever an ingenious man, found a way to carry out one of his own precepts: "First remove fear from your mistress, for cowardice is the mother of cruelty." At last Phyllis was kind.

Thereafter the passion which swept the two lovers made them dangerously indiscreet. Young Lord Brudenell, Anna-Maria's brother, told Reresby one night over a bottle of wine that "coming hastily through the dining room the evening before he saw two tall persons in a kind posture, and he thought they looked like the duke and his sister, but he would not be too inquisitive for fear it should prove so." Some time later, the Earl of Shrewsbury, faced with a comparable situation, became inquisitive, and that night "my Lord Brudenell was sent for from the tavern very late to his sister's chamber to [make] her and my Lord Shrewsbury friends, they having had a great quarrel of jealousy concerning the duke." Brudenell proved to be a first-rate diplomat, and Anna-Maria's power over her husband was so great that even after the quarrel he remained for some time longer at York. The Duchess of Buckingham was the only one of the company who (said Reresby) "perceived nothing at that time of the intrigue that was carrying on between her husband and the Countess of Shrewsbury"— or saw, and wisely pretended not to. Reresby himself saw and trembled. When the Buckinghams first came to York, Reresby had summoned his young wife to wait on the duchess, but when he became aware of the duke's successful intrigue, he promptly sent her away, "it being no good school for a young wife." Like Shrewsbury's, his was a May-and-December marriage.

Heedless Buckingham was ecstatic. "Joy would have killed me," he wrote, "but that I could not die upon the lips of my life." One of his undated, unfinished poems fits easily into this summer of his content:

> *A thousand blessings on thee, gentle moon,*
>   *And on thy silver light;*
> *Thou makest my evening, morning, and my noon;*
>   *The sun begins my night.*
>
> *Twice hast thou been so wonderfully good*
>   *To make me meet my sacred she;*
> *Like thy fair image in some beauteous flood,*
>   *Methought she walked along with thee.*

Alas, no moon goddess could linger long upon this sublunary sphere. In August the Cardigans and Shrewsburys departed, heading for their several estates, and the bereft lover took himself and his grief to his manor of Worthrop, Northamptonshire. There, early in September, he received word of a great fire which threatened to reduce to ashes "the whole city of London within the walls." Rousing himself from his dreams, Buckingham alerted his deputy lieutenants, warned them of the dangers of insurrection in such a troubled time, and galloped to London to put out the fire.[17]

III

PERSONS OF QUALITY
1666–1667

WHEN BUCKINGHAM arrived in London, the fire was over, and the City lay prostrated by the greatest calamity in its history. Westminster, the Covent Garden district, and the Strand with its palaces were untouched, but beyond Temple Bar a wilderness of smoking rubble stretched eastward to the Tower, with the ruins of St. Paul's and the shattered steeples of eighty-four churches rising from the desolation.

With its capital half destroyed, its Fleet shattered in a series of desperate battles, its manpower depleted by plague, its trade ruined, and its treasury empty, England was at its lowest ebb in the autumn of 1666. The Plague, now dying out, could be passed off as an act of God; the fire (everybody agreed blindly) had been set by French Catholics in concert with Protestant fanatics; but for everything else there must be better scapegoats. The King and his ministers laid all the blame on the malcontents in the House of

Commons, who had failed to vote enough money for the proper conduct of the war; the malcontents—a loose coalition of republicans, out-of-office demagogues, and tight-fisted country gentlemen—accused the King's officers of theft, waste, and incompetence. Both sides were right. When Parliament convened on September 18, 1666, everyone was in a belligerent mood.

Buckingham, too, had a chip on his shoulder. For some time he had fretted at his political unimportance. His advice on the conduct of the war and the proper way to handle Parliament had been brushed aside. He fancied himself a military man; he had served in the French army besieging the Spaniards at Arras and Valenciennes and had fought valiantly at the Battle of Worcester, where the King's Scots allies were routed by Cromwell. Now he himself was passed over, and he saw the armed forces commanded by men he considered incompetent: the Duke of York and Prince Rupert, the King's cousin. To add to his irritability now, he was passionately in love, and his mistress was a married woman.

Since, a year and a half later, Pepys could write that Lady Shrewsbury "is at this time, and hath for a great while been, a whore to the Duke of Buckingham," there can be no doubt that the lovers met as often as possible. The fact that there was very little gossip about them during that year and a half argues that Anna-Maria had learned discretion. The impetuous duke cared nothing for the world's opinion; he lived for the present, and *carpe diem* was his slogan. He found no joy in the memories of delight. "I can no more live by past favors," he wrote, "than the air can be enlightened by the beams of yesterday." "Love is like

a hectic fever, at first hard to know and easy to cure; afterwards easy to be known and impossible to be cured." [1]

In a more pragmatic age, the cure for the fever would
have been a double divorce followed by a marriage. But
the duke and his mistress labored under a double prohibition. In seventeenth-century England, divorce (with permission to remarry) was theoretically possible, but only by
an act of the House of Lords and on grounds of blatant
adultery. No such divorces had been granted since the time
of Henry VIII. Moreover, Anna-Maria was a Catholic;
even if there had been a double divorce she could not have
married her lover and remained in the church. There was
no use fighting against the rigid taboos of church, state,
and society; the two lovers could only seek to evade them,
occasionally deceiving their marital partners for a hectic
hour of passion.

Those hours were not easily arranged. For a bachelor or
a semidetached husband (who kept his wife in the country)
to fornicate with a casual wench was easy enough. Such
men lived in private lodgings and were visited by their
doxies early in the morning. "Remember five o'clock to-
morrow morning," said Etherege's Dorimant to his newest
conquest, Bellinda, who trembled as she remembered and
promised to come.[2]

But the Duke of Buckingham had his wife living with
him at Wallingford House. As a Lady of the Bedchamber
to Queen Catherine and one of Her Majesty's best friends,
she had every reason to remain in town. When the Earl of
Shrewsbury brought his family to town, he stayed either
with his wife's people at Cardigan House or with his
cousins, the Howards, at Arundel House in the Strand; at

either place Anna-Maria was surrounded by servants and kinfolk. Of course, since Her Grace of Buckingham was resigned to the duke's amours, it is not likely that she caused the lovers much trouble; still, they could hardly use Wallingford House as a trysting place. Lord Shrewsbury was a much tougher proposition; he was "a Person of Quality," he was jealous, and, of course, he wore a sword. Under such conditions only the most devious journeys could end in lovers' meetings. Samuel Pepys, Clerk of the Acts to the Navy, was enamored of a poor carpenter's wife and could visit her at home, find occasion to send the cuckold abroad for an hour, and have his *"plaisir* of *elle,"* but Bucks could not readily send the Earl of Shrewsbury on errands.

The lovers had to beware of Harry Killigrew, too. By this time he had completely reversed himself. "Without ever considering that he was the author of his own disgrace, he let loose all his abusive eloquence against [Lady Shrewsbury]; he attacked her with the most bitter invective from head to foot; he drew a frightful picture of her conduct, and turned all her personal charms, which he used to extol, into defects." Grammont blamed his behavior on the fact that Anna-Maria refused to see him, and "pretended even not to know him." But the fury of a congenital liar caught out in a lie is worse than that of a woman scorned.

Obviously Buckingham could not challenge Killigrew without giving away his own interest in the lady. Anna-Maria complained to her husband and her kinsmen, but no one cared to cross swords with the rascal, who was notorious as a duelist. Fortunately, at this juncture Killigrew made the mistake of slandering the King's *maîtresse en titre*, Barbara Palmer, Countess of Castlemaine. He was quoted as saying that Lady Castlemaine had been "a little lecherous girl when she was young." This statement happened to be true. At the age of fifteen—three years before she married Roger Palmer, a law student—Barbara Villiers had been the mistress of Philip Stanhope, Earl of Chesterfield, the first in her long succession of lovers.

Someone repeated Killigrew's sneer to Lady Castlemaine. Her protests and outcries to her family and friends brought summary vengeance upon the scandalmonger. The King banished him from Court and ordered the Duke of York to dismiss him from his post as Groom of the Bedchamber. Thereafter, perhaps because he blamed Buckingham (Lady Castlemaine's cousin) for his banishment, Killigrew's animosity towards Bucks and Lady Shrewsbury deepened into passionate hatred. For the moment, however, he was silenced.[3]

Husbands and rejected suitors were the thorniest brambles in the path of illicit love. Religious differences seem to have mattered hardly at all; yet Anna-Maria was a Catholic, and Buckingham, like most seventeenth-century Protestants, distrusted the Catholic Church and all its ways. He was particularly suspicious of the confessional. " 'Tis dangerous," he wrote, "for priests to know the sins of others, for 'tis an easy step for sin out of the memory into the will." "It cannot choose but make priests lascivious to feel thus the privy parts of women's souls." "I should be afraid that she should not deny the secrets of her body to whom she discovers the secrets of her soul." "Upon this condition of absolving a woman from a thousand old sins, 'tis easy to persuade her to commit one new one." "I would rather have confession made of our good deeds, for every man would strive to have something to say for himself." The duke could be very sententious on sin.[4]

He had no trouble with his own conscience. He claimed to be a good Christian; actually he was a deist, founding his theology upon reason rather than revelation. His belief that any man, permitted the free and uncontrolled use of his reason, could study the Scriptures and find out "the certain meaning of Christ and his apostles" brought him intellectually very close to the Nonconformists. To Bucks the great enemies of the Protestant religion were "papists and atheists" and all prideful men who opposed "the empire of reason." This empire was founded upon "a true and perfect liberty of conscience." [5]

All this was very pretty; it made every man his own interpreter of Scripture and his own judge of right and wrong. Now by coveting his neighbor's wife and lying with her, Buckingham had (apparently) sinned, and he fully intended to repeat the sin whenever he got a chance. However, since he claimed liberty of conscience, he could justify his behavior by reason. He could, for example, imitate that great sinner, King Charles, who said once that God would not "make a man miserable only for taking a little pleasure out of the way." God, too, was reasonable! For the rest, as Buckingham wrote philosophically, "the wounds of conscience by washing and keeping clean will cure of themselves." Morals are relative to time, place and sophistry.[6]

Bucks spent very little time examining the state of his soul. There was always something new to engage his versatile energies. For example, in 1666 his little circle of literati gained some useful recruits. One, young John Wilmot, Earl of Rochester, was rapidly becoming famous for wit and obscenity. He was a handsome devil, quite an amorist, and one of the best song-writers of a lyric age. Another was slender, fair-haired George Etherege, whose first play, *The Comical Revenge*, had been a hit in March, 1664, and who was languidly working on another. A third, John, Lord Vaughan, was a malcontent member of the House of Commons and a dilettante poet. Then there was boastful Sir Robert Howard (Dryden's brother-in-law), who cried himself up as the greatest poet, playwright, and politician in the world. Like Sir Charles Sedley ("Little Sid") and moon-faced Lord Buckhurst, these men were all interested in the stage, and some were eager to get fame as dramatists. Stimulated by them, Bucks set to work revising Fletcher's *The Chances*, a lively old comedy spoiled by a weak ending. This work kept his idle hours filled during the better part of the autumn.

But most of his energy went into politics. The ministry was tottering; a vigorous push might overthrow it. Contrary to his usual custom of coming late to the House of Lords and staying only briefly, Bucks "was now always present with the first in a morning and stayed till the last at night." He had strong friends in both Houses. "He invited them to his table," said old Clarendon, "pretended to have a great esteem of their parts, asked counsel of them, lamented the King's neglecting his business and committing it to other people who were not fit for it; and then reported all the license and debauchery of the Court in the most lively colors, being himself a frequent eye and ear witness of it." [7]

It was an odd way to get preferment, but politically Buckingham lived in an odd world. There was no such thing as a "loyal opposition"; those who dared oppose the King's wishes were called wilful men and rogues. Technically, the King, counseled by the two Houses of Parliament, made the laws; the King and his ministers enforced them. Actually, the House of Commons had one great source of power: it alone could initiate bills for taxes. If it refused to grant funds, the King was helpless. What with wars and inflation, the cost of government had mounted steadily, and the grumbling House of Commons grew more and more difficult to deal with. Bucks planned to build up his influence with Commons and trade it to the King for a post in the ministry.

The King's ministers were his personal servants, accountable only to him, although in extreme cases the Commons could impeach them before the House of Lords. He appointed and sometimes consulted with a Privy Council of some thirty men, of whom half a dozen were members of the Committee on Foreign Affairs, the "cabinet" or "cabal," which did the actual work of governing. In 1666 this cabinet was made up of the Duke of York, the Duke of Ormonde, Lords Clarendon and Southampton, and the two Secretaries of State: Sir William Morice and Henry Bennet, now Baron Arlington. Sometimes Prince Rupert and the Duke of Albemarle were invited. For four years Buckingham had been a Privy Councilor, but he had never been invited to join the "cabal."

Ever since the Restoration, Bucks had used all his wiles to win the King's favor and become a leader in the government. He had long been a Gentleman of the Bedchamber

—salary £1,000 a year, when it was paid. There were twelve Gentlemen—all of them "of the prime nobility in England"—who took turns waiting on his Majesty for one week out of each quarter. There were also twelve Grooms of the Bedchamber, men of gentle birth but lesser rank. One Gentleman and one Groom always served together. They helped the King dress in the morning, and when the Groom of the Stole was absent it was the Gentleman of the Bedchamber who had "the office and honor to present and put on his Majesty's first garment or shirt every morning, and to order the things of the bedchamber." Thereafter, during the day, the Bedchamber servants clung close to their master, attending him even when he went "to ease himself." There were dozens of pages, equerries, valets, physicians, and other supernumeraries about, but the Gentleman and the Groom were the King's intimate friends as well as his servants. They walked with him in St. James's Park, bowled or played tennis with him, hunted with him at Windsor, served him on bended knee when he ate in public, ate with him in private, pimped for him at need, and guarded his bedchamber door to ensure privacy.

Late at night, when the King was safely tucked away behind the curtains of his great four-poster bed, the Gentleman of the Bedchamber prepared for the night in another room. The Page of the Back Stairs lighted his way to the King's bedchamber, where a pallet awaited him close to the royal bed. (The Groom slept in the Antechamber.) Once inside, the Gentleman closed the door, turned the great brass knob, and settled down for the night. Sleep was not easy. Since the King loved warmth, a grate filled with Scotch coal was kept burning. Then a dozen of the King's spaniels usually slept in the room and were often restless, while four or five clocks chimed the quarter hour all night long.[8]

Although the Gentleman's duties were often onerous, he had the best of opportunities to beg favors, pensions, or privileges for himself, and to influence the King politically. Unfortunately that influence was never lasting and could always be countered by the autocratic Chancellor in a meeting of the cabinet. Buckingham called him derisively "the King's Schoolmaster."

Although all the ministers of state were in some degree dangerous to an aspiring politician, Buckingham was not concerned about Morice and Arlington, two nonentities (he thought), or Southampton, something of a doddering old fool. Clarendon was his greatest enemy and must be destroyed. Ormonde, who had no patience with modernism and "liberty of conscience," must be removed from office. He was an honest, loyal gentleman, but he was Clarendon's close friend, and two years earlier he had helped defeat Buckingham's ambition to become President of the North. Moreover, his second son, Richard, Earl of Arran, had married Buckingham's niece and presumed heiress, Mary Stuart, and Ormonde had been very inquisitive about the settlement of the duke's estates.

Bucks was slow to realize the enmity and cunning of Lord Arlington. Henry Bennet, who had begun life as a simple country gentleman, had performed many duties at the Court of Exiles, including a four-year term as Resident in Spain. Poverty-poor at the Restoration, in six years he had acquired a barony, a considerable estate, a mansion (Goring House), and a rich Dutch wife, whom he had married in April, 1666, when he was forty-eight. He "had the art of observing the King's temper and managing it beyond all the men of that time." He was capable, cautious, and industrious. His smooth, bland face hid his true feelings perfectly. The King thought him loyal and honest and was slow to recognize that he was unscrupulous and self-seeking. Since Arlington wanted to become chief minister (preferably as Lord Treasurer), he too hated Clarendon, but he feared the Duke of Buckingham more.[9]

Buckingham's first chance to assert himself came early in October, when the House of Commons was angrily probing into the finances of the Navy Office. He made "a wild motion in the House of Lords . . . for all men that had cheated the King to be declared traitors and felons." To prevent "cheats and abuses in the revenue, he moved for leave to bring in a bill making it death for anyone thus to act in the future." Laughing heartily, the House told him to go ahead. Bucks wrote his bill, and was persuaded not to offer it.[10]

Two weeks later he found a better way to demonstrate his power and make trouble for the government. A bill to prohibit the importing of Irish cattle—dead or alive—had been knocking about for over a year. On October 16 it came up again in the House of Lords. In principle and purpose it was a thoroughly bad bill, but the English cattle raisers, consulting only their own purses, were mad for it. They were joined by the malcontents, many of whom hated Ormonde, a considerable landlord in Ireland. Other supporters of the bill—notably Lords Ashley and Lauderdale—had even worse reasons. Ashley was a slender little man with a long, pale face and burning eyes. He was an artful politician, an expert at changing sides, and a thoroughgoing opportunist. Lauderdale, High Commissioner for Scotland, was a burly, red-faced Scotsman with a tongue too large for his mouth. Apparently stupid but actually very shrewd, he had worked out with Ashley a neat scheme to get rich by importing cheap Scotch cattle and selling them at high prices. As for Buckingham, the fact that the ministry opposed the bill was enough. Politicians have no use for principles. He devoted all his eloquence and biting wit to the support of the bill.

Thomas Butler, Earl of Ossory, a new member of the upper house, listened to the debates with mounting anger. He was a hotheaded young Irishman, impulsive and passionate, eldest son of the Duke of Ormonde, and Lord Arlington's brother-in-law. He took as personal affronts Buckingham's attacks on the ministry and the Irish. One day he blew up. In the course of debate, Bucks taunted Lord Clarendon by insisting that "whoever was against the bill was there led to it by an Irish interest or an Irish understanding"—in brief, Clarendon, who had no Irish estates, was a fool. Clarendon retorted angrily, and the debate broke up in disorder.

Afterward Ossory invited Buckingham into an anteroom and told him hotly that he had used "many loose and unworthy expressions which reflected upon the whole Irish nation, and which he himself resented so much that he expected satisfaction, and to find him with his sword in hand." This was a flagrant breach of Parliamentary privilege (and a neat way to kill off the opposition), but, according to the code of the day, Bucks had to accept the challenge. Naming the meetingplace as Chelsea Fields (which Bucks said later "he understood to be the fields over [the river] against Chelsea"), and the time an hour thence, the duke went home and changed his sword. Then he took a boat across the river and hastened to the designated spot. There he was found a couple of hours later by Guardsmen sent to prevent the meeting. Meanwhile Ossory had gone to Chelsea Fields on the north side of the river, where he simmered and fumed until he saw some people coming. Fearing they had been sent to arrest him, he retreated to London.

The story flew about the town, growing wilder with each relation. Next morning, to put the record straight, Buckingham stood up in the House of Lords and told his side of the story: how Ossory had "charged him with many particulars which he had spoken in the House" and challenged him to fight. Although Bucks asserted that he did not "hold himself obliged to do so in maintenance of anything which he had said or done in Parliament, yet that it being suitable and agreeable in his nature to fight with any man who had a mind to fight with him," he had accepted the challenge.

Ossory was in a difficult spot: if he admitted challenging the duke for words spoken in Parliament, he made himself liable to severe penalties. Therefore he insisted that he had been angered by "some sharp railleries and unhandsome reflections the duke had made upon his relations" in a private conversation, and called upon Lord Arlington to bear him out. Arlington bore witness in a smoothly pious speech which stirred Bucks to an angry reply, and hot words flew until the Chancellor intervened. Then Ossory and Bucks were ordered to withdraw while the House debated.

A ridiculous wrangle followed. The majority of the members proposed sending Ossory to the Tower. His friends claimed the offense was equal on both sides, because Buckingham had accepted the challenge. The duke's "unfriends," refusing to believe that the mistake about Chelsea Fields had been an honest one, defended Buckingham in mockery, saying that he had committed no fault, for "it was very evident that he never intended to fight," and so had "prudently mistaken the place that was appointed by himself." The duke's real friends rose to the bait, and to save him from the charge of cowardice urged that he should be punished as severely as Ossory!

Finally, after laying a command on Buckingham and Arlington "that they remain in friendship and act nothing to the breach of the peace in relation to what words passed this day between them in the House," the Lords sent Ossory to the Tower and committed Bucks to the custody of the Gentleman Usher of the Black Rod. This was equivalent to house arrest.[11]

Had the duke deliberately avoided a duel? Many people thought so, including Lord Clarendon, our chief (and most prejudiced) informant. However, Buckingham had amply proved his courage during the Civil Wars. There was the time, for example, when he and a few followers were in hiding after the failure of Lord Holland's rebellion, in 1648. They awoke one morning at St. Neots to find the house surrounded by Cromwell's soldiers, with a troop of horse drawing up before the gates. Bucks barely had time to get his small party armed and mounted; then he ordered the gates opened, charged the enemy, killed their commander with his own hand, and slashed his way to safety.

He was still one of the best swordsmen in England, but he was no longer young and reckless. As the receiver of a challenge his position was extremely difficult. If he refused to fight, he was a coward; if he fought and lost, he was disgraced—or dead; if he won, he could be charged with committing a felony. Whatever course he took, he had nothing to gain and much to lose. Perhaps he avoided the meeting —a highly irregular affair without duly appointed seconds —hoping that Ossory's temper would cool.

Two days after they were committed, the two lords were released. Ossory was still belligerent. On November 19, during another debate over the Irish cattle bill, the young Hotspur told Lord Ashley that he talked "like one of Oliver's council." Ashley had been a member of Cromwell's Council, but he hardly cared to be reminded of the fact. He flared up at once, demanding satisfaction. Buckingham got into the battle of words, drawing Ossory's fire on his own head. Again the House had to reprimand Ossory, and force him to apologize to Ashley and Buckingham.[12]

Everyone was short-tempered and truculent that autumn. Parliament passed the Irish cattle bill and then dilly-dallied over money bills until the King almost lost *his* temper. When a bill for supplies was finally passed, a rider was attached providing for a committee to audit the government's accounts, and the King was really angry. Meanwhile, his ministers quarreled among themselves, the Dutch war limped along, the Fleet rotted at anchor, and unpaid seamen rioted in the streets.

Rightly or wrongly, King Charles blamed Buckingham for Parliament's misbehavior. He was sure that the duke "must have very ill intentions." In the House of Lords Buckingham had said that "the King paid fifty in the hundred to the bankers," and wondered how the war could be "managed at this rate," and "contradicted the Duke of York when he affirmed the contrary." Constantly he cried out against the government, sought popular favor (said the King, indignantly), and "spoke for the seamen's having their pay"—when anyone could see that there was no money to pay them with.

No doubt Buckingham's sense of justice was outraged at the sight of the Court living in luxury while discharged sailors starved unpaid, yet it is certainly true that he seized upon the situation to build himself up as a popular leader. He too lived in luxury. On November 15, Pepys saw a grand ball at Court, with ladies "most excellently dressed in rich petticoats and gowns, and diamonds, and pearls," and among the gentlemen who danced was the Duke of Buckingham, very richly dressed.[13]

Toward the end of November, Bucks threw another wrench into the gears of government. Earlier in the session, when a bill for "the illegitimation of the children of Lady Anne Roos" was read in the House, Bucks had paid it little attention, although Lord Roos (a drunken reprobate) was his second cousin. Lady Anne, daughter of Henry Pierrepont, Marquis of Dorchester, had married John Manners, Lord Roos, son of the eighth Earl of Rutland. Lady Anne endured a brief period of marriage and then deserted her husband. After an absence of many months, she returned to him "in so gross a condition that it appeared that she had kept company too much." When her husband discovered that she was with child and asked "who got it?"

she was unable to remember, but answered happily that "whoever got it, if it proved a boy, as she believed it would, he should be Earl of Rutland." It proved a boy.

The circumstances were certainly suspicious, and Lord Roos had no trouble getting a decree of separation from the ecclesiastical courts. However, unless his new bill was approved, Lady Anne's son, aptly named Ignotus, would legally bear the surname of Manners and would inherit the Rutland titles and estates. Both families concerned favored the bill. The Marquis of Dorchester had disowned his daughter (who had continued her sinful ways), and now he openly "gave a free consent to the bill and desired that it might pass." It was opposed only by some timid lords who feared the precedent it might set.

The bill was getting along nicely until Bucks saw a chance to use it for his obstructionist tactics. On November 9 he rose to protest against the whole business on the technical ground that Lord Roos had usurped a title which belonged to him in right of his mother, Katherine Manners, the only child of the sixth Earl of Rutland. Actually the Barony of Roos belonged with the Rutland titles, and like them descended only in the male line. Lord Roos, as the eldest son of an earl, used it as a "courtesy" title. Buckingham had no case; his only interest was to muddy the legislative waters and demonstrate his power. He succeeded in both aims and managed also to get himself cordially hated by both Rutland and Dorchester.[14]

On December 19, when the members of Parliament were all tired, testy, and eager to get home for Christmas, there was a conference between committees of the two houses in the Painted Chamber at Westminster Palace. Bucks was one of the "managers" of the Lords' committee, of which Dorchester, a short, elderly man, was a member. As the members sat down there was much crowding and shoving for places around the table. Buckingham crowded Dorchester with his elbow; Dorchester pushed him away.

"Are you uneasy?" asked Bucks.

"Yes," said Dorchester fiercely. "You durst not do this elsewhere."

"Yes, I would," retorted Bucks. "I'm a better man than you."

"You lie!" screamed the marquis.

Bucks blew up. Snorting fiercely, he struck off Dorchester's hat, "took him by the periwig and pulled it aside and held him," while the frantic marquis pulled and clawed at the duke's hair. Then "my Lord Chamberlain and others interposed" and stopped the fight. The House sent both lords to the Tower.

It was noticed that "as the duke passed through the City to the Tower, the people made acclamation, not as he was a prisoner, but to show their respect for him, for he was become very popular by his aversion to Hyde"—Lord Clarendon. That afternoon also, by an odd coincidence, there was a riot in the City, with a thousand discharged seamen in arms. The Duke of Albemarle had to call out his Guards to clear the streets. The King's ministers put two and two together and firmly believed that Buckingham had caused the riot.[15]

Three days later the duke and the marquis were discharged from the Tower and "reconciled." Now a nobleman who had offended the House of Lords was presumed to have offended the King also; he was expected to wait upon his Majesty and humbly beg pardon. Wilfully or carelessly, Bucks ignored this formality and "presumed to appear in his Majesty's presence on Christmas Day, for which he was immediately forbidden the Court." Although he then made the proper apologies, he lay under the King's displeasure for some weeks. He appeared quite unconcerned, knowing, perhaps (as a cynical enemy wrote), "the infinite good nature in His Majesty to pardon such offenses." (To Lord Arlington it seemed that the time was ripe for a blow that would rid him of his rival.)

The year ended in fears and confusion. "A sad, vicious, negligent Court," wrote Pepys, "and all sober men there fearful of the ruin of the whole kingdom the next year, from which, good God, deliver us!" As for the government, "there are scarce any two that dare trust one another," wrote a courtier, "but every man is jealous of his neighbor, and those in power practising to supplant one another, and wants and debts increasing." [16]

Things were no better after the holidays. Parliament continued in session until February 8, 1667. Buckingham attended regularly, pounding away at Lord Roos until that unhappy gentleman dropped his title for the nonce to get his bill passed. Although, as one of Buckingham's "unfriends" wrote, the duke continued to behave "with great insolency," he did nothing further to arouse the King's anger. (Behind the scenes, Lord Arlington set in motion the machinery of a complicated and diabolical plot.) [17]

In January Bucks polished off his alteration of *The Chances*, the story of two wild gallants and their misadventures while seeking a famous Bolognese prostitute. By completely rewriting the last two acts he made the whole a closer-knit and more effective comedy. One new character, the Mother of the Second Constantia (the prostitute), shows not only Buckingham's acquaintance with the sub-world of Restoration bawdy houses but also his skill at character drawing. The Mother, a bawd (procuress), is brilliantly conceived as a woman of precious and stately speech. Under pressure from her daughter to flee the country, she refuses to "depatriate," and protests, "I'll ne'er depart from the *démarches* of a person of quality; and let come what will, I shall rather choose to submit myself to my fate than strive to prevent it by any deportment that is not congruous, in every degree, to the steps and measures of a strict practitioner of honor."

With the famous Charles Hart as Don John, the wilder of the two gallants; with Mary Knepp, an excellent singer, as the First Constantia, a distressed lady; and with witty Nell Gwyn as the Second Constantia, the comedy was performed at the King's Theatre in Covent Garden to great applause. Pepys saw it on February 5 and wrote, "A good play I find it, and the actors most good in it . . . the whole play pleases me well." In his epilogue, Buckingham apologized for his "fag-end of a play," and, with a sly reference to his state of Courtly disgrace, begged the audience not to tempt the author to further writing,

> *For he knows ways enough to be undone,*
> *Without the help of poetry for one.*

By the end of January, Buckingham's sentence of banishment had been lifted, but he made no attempt to return to Court and take up his duties there. Lady Shrewsbury had gone to her father's house at Deene, Northamptonshire. As soon as Parliament was prorogued, and without taking formal leave of the King, the literary politician and lover hurried off to his manor at Worthrop, conveniently close to Deene. (In London, Lord Arlington's plot was already in operation.)

EPISODE IN VILLAINY

1667

UCKINGHAM'S HISTORY gave King Charles every reason to believe that he was up to no good. Not only had he deserted the royalist cause in 1657 when he came back to England and married Mary Fairfax, but also, during the later years of Cromwell, he had been on intimate terms with Colonel Lilbourne and Major Wildman, leaders of the Levellers, a party of wild-eyed republicans. At one time Lilbourne, grateful to Bucks "for extraordinary benefits and favors," praised him as a man of "reason, sobriety, civility, honor, and conscience"—forsooth! (Lilbourne was dead, but Wildman, a dangerous radical, lived on, safely tucked away in Pendennis Castle, Cornwall.) Furthermore, since the Restoration Bucks had talked for liberty of conscience, worked for popularity with the masses, plotted with the malcontents in Parliament, and, worst of all, had treated fanatics—such wicked people as Baptists and Quakers—with leniency, instead of hanging

[70]

them out of hand as a good officer should. Everyone was certain that he had stirred up the discharged seamen to mutiny, and the King had information that he associated with men of "mean condition, but of very desperate intentions." [1]

Still the King could not bring himself to believe that his old friend was guilty of "treasonable practises." Neither could Lord Arlington, but that aspiring minister never let his beliefs determine his actions. He wanted to get rid of a dangerous rival. His problem, then, was to find proof of treason and so bring the heedless duke to a headless end.

Unable to find that proof, Arlington proceeded to manufacture it with the aid of a parcel of hired informers. He took none of his ministerial colleagues into his confidence, and, indeed, there was no reason why he should. As Secretary of State he was responsible for the internal security of the nation; he spent thousands of pounds annually for spies and informers whose function it was to ferret out treason and give warning of uprisings in embryo.

The government lived in deadly fear of revolts. By the nature of their beliefs the Nonconformists were all, in some degree, tinged with political radicalism. Persecution only made them worse; they were numerous, vocal, and stubborn. The fanatics among them were theocrats, anarchists, republicans, and the like—a dangerous lot in a monarchy. Moreover, England was full of Cromwell's disbanded soldiers, tinder to a spark of insurrection, and over in Holland there were famous republican leaders living in exile and dreaming of the promised land. Some of the fanatics schemed grandiose plots—and ended up behind bars with thousands of their kind. The jails were filled with plotters, most of them arrested on suspicion. Since informers were paid on a piece-work basis, they often acted as *agents pro-vocateurs*, or "decoy ducks," tricking their victims into treasonable talk and sham plots.

The informers that Arlington hired for his plot against Buckingham were reasonably literate, and their letters give us a pretty story of unabashed villainy. The chief informer was one William Leving, a snuffy, pock-marked fellow who always wore a brown periwig, insisted upon being called "Captain," and answered also to the names of Leonard Williams and William Ward. At one time in his checkered past he had been a fanatic. Captured during a minor revolt in Yorkshire in 1664, he had saved his neck by informing against his fellow rebels. Sir Roger Langley, Arlington's chief agent in Yorkshire, thinking Leving "might be of good use" to his patron, had sent the turncoat to Arlington, who found him very useful indeed.[2]

In the autumn of 1666 Leving was in Ireland, trying to catch an annoying outlaw for the Duke of Ormonde. Summoned home in December, he brought with him a recruit, another turncoat named George Middleton, alias Fawcett. Middleton seems to have been a young man of rather engaging manners and appearance. Leving swore that he and Middleton together could do Arlington's "business." "We will engage our lives for it," he wrote, "and when we shall think it convenient to execute anything, Ensign Langley [Sir Roger's son] has promised to assist us with soldiers." The nature of Lord Arlington's business was not stated, but it soon became clear enough.[3]

Arlington was too canny to commit anything to paper or to work out the details of the "business" himself; that duty fell upon another of Buckingham's enemies, Sir Roger Langley, a former high sheriff of Yorkshire and a rabid fanatic-baiter. Sir Roger was not content to have only Leving and Middleton and tried to recruit a third informer, William Frear, alias Fryer, who had once worked with Leving. Months later Frear admitted that he had been approached but piously denied taking any part in the plot. Sir Roger, said Frear, first swore him to secrecy, "and then told him the Duke of Buckingham was a proud, ambitious man, and sought by all means to make himself greater, and was privately the King's enemy." Surely, said Sir Roger, Frear must know "something whereof to accuse him, and if he would undertake to witness against him, he should be well gratified." He conveyed to Frear the impression that men of high rank were backing the affair. "They had considered what each witness would say, and he might know his part from the rest, if he would submit to be one of the witnesses." Frear said that he refused to play and ran to Lord Arlington, who told him drily that "he was an obstinate fellow, and he perceived would not be persuaded to his advantage." [4]

Frear remaining obstinate (although he got into the act later), Leving and Middleton went it alone. Sir Roger had promised them £100 each for their testimony, enough to pay for swearing away the lives of a dozen dukes. They took about three weeks to collect their evidence and mature their plans, "in which time they ordinarily consulted with my Lord Arlington, who told them they must put in writing what they would accuse the duke of before he would make it known to the King." The Secretary was taking no chances.

The informers had decided that the best way to get at Buckingham was through one of his radical associates. Who of these was more vulnerable than Doctor John Heydon, the half-cracked astrologer? He had once been accused of writing a seditious book; he was known to frequent Wallingford House and to boast of his intimacy with the duke; and in prefaces to his books he had praised Bucks in the language of a subject addressing his king. All kinds of subversive stuff might be found (or planted) among his papers, and under torture he would confess whatever my Lord Arlington wished.

Middleton, the Irish informer, made Heydon's acquaintance and soon became so much his friend that the silly astrologer even trusted him with letters to be delivered to Bucks—letters which, of course, the spies read and copied. As Middleton deposed later, Heydon boasted of his greatness with the duke, hinted of revolution, and bewailed the chance he had missed to raise the discharged seamen and storm the Tower when Bucks was a prisoner there in late December. The moment had been lost "by reason the duke was set at liberty so suddenly," but there would come a time! Heydon hinted that the duke had urged him to take the lead in stirring up a revolt. Once it was well under way, Buckingham would come forward to take command.[5]

The spies rubbed their hands and took it all down, adding a few twists of their own. Then, on January 24, 1667, armed with Lord Arlington's warrant, the informer Leving and a provost marshal descended upon Heydon in his East Smithfield lodgings, arrested him and everybody in the house at the time, seized his books, papers, money, watch, and sword, and hustled him off to the Tower. (Middleton got the watch and sword as his share of the loot; poor Heydon never saw them again.) Later that day the two informers delivered all their papers to Sir Roger Langley, "and then they all went and delivered them to my lord"—Arlington. The arrest was made quietly; Buckingham, still in London at the time, knew nothing of it.[6]

After a week or so—great men must not be hurried—Arlington "examined" Heydon in the Tower. By the usual combination of threats and promises, it should have been easy to force all kinds of confessions from the terrified "Secretary of Nature." The evidence against him was damning. There were copies of several letters to Buckingham, and "one or two" originals, sealed but not sent, had been found among his papers. In one letter Heydon gave Bucks "the style of Prince, and mentioned what great things his stars promised to him, and that he was the darling of the people, who had set their hearts and affections and all their hopes upon his highness." Then there were the informers' sworn statements that for four years Heydon had been Buckingham's privy councilor, and that, at the duke's orders, he had sown sedition in the navy and engaged seamen in a plot to seize the Tower. To this last, "some of the persons taken up" with Heydon (his landlady, Joan Chidley, and two or three badly frightened sailors) bore witness—or at least said what they were told to say. There was also an unsigned letter to Heydon, apparently commissioning him to cast the King's nativity. When King Charles saw this letter some time later, he declared that it was "every word in the duke's own hand." Finally, to cap everything, it turned out that for several weeks Heydon had been living among Quakers. He was damned by association.[7]

But Heydon, sustained by his faith in God and Buckingham, refused to confess. He admitted that he had known one of his fellow lodgers to be a Quaker, but he swore that he had never been with Quakers before, and assured Arlington that "if God, the King, and you be merciful to me this once, I never will come amongst them again!" He denied all thought of treason, defended Buckingham mightily, could not remember what was among his papers, but insisted that he had received only one letter from his patron, written "about two years since," when the duke delivered him from debtors' prison. Close confinement and even torture only made him more vehement in his denials.[8]

While Arlington bullied Heydon, the informers scratched their heads for more evidence. On February 12 Leving remembered that two years ago he had held a conversation with Henry North, Buckingham's personal informer in Yorkshire—every great man had a tame rogue in pay. North, said Leving, had told him that Bucks was not an enemy to the fanatics, that he (Bucks) was "against the bishops and Common Prayer," and had bidden North assure the Nonconformists that he was their friend.[9]

With this slim thread of evidence woven in, the net was ready. However, Arlington gave Heydon another week or so, hoping for a confession. Then he could wait no longer. Informers were tricky fellows, and there was always a chance that news of the conspiracy might leak to Buckingham's friends. On February 25 he laid all his evidence before the King and the Privy Council.

His Majesty was appalled; this was more than he had sus-

pected. Worst of all was the letter commissioning Heydon
to cast the King's nativity. By an ancient statute, to draw
up a royal horoscope was an overt act of treason, punish-
able by death for the astrologer and his patron. A horoscope always included a prediction on the life span of the
subject, often the exact date and hour of his death. It would
be extremely dangerous to let disaffected men know when
their King was due to die; they might see to it that the prediction came true, blaming a murder upon the stars. Moreover, although astrologers could not control the actions of
heavenly bodies, men bent on treason could control astrologers! King Charles had no faith in horoscopes, but he
had a healthy fear of treason.

The next day Arlington wrote gleefully to the Duke of
Ormonde (who already had some inkling of the plot), "By
the taking of a seditious astrological (Dr. Heydon by
name) before the Parliament rose, we discovered some dangerous and foolish practises the said doctor had with the
Duke of Buckingham, for which his Majesty, without naming the cause, declared yesterday in council that he sus-
pended him from the council, with intention to take from
him likewise his place of Gentleman of the Bedchamber,
and putting him out of all commissions [Lord Lieutenant,
Justice of the Peace, etc.]. Afterward he commanded me
likewise to draw up a warrant for the seizing him by a
Serjeant at Arms and putting him a close prisoner in the
Tower, which is now under execution, though not known
abroad yet." Orders were sent out also to seize Henry
North, the Yorkshire informer, "for treasonable practises,"
and commit him to the Tower.[10]

Even as Arlington was writing, Serjeant John Barcroft

was riding for Worthrop with his mace across his saddle and two men at his horse's heels. The plan was to arrest Buckingham before any of his friends at Court could give warning, and Barcroft rode so fast that by the evening of February 28 he was only five miles from Worthrop. Then, in the gathering gloom, a six-horse coach attended by half a dozen outriders overtook him. As Barcroft learned later, Lady Shrewsbury was seriously ill at Deene; the Duchess of Buckingham "had watched the night before" at her bed-side, and now was on her way home. One of her attendants recognized Barcroft, suspected the significance of the mace he bore, and warned the duchess. Her Grace let down the coach window to greet the Serjeant; then she ordered full speed ahead. The coach rumbled off at a pace too great for Barcroft's tired horses and got to Worthrop half an hour before him.

When he arrived, he found the foregates barred and the mansion shut up like a fortress. For nearly an hour he parleyed with Brian Fairfax, who stoutly denied that the duke was within, insisted that the duchess had gone to bed, and flatly refused to admit the Serjeant. Since Fairfax was backed by dozens of armed servants, Barcroft was forced to give up and ride to nearby Stamford for the night. Soon after he left, Buckingham made his escape.

At eight the next morning Barcroft returned, reinforced by the mayor of Stamford, two aldermen, and a justice of the peace. This imposing army was admitted without question, but my lord duke had flown. Angrily Barcroft demanded to see "the duke's closet" and all his papers. Fairfax (a humorist) showed him to "the house of office"—an inside privy—where there was "a close-stool and above a thousand of billets"—sheets of paper. At last the furious Serjeant found the duke's study, but all his papers had been cleaned out except "some tunes pricked on several papers . . . with the duke's own hand."

All that day the Serjeant wandered about the country-side, hearing of his quarry now and then, but never catching up with him. At last, convinced that the duke had gone to London, he gave up. The next day he set out for town to tell my Lord Arlington.[11]

Bucks had fled because of caution, not a guilty conscience. He was well aware that his ministerial enemies could clap him into the Tower on trumped-up charges, deny him the right of habeas corpus, and keep him locked up indefinitely. Since he had no notion of what he was charged with, it was only wisdom to evade the King's officers as long as possible and try to find out what was going on. Therefore he drove to London as fast as his coach could travel. Once there, he took refuge in the house of a friend, Sir Henry Belasyse, got in touch with his other friends, and set inquiries afoot.

All the next week, rumors of Buckingham's disgrace ran about Whitehall. On March 8 the King published a proclamation commanding Bucks to surrender himself and answer charges that he had "held and maintained secret correspondencies by letter and other transactions tending to raise mutinies in His Majesty's forces and stir up sedition among his people." Buckingham's enemies had a gay time at his expense. One of them wrote to Ormonde, "this affair, if in print, were superior to all the ridiculous characters my lord of Bucks described in his play called The Fopps [*The Chances*]." The Court was especially amused at the idea of the great duke consorting with a mean little astrologer and having him cast the King's nativity. Perhaps it was all one of the duke's jests, "if there be jesting with the statute law, though not of long time put in execution." [12]

Jest or earnest, everyone was sure that Buckingham was done for as a courtier. The King gave his Bedchamber place to John Wilmot, Earl of Rochester, and his lieutenancy in Yorkshire to Richard Boyle, Earl of Burlington. The Ormonde family was so certain of Buckingham's doom that they feared his estate, as usual in cases of treason, would be confiscated by the King. Therefore they sent the Earl of Arran posthaste to England, so that he could "in behalf of his wife [Buckingham's niece] humbly put His Majesty in mind of her innocence and of the merit of her father"—James Stuart, Duke of Richmond.[13]

While the vultures gathered, Buckingham's friends ran around in circles; his wife came to town and took lodgings in St. Martin's Lane; and from the Tower (on March 13), Heydon wrote and smuggled out a letter to Stephen Montague, Buckingham's auditor. Incoherent and hastily scrawled, it bears the mark of a brave spirit, if no great intelligence:

"Mr. Montague, my service, salute you, wishing health. The false reports raised against my lord I will prove to be devices of a villain that was hired to inform against him, and a plot to put me first into the Tower, and forge letters under his and my name corresponding, &c. My lord duke is wronged, and with my life I will let the world know it. I pray, let not my lady be afraid, for when his Majesty hears the truth the duke will be restored to more favor than ever, and his enemies ashamed of their actions. Let me hear your answer by this or another faithful person, for the duke is most unjustly abused and I am undeservedly a close prisoner, tortured in the dungeon to speak their desires against him; but death shall close up the scene before I will be found to damn my soul for a witness to their wicked designs. My last word shall be, the duke is innocent, for I know nothing against him!"

Montague was a cautious man, newly appointed to his post, and not yet as fanatically devoted to his master as most of Bucks' servants were. Heydon was "a close prisoner"—i.e., kept incommunicado—and it was dangerous to write to him or even receive a letter from him. Nevertheless, his letter was the first real clue to the conspiracy, and the duke must have it. With commendable caution, then, Montague made a copy of the letter and delivered it to a jailer at the Tower. Having done his duty as a citizen, he carried the original to the duke's secretary, Martin Clifford, at his lodgings in the Savoy.

Eventually the jailer's report reached Arlington, who summoned Montague to Goring House for an explanation. (Afterward Montague wrote out a word-by-word account of the interview.) Arlington, peevish at missing the original of the letter, was very severe with the auditor. It was important for his plot that Heydon be kept from communicating with Buckingham.

"What is the reason you did not bring the original to me or some other of the Secretaries?" he demanded.

"Under favor, my lord," said Montague, "I did look upon it that it mought one day be of use to my lord duke, and truly, for my part, I was glad to see the contents of it."

"Why, what was the contents of it?"

"It tended to vindicate my lord."

"As if a guilty or condemned person's words or writings can avail to clear another," Arlington snapped.

"My lord, I humbly conceive that when a person is sent to prison it is in order to a further trial. And I did not look upon Heydon as yet as a guilty or condemned person, and therefore did hope his words or writings mought avail my lord duke."

"You must teach me!" said Arlington angrily, and proceeded to berate Montague, threatening him with dire punishment for corresponding with a prisoner. But it was an idle threat, and he got no change out of the sturdy auditor. Anyway, the letter was now out of Arlington's reach. Clifford (said Montague) had turned it over to one of the duke's noble friends, either Charles, Lord Buckhurst, or Aubrey de Vere, Earl of Oxford.[14]

Unfortunately, rattle-brained Heydon had mentioned no names. Who was the villain hired to inform against him? Fighting fire with fire, the Buckingham party seems to have hired another informer, "Captain" John Gryce, a talkative fellow who was out of employment at the moment. It took Gryce some weeks of digging around before he found a clue. The master plotter, Leving, had gone off to Yorkshire to hunt for Buckingham, taking with him William Frear, who was certainly in the plot by now, despite his later denials. In April the two rascals talked big to the postmaster of Bradford, Yorks, offering to pay for information leading to the duke's arrest. "They wanted not for money," they said. "If they did, Sir Roger Langley would supply them." (In August, 1667, the postmaster wrote out a deposition about them, but by then the episode was ended.) [15]

While his friends labored, Buckingham wandered about London, having a wonderful time. He always throve on excitement, and danger quickened his senses. He had a number of hiding places about the city, and whenever the Serjeants "came where he was known to have been but an hour before, he was gone from thence, or so concealed there that he could not be found." A master at disguise, he loved to roam the streets late at night. It was rumored that he had been "taken by the watch two or three times . . . but so disguised that they could not know him" and so let him go. [16]

His friends were doing their best to soften the King. They defended him so boldly that men came to say "the King believes better of him than formerly." If so, it was not much better. The King replied to one earnest solicitor by charging passionately that Bucks was "the cause of this continued war" with the Dutch, because he had so weakened the power of the government in Parliament. To an extent, the King was right. As warm weather came on, the Dutch Fleet sailed boldly forth, while the English ships, frozen by Parliament's parsimony, lay helpless and unready at anchor. [17]

Early in May (at a guess) Gryce found Middleton, the Irish informer. Now for a while we move half in the realm of speculation. Two women entered the picture: Mistress Fr. (for Frances) Damport and her daughter, also Fr. Damport. It is very likely that these two were the mother and older sister of Elizabeth Davenport (the name was often spelled Damport), the famous "Roxalana" of the Duke's

Theatre, who in 1662 became the mistress of Buckingham's friend, the Earl of Oxford. (Oxford had a son by her, and gave her an allowance.)

In 1667, Frances and Elizabeth Davenport (the sisters) were playing at the King's Theatre. The Dramatis Personae of Orrery's *The Black Prince* has "Valeria—F. Damport," and "A Lady—Betty Damport." Frances was not much of an actress; in 1668 Pepys recorded his pleasure that she had left the stage "to be kept by somebody . . . she being a very bad actor." Perhaps she was not too bad to play a rôle in a counterplot.

From an undated statement (probably written in 1673) by Mrs. Damport, the mother, we learn that Gryce brought Middleton to her house "with intention to make a match between her daughter [Frances] and the said Middleton." This sounds like a trick by Gryce and the Buckingham party to get Middleton to talk. If so, it succeeded. In the presence of Mrs. Damport, Middleton said "that he had received £100 from my Lord Arlington to bear witness against the duke for having the King's nativity cast by Heydon, and to testify that he heard the duke speak treason against the King and the government." He also implicated Frear, who, he said, had received £60 "for to join with him in bearing witness against the duke, and was promised £500 more when the business was effected."

Now we may imagine Captain Gryce and three of Buckingham's young friends—Lord Buckhurst, Sir Henry Belasyse, and Mr. Gervase Pierrepont—bursting in on Middleton one night at the Damports' with their swords drawn. The sight of so many naked blades was too much for the Irish informer; as the following deposition indicates, he hastened to retract his testimony: "The 19th of May, being about nine of the clock, Mr. Middleton was heard to say these words, (viz.) that he had been often and several times in the Duke of Buckingham's company, but never heard him speak anything prejudicial to the King or government, and that for his part, neither man nor woman, in public or private, had ever heard him speak anything against the Duke of Buckingham, nor would not, for he knew nothing of his concerns." [18]

The deposition was signed by the three gentlemen, Captain Gryce, Mrs. Damport, and her daughter Frances. Middleton himself failed to sign, probably because he could not write. No matter; the evidence of six credible witnesses was sufficient. However, his retraction was not, of itself, enough to clear Buckingham. In the seventeenth century, a man accused of a crime was considered guilty until he proved himself innocent. Bucks still had to disprove Leving's testimony and clear up the business of his supposed letters to Heydon. The next problem was to find Leving.

But the long arm of the law had fastened on that rascal and tucked him safely out of sight. Early in May, just to keep in practice, Leving and Frear had robbed a house near Leeds. Leving was caught red-handed and sent to York Castle, whence he wrote despairing letters to Arlington, protesting that his theft had netted him only 4s/6d. (the theft of 5s or more constituted a felony). Frear escaped to London and the protection of Lord Arlington. The Secretary was in something of a quandary; his tame rogues had run wild. At last he had Frear arrested on the charge of "seditious practices" (to protect him against a Yorkshire indictment), and ordered Leving brought down to Newgate, where he too would be safe from the jurisdiction of the Yorkshire courts. The evidence of informers under indictment for robbery would be tainted enough, but if they were convicted it would be worthless.[19]

Buckingham continued to dodge about London, but he was wearying of the game and worried by the rumors which reached him. He heard that "the King resolved to proceed against him for his life, and that his estate was begged and given"—to the Earl of Arran. Moreover, he was missing all the fun. The Dutch war had grown hot again; the militia of every county had been alerted against forays and a possible invasion, and here was the great duke, who should have been heading an army in Yorkshire, a fugitive from the law! Affairs reached their climax on June 12 when the Dutch Fleet sailed insolently up the Medway, broke a chain across the river, burned a squadron of helpless ships of war, and withdrew unscathed, towing one great ship, the *Royal Charles*, behind them. All England burned with shame and cursed the Clarendon ministry.

The impatient duke decided to come out of hiding. First, however, he sent Martin Clifford to ask Lord Clarendon for an interview. The stiff-necked chancellor refused to see Bucks and suggested that he give himself up and then petition the King for pardon. Bucks rejected this advice and sent Sir Robert Howard to the King with a letter containing protestations of innocence and a plea for an audience; he was sure that he could talk himself out of the charges against him. But the royal dignity could not be flouted by a subject who refused to obey proclamations. For the King to give Buckingham an audience would be, as Clarendon said, "a thing dishonorable to him after so long a contest."[20]

Nevertheless, the King was showing signs of being bored by the whole affair, and Arlington was deeply worried. He had heard of Middleton's retraction and had sent out an order for his arrest, but the provost marshal who received the order was at Gravesend, looking out for Dutch invaders. Then came news that Middleton had smallpox, and his life was despaired of. Arlington began to run for cover, assuring Buckingham's friends "that he knew nothing of the business, but that the whole prosecution was made by the information and advice of the Chancellor!" [21]

On June 26 a proclamation appeared, calling Parliament to meet a month later. Now, with the power of his party to aid him and, if need be, pluck him out of the Tower, Bucks decided to take a chance. First he sent the King a flamboyant letter:

> *"May it please Your Majesty,*
> *Though I could not but be afraid of your Majesty's anger, yet I dare trust your kindness, and now I understand that your Majesty thinks your honor is concerned in my surrender, I will have no longer consideration of myself, since that comes in question; but as soon as I am in a posture fit to appear before your Majesty I shall come and throw myself at your feet, to be disposed of as your Majesty shall think fit."*

Then he surrendered himself to Secretary Morice.

His journey to the Tower was a triumphal procession. On the way, he stopped to dine at the Sun Tavern in Bishopsgate Street with a jolly company: Lords Buckhurst, Rivers, and Vaughan, and Tom Porter, the playwright. They were all "mighty merry," and Bucks sent word to the Lieutenant of the Tower, "that he would come to him as soon as he had dined." A great crowd gathered outside the tavern, and after dinner the duke "showed himself with great ceremony from the balcony" to receive their applause. Then, in leisurely fashion, he ambled off to the Tower.[22]

Three days later he was "examined" by Lord Arlington, Secretary Morice, Sir William Coventry, and Sir Thomas Clifford. He was nonchalant and flippant, as if he found the procedure amusing. Arlington's plump face was serious; his conduct of the examination was a prize example of oily hypocrisy. So that he could ask his questions "in method," he had them all written out, and after each answer he turned gravely to his colleagues and said, "Write that down." He began by asking if Buckingham knew Heydon, and if the astrologer was "any relation" to him.

"What do you mean by relation, my lord?" said Bucks. "Do you mean whether he be akin to me or no?"

"No, my lord. If he were your footman we might call that a relation."

"Oh, then you mean whether he were my domestic servant or no?"

"Yes, that is the question."

"Why then, to that question I answer no."

"Write that down," said Arlington to his colleagues. Then, "Did Your Grace ever trust him with anything?"

"Well, my lord," said Bucks, "I don't know what you take him to be, but the first time I saw him I took him to be so silly a fellow that I would not think it fit to trust him with a tallow candle."

"Pray," said Arlington to the others. "Write down all this likewise." He inquired then about a correspondence between Buckingham and Heydon, and touched delicately on the troubles with the seamen at the time of the duke's last stay in the Tower in December, 1666, saying after each answer, "Write that down." Then he came to the key question, "Did Your Grace ever write a letter to him?"

"I have heard that I writ a letter to him," said Bucks, "and that your lordship has it. But if I were to die this minute, and were to be forgiven my sins upon condition of speaking truth in this matter, I should swear that I never did write to him, and I am so confident of this that I will lay your lordship £100 if you please that I never did."

Arlington, always cautious, ignored the offer. He asked one more useless question and then concluded everything with a humble offer from his "brethren" and himself "to do Your Grace any service with his Majesty that you shall please to command us." On this happy note the examination ended, and Buckingham was ushered back to his apartments.[23]

Arlington was in no haste to bring matters to a head; he would gladly have kept the duke in the Tower forever. While Buckingham fretted, his friends brought pressure to get him a hearing before the Privy Council. Sir Robert Howard, always positive, declared passionately that "he would be content to lose his head if he did not prove that the witnesses examined against the duke were bribed and perjured." Even Lady Castlemaine, moved more by hatred of Clarendon than love of her cousin Buckingham, interceded for him with the King. With her usual violence, she told His Majesty that he was a fool, and that "if he was not a fool he would not suffer his businesses to be carried on by fellows that did not understand them, and cause his best subjects, and those best able to serve him, to be imprisoned." Although the long-suffering King retorted by calling the great lady "a whore, and a jade that meddled with things she had nothing to do with at all," he agreed to give the duke a hearing.[24]

On July 8, Buckingham, dressed with his usual splendor, was brought before the Privy Council. The King presided at the head of the table, his heavy face set in sardonic lines. Since the hearing was open to the privileged, several malcontent members of Parliament stood along the walls to see that their leader had fair play.

Middleton, the chief witness, had died just two days earlier, and Arlington was too uncertain about Leving and Frear to bring them forward at this time. All he had to offer, then, was an accumulation of paper evidence. The attorney general read the charges, the examinations of Heydon and the "witnesses," and the letters said to have passed between Bucks and Heydon. Throughout the hearing, Buckingham "did carry it very submissively and pleasingly to the King, but to my Lord Arlington, who do prosecute the business, he was most bitter, and sharp, and very slighting." Accused of the crime of popularity-hunting, he retorted, "Whoever was committed to prison by my Lord Chancellor or my Lord Arlington could not want being popular."

Bucks denied "most of the particulars contained in the examinations," and evidently the Council believed him. He admitted acquaintance with Heydon, who "came often to him, and pretended skill in horoscopes but more in distillations, in which the duke delighted and exercised himself." Yes, he had received some begging letters from Heydon, but not those now read in his presence. Certainly he had never written to the astrologer; he looked upon him "as cracked in the brain and fit only to be laughed at." Poor, faithful Heydon!

At last the mysterious letter—"in the duke's own hand" —commissioning Heydon to cast the King's horoscope, was produced and shown to Buckingham. After one quick glance he said to the King, "Sir, this is none of my hand, and I refer it to Your Majesty whether you do not know this hand." The King took the letter, somewhat shaken by the duke's confidence. If it was not his hand, whose was it? "Why," said Buckingham, "it is my sister of Richmond's, some frolic or other of hers of some certain person; and there is nothing of the King's name in it, but it is only said to be his by supposition." The King took a second look, and then, "much out of countenance," agreed that he had been mistaken, "and confessed that it was the duchess's hand." [25]

With this the whole case against Buckingham collapsed. The carefully constructed plot came to a trivial and—for both sides—an unsatisfactory end. Arlington was cheated of his victim; Buckingham was cheated of a trial by jury, a ringing "not guilty," and the cheers of the multitude. Instead he was sent back to the Tower to await the King's pleasure.

What was in the famous letter and how the informers got hold of it are still unsolved mysteries. It was not unusual to send unaddressed, unsigned letters by a messenger and to write them in a style so cryptic as to baffle the uninitiated reader. Buckingham's sister, the Duchess of Richmond and Lennox, was a Lady of the Bedchamber to the Queen Mother. She flitted back and forth across the Channel, consorting with the great on both sides of the water, and was always happily mixed up in some harebrained intrigue or other. Probably she wrote her brother a vague, confused letter about some nameless "certain person," and the letter fell into the hands of Leving and his pals. Recognizing the similarity of hands (Bucks and his sister had been taught by the same tutor), they forged Heydon's name on it and passed it off as a letter from Bucks to Heydon. The whole affair is very obscure; even Buckingham seems to have been confused by it. Some years later, reverting to this episode, he said to the House of Commons, "I had a letter from a sister of mine, which was alleged one from [to?] Dr. Heydon, a conjurer, but through his name any man might see Richmond and Lennox." Perhaps the conspirators did some erasing before committing forgery.[26]

Because there was no formal trial, the stain on Buckingham's reputation was never wiped out; for years his supposed association with astrologers was a subject for jesting. But for some of the lesser actors the play was no comedy. Middleton was dead. Leving was sent back to Yorkshire to stand trial, but Arlington gave him a warrant for a pardon if he was found guilty of felony. He died under suspicious circumstances on or about August 5, 1667, in York Castle. Frear was sent to York later, in spite of his plea that he would be in danger of being "poisoned by the same that did it to Mr. Leving." He too was pardoned, although he remained in prison during most of the autumn. (On October 24 he told one of Buckingham's agents the whole story of his association with the plot.)

The date of Heydon's release from the Tower is not recorded. In 1668, some time after he was freed, he wasted much time and eloquence pleading for the return of his confiscated valuables. Then he married the widow of Nicholas Culpepper, the famous herbalist, and became a respectable citizen. As for the bit players—Heaven alone knows what happened to Henry North, the Yorkshire informer; Joan Chidley, Heydon's landlady; and the poor sailors arrested with Heydon!

Buckingham was released on July 14. Burning for revenge against the ministers who had caused him so much trouble, he hastened to St. Martin's Lane, where his faithful wife awaited him.[27]

V

EXIT THE HUSBAND
1667–1668

FOR SOME TIME after Buckingham's liberation a variety of affairs kept him too busy to plan his vengeance. He was still officially in disgrace—not for plotting treason, but for refusing to obey the King's proclamation. For a while he was occupied moving his family from St. Martin's Lane to Wallingford House, preparing for the coming session of Parliament, and working to get back his posts and commissions. And, of course, he had to see Anna-Maria as soon as possible—probably for the first time in nearly six months. Fortunately, there was nothing for him to do in Yorkshire. The Dutch war had dwindled to a series of skirmishes, and peace negotiations were under way at Breda.

On the afternoon of July 20 Bucks took his wife and Anna-Maria to the Duke's Theatre. The two ladies were quite good friends by now, the duchess (unless we assume that she was deaf and blind) making a virtue of iniquity.

The three sat together in a box, and, by ill chance, Harry Killigrew sat right next door to them. Still out of favor at Court because of his attack on Lady Castlemaine, Killigrew was bitter and frustrated, ready to discharge his venom at the first opportunity. When he saw Lady Shrewsbury with Buckingham he let loose his malice in "abusive eloquence" loud enough to be heard all over the theatre. Buckingham gave him a hard look; Killigrew "made mouths" and "spake scurvy language at him," mingled with slurring comments on Lady Shrewsbury. Quietly Bucks "told him he might govern his tongue and his face better."

The soft answer increased Killigrew's wrath. Spying Lord Vaughan in the pit, he left the box, sought him out, and asked him to carry a challenge to the duke. Vaughan refused. Still burning, Mad Harry returned to his box and, without warning, struck Buckingham twice over the head with his sheathed sword. Then he ran away "most nobly over the boxes and forms, and the duke after him, and cut him well-favoredly, he crying, 'Good, Your Grace, spare my life,' and fell down, some say to beg for his life, but certainly the duke kicked him." The house was in an uproar, the duchess "swounded," Lady Shrewsbury was "hugely frighted," and Buckingham lost his blond periwig in the scuffle.

Killigrew was not seriously hurt. When he came to his senses and realized what he had done, he saw no safety except in flight. He begged one of the undersecretaries of state for the loan of thirty pounds—"which if not given will be followed with a jail and a million of other miseries" —and then fled to France. The King ordered that "when taken he should be sent to the Tower, and that he should be forever banished from Court." Three months later, in a more forgiving spirit, His Majesty wrote to his sister, Henrietta, Duchess of Orleans, in France,

"For Harry Killigrew, you may see him as you please, and though I cannot commend my Lady Shrewsbury's conduct in many things, yet Mr. Killigrew's carriage towards her has been worse than I will repeat; and for his démêlé with my Lord of Buckingham, he ought not to brag of [it], for it was in all sorts most abominable. I am glad the poor wretch has got a means of subsistence, but have one caution of him, that you believe not one word he says of us here, for he is a most notorious liar and does not want wit to set forth his stories pleasantly enough." [1]

Buckingham came out of the brawl with heightened reputation and much praise for having behaved "as became a man of honor." The only serious damage was to Lady Shrewsbury's battered reputation. The gossips remembered Killigrew's luscious descriptions of her "secret charms" and rightly blamed the quarrel on his jealousy of the duke. Although Anna-Maria's kinsmen (and presumably her tongue-tied husband) were greatly "offended," Killigrew was soon beyond the reach of their timid swords. It was all very well for them to bluster and brag, but, with all the strength of her passionate nature, Anna-Maria wanted revenge.

Buckingham had neither time nor inclination to pursue and punish his old drinking companion. Parliament met on July 24 and four days later was prorogued to October. On July 28 Abraham Cowley died at his home at Chertsey.

There can be no doubt of the duke's love for his old friend. Some time later he wrote in his Commonplace Book, "If those that are dead retain any sense of their friends below, he dies still by my grief, as I die continually by his death"— a conceit worthy of the great poet himself. Cowley's body was carried to Wallingford House where it lay in state for a week. Nearly a hundred "coaches of noblemen and persons of quality" followed the hearse to Westminster Abbey, where Cowley was buried next to Chaucer and Spenser. Buckingham, who paid all the costs of the splendid funeral, erected a marble monument to his friend, and King Charles, who had neglected the living poet, was heard to say that "Mr. Cowley had not left a better man behind him in England." Praise costs so little.[2]

As soon as possible, Buckingham set out to find and punish the ringleader of the conspiracy against him. He was morally sure of Arlington's guilt. If he could have read Leving's letters—safely hidden in official files—he would have been positive. While his agents searched England for the informers Leving and Frear, Bucks sought the help of his enemy, Lord Clarendon. He asked the Chancellor "to deal freely with him concerning the Lord Arlington, whom he knew to be an enemy of both of them." It was his intention, he said, to have Clarendon "examined upon that conspiracy." Clarendon refused to be questioned about anything said or done in Council and assured the duke that to the best of his knowledge there had been no conspiracy, "nor did he know that the Lord Arlington had done anything in the prosecution but what was according to the obligation and duty of his office."

From anyone else this could have been taken at face

value as the statement of an honest, if not very bright, official with nothing to hide. To Buckingham, blinded by his long hatred of the Chancellor, it sounded suspicious. Could it be that Clarendon was the mastermind? Most of his friends thought so, and the malcontents in Parliament were quite positive. In a satire written at this time, the republican poet, Andrew Marvell, took a fling at Clarendon:

> *See how he reigns in his new palace culminant,*
> *And sits in state divine like Jove the fulminant.*
> *First Buckingham, that durst 'gainst him rebel,*
> *Blasted with lightning, struck with thunder, fell.*

There was also the damning fact that the Earl of Burlington, who still held Bucks' Lord Lieutenancy, was connected with Clarendon through the marriage of one of his daughters to the Chancellor's younger son.

Wily Lord Arlington fed Buckingham's suspicion with flattery and lies. (This was in August; Leving was dead, and Frear, whose testimony gave convincing proof of Arlington's guilt, was not located until October 24.) Repeating his assertion that "the whole prosecution was made by the information and advice of the Chancellor," Arlington avowed his own friendship for Bucks, desired to be of service to him, and begged his protection against their common enemy, the Chancellor! Sometime earlier Clarendon had refused to be present at the examination of witnesses against the duke—because, he said, if the matter ever came to a trial before the House of Lords, he would have to preside as High Steward. Now, leaving out the context, Arlington told Bucks "that the Chancellor had said he was to be High Steward at the trial of the duke"—as if it were all prearranged.

Most of Buckingham's friends were Clarendon's bitter enemies—among them Lords Rochester and Vaughan, Sir Thomas Osborne, Sir Robert Howard, and Sir George Savile, whose uncle, Sir William Coventry, was passionate in his hatred of the Chancellor. These men were far more interested in destroying Clarendon than in helping Bucks find the truth about the conspiracy against him. Between their urgings and Arlington's suave lies, Buckingham, half-convinced, was brought to a reluctant and doubtful friendship with Arlington and set up as the leader of the anti-Clarendon faction.[3]

The old Chancellor's fall was long overdue. Arrogant and domineering, he had few supporters left. His best friend, Lord Treasurer Southampton, had died in May, 1667. His next best friend, the Duke of Ormonde, was in Ireland. Only his son-in-law, the Duke of York, was powerful enough to help him. The other ministers were happy to see him made the scapegoat for all the failures of the last two years: the bloody, expensive, and indecisive war with Holland, the record of waste and incompetence in the Fleet, and the shame of the Medway disaster of June 12.

The King himself was honestly glad to get rid of his "schoolmaster." Time and again, Clarendon had interfered with his pleasures: women, plays, sauntering, talking, and hunting. Charles loved his ease and his hobbies; he was happier in a laboratory or a lady's boudoir than in a council chamber. Clarendon was forever demanding that he pay attention to "business," which he hated, and lecturing him sternly on his duties as a king. The story goes that once upon a time the King saw a notorious muckraker in the pillory and learned that he was being punished for libeling Lord Clarendon. "Od's fish!" cried his Majesty, "Why did not the fool go on libeling of me? He must now certainly suffer for libeling this great man."[4]

On August 30, the King relieved Clarendon of his symbols of office and threw him to the hungry House of Commons. Sir Orlando Bridgman, a staid lawyer, replaced him, with the lesser title of Lord Keeper.

The broken-hearted ex-Chancellor retired to his new mansion (the mob called it "Dunkirk House" in reference to supposed bribes for the sale of Dunkirk to France) and sat there groaning over the King's ingratitude and his own gout. His intention, he said, was to retire to the country and live a private life, but he was too proud to go at once. His enemies, moved both by hatred and the fear that he might return to power, talked of impeaching him for high treason as soon as Parliament met. All through September Clarendon waited for the other shoe to drop.

On September 15 Arlington and Sir William Coventry brought Buckingham "to a reconciliation with His Majesty." A few days later the King declared in Council that "upon the humble submission made by the Duke of Buckingham" he was pleased to restore him to his places in the Council and the Bedchamber. "Whereupon his grace was immediately called in, and having kissed his Majesty's hand, took his place at the board accordingly." That night he waited on the King at dinner, more in favor than ever. As Bucks wrote, in his usual ironic vein, "A Prince's anger is like thunder: it clears the air a great while after."[5]

However, there was one cloud in Buckingham's sky. For nearly two months Anna-Maria had been sulking, complaining about that wretch Killigrew, and suffering from the slings and arrows of outrageous gossip. On September 16, accompanied only by her maid, she "took to her heels, and they say is gone either into a monastery [i.e., a convent] or to kill Harry Killigrew herself, since none of her relations will undertake it." According to another gossip, she left three letters in her bedroom, "one for her lord [Shrewsbury], one for her mother, and one for her ghostly father. From which some conjecture that she had taken up a resolution of retiring from the world and living a recluse." Although Lord Shrewsbury sent messengers to Dover and Rye "to stop her if possible," she crossed safely to France, where she remained for the next eight months in a convent—probably with the Benedictine nuns at Pontoise, fifteen miles from Paris. Luckily for Killigrew, she did not come upon him in Paris.[6]

Did Buckingham have anything to do with Anna-Maria's flight? The Earl of Shrewsbury seems to have thought so. But, five years later, in a formal statement made upon his honor, the duke declared that "it is generally known that the Countess of Shrewsbury parted from her husband because she thought her honor was not vindicated upon one who had done her a public and barbarous affront"—i.e., Killigrew. Slander must be promptly washed out in blood, otherwise, in the eyes of the world, it was not slander but truth! Since Anna-Maria's husband refused to pursue Killigrew and slay him, the injured wife was forced to retire from the world until the gossip blew over. A convent was an ideal retreat: it covered a multitude of sins.

Two items in Bucks' Commonplace Book suggest that he knew of her plans and disapproved. One is a drily cynical remark, "My mistress is going to sea; I would find out somebody to insure her." The other is a rather bad poem addressed to the ship which is to carry a bright and glorious "freight" on a voyage. The freight, of course, is the poet's lady-love, ironically described as the "pious wife." [7]

On the whole, Anna-Maria's absence during the autumn of 1667 may have helped Buckingham's rise in politics; her presence could have distracted him. He was the man of the hour, and the King, eager to make up for the past, "bid him ask what he pleased and he would grant it." Clarendon's dismissal had left a gap in the ministry, and Bucks was the logical man to fill it.

When the malcontent members came to town for the October session of Parliament, they sought out the duke, hailing him as a martyr to the malice of the ex-Chancellor. His popularity grew apace—even the mob loved him, said Pepys, "as one that will enquire into faults." Rashly, Buckingham boasted to the King that "Parliament was as wax in his hands, to be moulded at will." Charles took him at his word, reinstated him as Lord Lieutenant of the West Riding, and, best of all, called him to the cabinet, the Committee on Foreign Affairs. The other members were the two Secretaries; the Duke of Albemarle; the new Lord Keeper, Sir Orlando Bridgman; the Privy Seal, Lord Robartes; and, of course, the Duke of York—when he chose to appear. [8]

Buckingham's enemies (and after them, all historians) complained that he had neither policies nor principles and that he spent his time in riots and revelry. As one early historian put it, Bucks had the talent to be a capable minister, but he was "diverted from business by an extreme degree of lewdness and such a resignation to his pleasures as rendered him trivial, though born as fit as any for solid affairs." Even Sir John Reresby, once his friend, complained that the duke was unfit to be a minister "by reason of his giving himself up to his pleasures, that (turning the night into day and the day into night) he neglected . . . all sorts of business." [9]

It is true that in politics, as in everything else, Bucks kept his amateur standing. The professional officeholders—such men as Arlington, Ashley, Lauderdale, Sir Thomas Clifford, and Sir Thomas Osborne—were single-minded, methodical, and industrious, eager for prestige and pelf. With their offices came fat salaries and even fatter pickings. Bucks could have had almost any office he chose, but he detested routine, fretted at details, and hated regular hours and paper work. He wanted to make policy, not administer it. To become ever more popular he neglected his personal affairs and spent money lavishly, wooing the multitude; consequently he grew poorer as his rivals grew richer. As for his pleasures (which were always described as venereal), they were such follies as hunting, racing, chemistry, music, literature, witty conversation, and, of course, love.

He had two fundamental policies. Domestically he believed in and worked for liberty of conscience. Whatever the political values of this policy, his conviction was sincere. "Nothing," he wrote, "can be more anti-Christian, nor more contrary to sense and reason, than to trouble and molest our fellow Christians because they cannot be exactly of our minds in all the things relating to the worship

of God." He wondered, indeed, whether men who prac-
ticed religious persecution, "ought not justly to be called
anti-Christians." For the seventeenth century this was a
radical belief.[10]

Since Bucks was a minister without portfolio, no one
(including himself) knew the precise limits of his powers,
and everyone feared to inquire. For the moment, he was
the King's favorite, a fact sufficient in itself. Therefore,
toward the end of the year, he managed to get the execution of the laws against Nonconformists relaxed, much to
the joy of those persecuted people. As one of them wrote,
Bucks "was a man for liberty. Under him the Nonconformists in London were connived at, and people went
openly to their meetings without fear." As the dissenters
prospered they became "mighty high," expecting soon their
day of triumph and reckoning with their oppressors. In
part, at least, because of Bucks' influence, the hundreds of
fanatics in jail were gradually released, and the government
gave up its pleasant custom of jailing "plotters" without
trial and ignoring writs of habeas corpus.

One of the first of the fanatics to come blinking into the
sunshine was the duke's old Leveler friend, Major John
Wildman. Bucks took him into his service and nominated
him for an important commission. In Parliament, Sir John
Talbot (a kinsman of Lord Shrewsbury) "did fly out and
was very hot in the business of Wildman's being named,
and took notice how he was entertained in the bosom of
the Duke of Buckingham, and that it was fit to be observed by the House and punished." Bucks paid no attention; Wildman, he said, was one of "the wisest statesmen
in England." But even the powerful duke could not per-

suade Parliament to name Wildman a Commissioner for Accounts.[11]

Buckingham's foreign policy was unabashed nationalism. Once he stated it fully in a printed *Letter to Sir Thomas Osborne.* "The undoubted interest of England," he wrote, "is trade, since it is that only which can make us either rich or safe; for without a powerful navy we should be a prey to our neighbors, and without trade we could neither have seamen nor ships. From hence it does follow that we ought not to suffer any other nations to be our equals at sea, because when they are once our equals it is an even lay whether they or we shall be the superiors." Since the Dutch were England's trade rivals, it followed, quite simply, "that we must never give them leave to be our equals at sea."

Bucks admired Louis XIV of France and refused to take Louis' imperialism seriously, even though he was moving steadily into the Spanish Netherlands—Flanders. The fact that Louis thought of himself as divinely appointed to rule all Europe and to bring heretics back into the Catholic Church—dead or alive—bothered the duke not at all. France had a large army but a small navy; therefore she could not harm England. However, if France and Holland joined forces they could invade and conquer England. Obviously, then, it was to England's interest to ally herself with France, help crush Holland, get some of the spoils of Flanders, and become truly mistress of the seas. "My aim in this," Bucks concluded, "is that the interest of England may be thoroughly searched out; and I can truly say for myself I never yet had any design but what I believed was for the honor, the greatness, and the prosperity of this nation." [12]

Very statesmanlike, but not quite the whole truth. Over Buckingham lay always the shadow of his splendid father, Great Admiral of England, Lord General, Governor of the Seas and Ships, Master of the Horse, Lord Warden, Constable of Dover, Constable of Windsor, Chancellor of Cambridge University—plus a dozen other resounding titles. The son, too, longed for glory and titles, particularly military. In all his planning for England he included something for himself—the command of an English army on the continent. He had led men to battle in Flanders and England, and in Yorkshire he had shown that he could organize, drill, and lead whole regiments. Now he wanted the prestige and excitement of commanding an army under the eyes of all Europe.[13]

The autumn of 1667 was a whirlwind of affairs. Bucks had little time to think about Lady Shrewsbury, and, since the gossips coupled no other woman's name with his, it is likely that he was faithful in his fashion. If he corresponded with her, no letters have survived. Anyway, he had no use for love letters. "Love in writing is only compliment, and seems too much studied to be natural." "To write one's love well is flattery to others; to do it ill is wrong to ourselves." At least he knew where Anna-Maria was. If Lord Shrewsbury knew also, he gave no sign. During this period of crisis in national affairs, he never once took his seat in the House of Lords. He kept a brooding distance from public life.[14]

Although Bucks took a leading part in the action against Lord Clarendon, the burden of the attack was borne by his friends in the House of Commons. Chief among these were Edward Seymour; Sir Robert Howard; John, Lord Vaughan, who was heard to say, "God damn him, he would do my Lord Clarendon's business"; and Sir Thomas Osborne, who had sworn before Parliament met that "the Chancellor would be accused of high treason; and if he were not hanged, he would be hanged himself." Osborne, a Yorkshireman, was Buckingham's close friend and protégé; he was handsome, clever, capable, ambitious, and unscrupulous—an ideal politician.[15]

Politics was a violent profession in the seventeenth century. The House of Commons accused Clarendon of every conceivable crime and drew up articles impeaching him for high treason. With a nice sense of justice, the members agreed that "the Duke of Buckingham should be made High Steward for his trial." They had the active support of Arlington and the tacit consent of the King to their proceedings. But when they asked the Upper House to commit Clarendon to the Tower, a majority of the Lords refused on the ground that the charges were not specific enough. Buckingham dissented violently, and he and twenty-seven other peers signed a strong protest against the decision. The two Houses tied themselves up in wrangles over privilege until November 29, when Clarendon, on the advice of friends, slipped quietly out of the country.[16]

He left behind a long, prosy petition, blaming all the failures of his government on others. *His* advice had always been sound! Bucks, who figured in the document as one of those councilors who turned "all things serious and sacred into ridicule," delivered the petition to the House of the Commons with the flippant remark, "The Lords have commanded me to deliver to you this scandalous and seditious paper sent from the Earl of Clarendon. They bid me present it to you, and desire you in convenient time to send it to them again, for it has a style which they are in love with, and therefore desire to keep it." [17]

Parliament had no qualms about kicking a man when he was down. To make sure that Clarendon stayed abroad, both Houses promptly passed an act for "banishing and disenabling" him, and ordered his petition burned by the common hangman—a great loss to literature. Bucks made up for it with a poem "On the Late Lord Chancellor," written for the amusement of the wits who gathered at Wallingford House:

> *To ale and toasts and the mirth of a catch,*
> *And all thy witty disputes with the watch;*
> *To meat without napkins, and trenchers of bread,*
> *Which in many a quarrel has been flung at thy head;*
> *To a sack by thy side, and a knife in thy pocket,*
> *In an old sheath that stinks like a candle i'th' socket;*
> *To thy pleasant walks to Westminster Hall*
> *In a dirty Term, and thy jostlings for the wall;*
> *To thy breakfast in Hell, with black pots by the tally,*
> *Thy return in a sculler, and dinner in Ram Alley;*
> *To the glorious Court of the Prince d'Amour,*
> *Where, if thou pretendst to be a councilor,*
> *Thou wouldst, even there, be but weight and a clog—*
> *Return, return, thou now stale pettifog!* [18]

The sneer at Charles II as the "Prince d'Amour" was typical of Buckingham's attitude toward the King, an attitude which he rarely bothered to hide. All through November and December, Parliament, supposed to be wax in

Buckingham's hands, showed that it was made of a tougher substance, refusing to vote supplies, quarreling over privilege, baiting the Navy Office, and investigating the miscarriages of the late war.

On November 17, Pepys heard a secondhand, but plausible, story about someone who "did lately speak with the Duke of Buckingham about his greatness now with the King, and told him, 'But, sir, these things that the King do now in suffering the Parliament to do all this, you know are not fit for the King to suffer; and you know how often you have said to me that the King was a weak man and unable to govern, but to be governed, and that you could command him as you listed. Why do you suffer him to go on in these things?' 'Why,' says the Duke of Buckingham, 'I do suffer him to do this that I may hereafter the better command him.'" Ten days later a courtier told Pepys "how the King is now fallen in and become a slave to the Duke of Buckingham," who "do hate the very person of the King, and would, as well as will, certainly ruin him." [19]

"Hate" is too strong a word; "despise" would be more accurate. In fact, Buckingham was scornful not only of his old friend Charles Stuart but of kings in general—with the exception of Louis XIV of France, whom he considered a man of intellect and action. In the duke's opinion, King Charles, an ardent yachtsman, was better fitted to be a sailor than a ruler. See his little squib, "The Cabin-Boy,"

Nay, he could sail a yacht both nigh and large,
Knew how to trim a boat and steer a barge,
Could say his compass, to the nation's joy,
And swear as well as any cabin-boy;

But not one lesson of the ruling art
Could this dull block-head ever get by heart.
Look over all the universal frame,
There's not one thing the will of man can name
In which this ugly, perjured rogue delights,
But ducks and loitering, buttered buns and whites! [20]

To Buckingham, the tall, swarthy King seemed to be a very lazy fellow as he loitered through St. James's Park, feeding his ducks and swans, or lazed about Whitehall, caressing his mistresses—the "buttered buns." And his constant complaints about his need for money—"whites"—must have been irritating to the duke.

Buckingham greatly underestimated his master. Although Charles was indolent and easygoing, in the long run he turned out to be the shrewdest crowned head of his generation. Recalled to a nation torn by religious and political wars, and with revolution always simmering beneath the surface, he had found himself upon the most difficult throne in Europe. He learned very quickly that if he wanted to stay on that throne he must please his people, whatever his own desires, and that if he wanted his way he must get it by oblique devices and double-dealing. He was tolerant, humorous, and democratic, yet he longed to be an absolute monarch, simply because absolutism was the easiest way of ruling. Whenever possible, he left government to his ministers and amused himself watching them fight with each other. He trusted no one completely. "Od's fish!" he declared, "When rogues fall out, the master is like then to know the truth." [21]

Buckingham was cynical about kings and kingship. "A crown," he wrote, "makes many flatterers, but it is the greatest itself." "I wonder why men do not rather kill themselves to leave a crown, than others to gain it." And again, "Angels laugh to see a king proud, as much as kings might do to see a player so." Surely he had Charles Stuart in mind when he wrote, "He's our King, true, but he's not Fortune's; we're both equally her subjects," and "Kings, as they love treachery and hate the traitors, so they love virtue, but hate and fear the virtuous." [22]

Intellectually Buckingham was better gifted than the King, but whether he would have made a better ruler is a debatable question. Certainly he himself thought so. However, if he could not be a king, he could at least rule one. He had studied his royal master for years and thought he knew the ways to "command him"—by keeping him flattered, entertained, and occupied with venery. He and his witty friends—particularly Rochester, Buckhurst, and Sedley—could take care of the flattery and entertainment well enough. As for the venery—Lady Castlemaine was rapidly losing her attractions for her royal lover; he was getting tired of her tantrums. Because Bucks thought "a gaiety of humor would take much with the King, he engaged him to entertain [as mistresses] two players"—Moll Davis of the Duke's Theatre, a popular singer and dancer, and Nell Gwyn of the King's Theatre, "the indiscreetest and wildest creature that ever was in a Court." Each lady was highly successful in her new career, and both became permanent members of the royal seraglio.[23]

Unfortunately, Bucks could not rule Lord Arlington by such means. The austere Secretary lived a blameless life and was rarely amused. His chosen field of action was foreign affairs, and when the restless duke tried his hand at treaty-making, Arlington, unwittingly aided by France, soundly defeated him. True to his principles, Buckingham wanted an alliance with France in a war against Holland, a share in the Spanish Netherlands, and English supremacy on the seas. Arlington, like most of his countrymen fearful of France, wanted an alliance with Spain, and when a treaty with that fading power fell through he leaned toward Holland and neutrality. France, busily annexing the Spanish Netherlands, asked only that England remain neutral in any war between France and Spain, and proposed a treaty so one-sided that even Bucks was repelled. At this juncture Arlington proposed a defensive alliance with Holland and Sweden against France, and the cabinet, perforce, agreed. While Louis XIV waited smugly for England to come to terms, the famous Triple Alliance was completed (January 13, 1668), to the joy of most Englishmen. Not, however, of all; in the general jubilation Sir Thomas Clifford, a Privy Councilor and a coming man, gave voice to a growing belief, "Well, for all this noise, we must yet have another war with the Dutch before it be very long." [24]

Buckingham's ardor for war was soon to be tested on a private battlefield. For nearly four months Lord Shrewsbury had been silent and forgotten. Now, early in January, he sent Buckingham a challenge. His motives are far from clear. If, as Grammont said, he "resolved to have redress for his injured honor," why did he wait so long? According to Richard Baxter, the earl believed that Bucks was keeping Lady Shrewsbury secretly. Bucks himself said later that the earl, "upon a groundless jealousy of the duke's having been the cause of her going away, was much incensed against him." This sounds like the ostensible reason given in the challenge.

But, behind the scenes, Shrewsbury's kinsmen had been at work. Again according to Bucks, "If the earl had been left to the goodness of his natural disposition, and had not been exasperated by others" there would have been no challenge. This is likely enough. Shrewsbury was a quiet man of about forty-five (five years older than the duke), with no reputation as a fighter, and, to judge by his past behavior toward such men as Jermyn, "Northern Tom" Howard, and Harry Killigrew, no stomach for a fight.

But most of the Talbot clan belonged to the anti-Buckingham faction in Parliament and at Court. Sir John Talbot, Shrewsbury's chief second, was a belligerent man, Lord Arlington's close ally, and one of Bucks' bitterest enemies. Shrewsbury's other second was another kinsman, Bernard Howard, eighth son of the Earl of Arundel. Both seconds were reputed to be skilled swordsmen and valiant fighters. We shall never know which one of the bloodthirsty challengers decided that the duel should be fought in the unusual French style, with three men on a side; in a wild, hacking mêlée someone was sure to get hurt. It looks very much as if the earl's kinsmen had egged him on as much for political as personal reasons, planning to fight beside him and make sure that Buckingham was slain.

Bucks seems to have thought of the duel as a plot against his life. As the challenged man, he knew, of course, who his opponent's seconds were to be. Ordinarily he would have picked as his own seconds some of his intimate friends —Lords Buckhurst and Rochester, perhaps. This time he chose two professional fighting men: Sir Robert Holmes, a sailor; and Lieutenant William Jenkins, a soldier and said to be an ex-fencing master.

It was not easy to keep secret the preparations for so elaborate a duel. Pepys heard afterward that the King "had some notice of this challenge a week or two ago." (From Buckingham? Certainly he had nothing to gain by fighting Shrewsbury, and a great deal to lose.) The King told the Lord General, Albemarle, to "confine the duke or take security that he should not do any such thing as fight." Somehow the orders were confused; the King thought Albemarle was taking care of the matter; Albemarle thought the King was doing so; and the whole business, said Pepys, "fell between two stools." Was the confusion engineered by Buckingham's enemies? [25]

On the afternoon of January 16 the six men met in a close near Barn Elms, with only their servants to witness the battle. (It is not true, as the gossips of a later generation said, that Anna-Maria, dressed as a page, held her lover's horse, and that afterward "the duke slept with her in his bloody shirt." She was still hibernating in France.)

Stripped to their shirts, and with swords at the ready, the two parties lined up, Bucks against Shrewsbury, Holmes against Talbot, and Jenkins against Howard. At a given signal they came together with clashing blades. After a few quick passes, Buckingham ran Shrewsbury through the body, "from the right breast through the shoulder," and then turned (as the code permitted) to help Jenkins. With one hand Howard beat aside the duke's blade and "ran furiously upon Jenkins and killed him"—instantly. By that time Talbot had received a painful wound in his sword arm and was out of action. With Holmes and Buckingham against him, Howard gave over. He was unhurt; Holmes had a cut on one hand, and Bucks "only a scratch on his shoulder."

The servants carried Shrewsbury to a house in nearby Chelsea while the surviving duelists scattered. Five days later the earl was taken to Arundel House in the Strand. He was dangerously wounded, "and yet," said a newswriter, "the chirurgeons make no question of his life, saying his wound doth now well digest, and that his spitting blood was a good sign of his recovery." To the Duke of Buckingham, this was very good news indeed.[26]

VI

RIVALS AND RIBALDRY
1668

ONCE AGAIN Buckingham had to go into hiding while his friends labored to save him. This time, however, warrants were out for his enemies, too. In the eyes of the law, if a duelist was slain all involved in the duel were guilty of homicide, and Lieutenant Jenkins was certainly defunct. Bernard Howard fled to France, while the powerful family of Arundel clamored for his pardon. Sir John Talbot lay close until his friend Lord Arlington could help him. Holmes had strong friends in the Navy. Lord Shrewsbury, too weak to be sent to the Tower, was subject to arrest, but he had a host of noble kinsmen to plead his cause with the King. It was impossible to pardon one without pardoning all.

From the King's point of view, it was most important that Buckingham be saved. Parliament was due to meet again on February 6, and the duke had promised that the maverick House of Commons would vote the King the funds he needed. There was a knowing whisper that "His Majesty, in consideration of the high provocation given the duke"—as the challenged party—"will restore him to that capacity that he may sit at the meeting of the Parliament." Sure enough, on January 27 the King signed a warrant pardoning Bucks for "all treason, misprison of treason, felony, etc.," in the killing of Jenkins and assaults on Shrewsbury and Talbot, "whether or not they died or shall die." That night, muffled in his cloak and disguised by a jaunty black periwig, Bucks stole to the Duke of Albemarle's lodgings in Whitehall to receive his pardon. Within the next few days warrants for pardons were issued to all the other survivors of the battle. The Earl of Shrewsbury was showing such hopeful signs of recovery that he was permitted to sit up in bed, and his case was "left to the managery of only one chirurgeon, which before was committed to two."

On February 2, Buckingham "appeared publicly at Court." When Parliament convened four days later, he was in his customary seat, as brisk as ever. That afternoon Pepys was amazed to see him sitting openly in the pit of the Duke's Theatre with Lord Buckhurst, Sir Charles Sedley, and George Etherege. The occasion was the first performance of Etherege's new comedy, *She Would if She Could*. At Court the merry duke was as much in favor as if nothing had happened. Cynical King Charles was not disturbed by such trifles as adultery and homicide. As he wrote drily to his sister some time later, "I am sorry to find that cuckolds in France grow so troublesome. They have been inconvenient in all countries this last year." Od's fish! If a man loses his wife, must he try to lose his life, too?

Only the godly (and the anti-Buckingham party) were scandalized by the flood of pardons. The ungodly, who made and enforced the moral code of the day, maintained that men of honor must be ready to fight at the drop of an epithet. As gentlemen, they were above the law. On rare occasions, when a duelist was slain his killer was tried for manslaughter, but he was always acquitted by a jury of his peers. Time and again the King found himself obliged to pardon duelists on some flimsy excuse or other. This time he declared in Council that his reason was "the eminent services heretofore done" by the five survivors— a neat way to save face. However, he added sternly that "on no pretence whatsoever any pardon shall be hereafter granted to any person whatsoever for killing of any man, in any duel or rencontre, but that the course of the law shall wholly take place in all such cases." [1]

Since few people cared about the death of an obscure lieutenant in the Guards, it seemed, all through February, that the duel would be little more than a nine days' wonder. But on March 16 the Earl of Shrewsbury, supposed to be convalescent, surprised everybody by dying. Although a new pardon was promptly issued to Buckingham, the surgeons, concerned for their reputations, hesitated to state the cause of Shrewsbury's death and called for a post mortem. The body was opened by one of the King's own surgeons in the presence of seven eminent physicians, three surgeons, and "several noblemen and persons of quality." Unanimously the men of science testified "that the wound was perfectly cured, that no impostumed or congealed blood was found in all his lungs or the chest of his body," but that "his heart had grown very flaccid, and his liver and entrails much discolored and decayed." This was not a putup job to clear Buckingham of responsibility; the good doctors were honestly puzzled by Shrewsbury's death.[2]

Of course Shrewsbury lost a good deal of blood when he was wounded. Since the usual treatment for wounds was a course of cordials, plasters, purges, and daily bloodlettings, the wonder is not that patients died but that any recovered. The fact that Shrewsbury lived under such treatment for two months after his lung had been punctured is a tribute to his stamina. It may be said that he was a victim of medical malpractice. Nevertheless, Buckingham gave him the wound which led to his death; therefore Buckingham killed him.

Respectable people called it murder. The world laughs at a cuckold until he bestirs himself to avenge his honor. Then if he kills his wife's betrayer, it sympathizes with him and condones his action as mere manslaughter. However, by the curious logic of civilized man, if the betrayer kills the cuckold, even in a fair fight, he is guilty of murder. It was Buckingham's bad luck to be known in his own generation and to history as the man who murdered his paramour's husband.

His own reaction to the fatal affair is nowhere recorded, but he was not the man to cry over spilt blood. One ironic remark in his Commonplace Book may be an echo of the duel. "Strange perverseness of custom!" he wrote, "We go into open fields to kill men, and into corners to get 'em. We run to see 'em die, and are not suffered to be present at their birth. It is perhaps that Nature itself tells us 'tis better to die than to be born."

The immediate effect on the duke's career as a politician was very slight. In the political firmament he shone still as the Commons' favorite son, even though, after Shrewsbury's death, the crop-eared old ex-rebel, William Prynne, called upon his fellow members to confiscate the estates of "the duelists (Duke of Buckingham, &c.) towards his Majesty's supply." Bucks remained popular with the Nonconformists, perhaps because soon after the duel "he celebrated a day of humiliation and seeking of God" at Wallingford House. He could be all things to all people. He had his private cabal of fanatics—Major Wildman, Dr. John Owen (Cromwell's chaplain), and others of the same kidney. (It was rumored that when he met with them he told the King that he was "with his wenches," an excuse quite credible to the "Prince d'Amour.") Fearful men agreed that Buckingham "thinks to arrive to be another Oliver, and the fanatics expect a day of redemption under him." [3]

But Cromwell himself could not have controlled a House of Commons which was "in a most broken condition, nobody adhering to anything, but reviling and finding fault." Buckingham's power had begun to wane the moment he dropped his opposition tactics and became one of the King's ministers. Now his little knot of supporters in Commons—Howard, Vaughan, Hollis, Temple, Osborne, and Seymour—became known as "The Undertakers," because, said Pepys, "they did undertake to get the King money." The tightfisted country members "would not hear them in the House," and the Court sneered at them, "seeing that they cannot be useful to them, as was expected." Matters were not improved when Buckingham's earlier boast that Parliament was as wax in his hands became known. Arlington, said the duke indignantly, had betrayed him.[4]

The wax was tough and stubborn. Commons quarreled and investigated, passed angry resolutions, and talked endlessly. A bill to relax the laws against Nonconformists and bring them into the Anglican Church was lost before it was offered, even though (as a courtier wrote sarcastically) the bill "had the honor of having the Duke of Buckingham for its author." The King's request for £500,000 was trimmed to a grudging £310,000, a mere drop in the vast bucket of his needs. Towards the end of the session, the Commons came almost to blows with the Lords over the trivial business of a suit by a merchant named Skinner against the East India Company, both Houses claiming jurisdiction. Bucks addressed a conference of committees in his most eloquent style, alternating logic with wit, appealing to reason and self-interest, all to no purpose. On May 9 the disgusted King prorogued Parliament, leaving a dozen major problems hanging in mid-air.[5]

All this time Anna-Maria was in France. Taking advantage of her absence, her husband's family, headed by the autocratic Sir John Talbot, seized control of her children, had guardians appointed for the young earl, and withheld Anna-Maria's jointure—her share in her husband's estate. Early in May she returned to England to look after her affairs. Discovering that she was barred from the Court and "disowned by her friends and relatives," she turned to Buckingham for assistance. Truly, as he said, "no man of honor could have denied a lady in her condition." The fact that he was still besottedly in love with her may have had something to do with his quick response.

On May 15, Pepys heard that Buckingham had brought Lady Shrewsbury home with him to Wallingford House. According to the gossips, when the duchess protested that "it was not for her and the other to live together in a house," the duke replied, "Why, madam, I did think so, and therefore have ordered your coach to be ready to carry you to your father's." This, commented Pepys, "was a devilish speech, but they say, true, and my Lady Shrewsbury is there, it seems." [6]

Pepys was an honest recorder, but he held only one end of a piece of string; we can barely guess at the knots and ravelings its length might reveal. Why did Bucks bring Anna-Maria to Wallingford House instead of setting her up in lodgings? Were the vengeful Talbots pursuing her, to clap her into a convent? Lord Shrewsbury was survived by one brother, two half-brothers, two sisters, one half-sister, a dozen nephews and nieces, and hundreds of cousins —a proud and powerful clan, naturally resentful of the scandal Anna-Maria had caused. Why did Bucks send his wife off to stay with her father at Nun Appleton? Logically, he should have kept her at home to give the appearance of propriety to Anna-Maria's visit. Was he trying to save the duchess from the foul breath of scandal? Grammont tells us that Queen Catherine was one of those most horrified by Bucks' duel with Lord Shrewsbury and its aftermath of pardons. Both the Queen and the duchess were short, plump, and homely; both were childless; and each was neglected by her husband in favor of a beautiful mistress. "This sort of parallel in their situations," said Grammont, "interested the Queen in [the duchess's] favor." If the duchess received Anna-Maria at Wallingford

House, would she lose the Queen's friendship? To all these questions Pepys has no answer.

We do not even know how long Anna-Maria stayed with Buckingham. Within a few months, at least, she came to some kind of an understanding with the Talbots, received the full amount of her jointure, and set up an establishment in King Street, not far from Wallingford House. The Talbots seem to have kept control of her children—her step-daughter, Mary, about twelve; and her sons, Charles, now eight, and John, three—but Anna-Maria evidently had permission to visit them, take them for outings, and the like. Thereafter the wicked duke and his paramour paraded their love openly, "in defiance of the laws of God and man" (as the Talbots protested later), and without taking "the usual care of such offenders to cover actions of guilt and shame." Theirs was no hole-in-a-corner affair; they had a wonderful time.[7]

Anna-Maria's love for Buckingham is beyond question. At twenty-six, she was a most attractive widow—as much for her jointure as her beauty. In spite of scandal, she could easily have found a second husband, her peer in rank and wealth. Because of childbed fever, female mortality was high, and there was a steady supply of widowers shopping for rich young wives. For her lover, then, Anna-Maria gave up marriage, family, and reputation.

At the Court of Charles II, however, a lost reputation was hardly missed. Anna-Maria became one of the demi-mondaines who swarmed about Whitehall, living in the palace itself, in nearby King Street, or in Pall Mall, where "most of the great men's misses [i.e., mistresses] have houses." It seems that Queen Catherine refused to receive her, but the Queen's levees were dull affairs anyway. Anna-Maria was still welcome in the Banqueting Hall, the Stone Gallery, the Groom Porter's, and the King's chambers. There were still all the delights of the town: shopping at the New Exchange, theatres, balls at Whitehall, drives in the Ring at Hyde Park, boating parties on the Thames, trips to Windsor and Newmarket with Buckingham, and nights of merriment and love.

Although Anna-Maria remained on excellent terms with the patient Duchess of Buckingham, most of her friends were drawn from those kindred spirits who had renounced respectability for love. Living precariously as "great men's misses," and always fearful of rivals, these ladies could be friendly, yet each was jealous of her own preserve. One of Anna-Maria's friends was the King's little cockney mistress, Nell Gwyn. Once upon a time, as the story goes, Nell planned a party for the King's birthday at her house in Pall Mall. Anna-Maria hinted to the King that she would like to be invited. His Majesty passed the hint on to Nell, who refused, saying, "one whore at a time was enough for his Majesty." [8]

If Anna-Maria's situation ever bothered Buckingham, he gave no hint of the fact. For him, love was all, or, as he put it, "Love is like Moses' serpent: it devours all the rest." He never bothered his head about his own sins. Perhaps he thought of them as only venial now, since adultery was usually defined as "the lying of a single or married man with another man's wife, and not the lying of a married man with a single woman." Anna-Maria was now a single woman! Besides, the King and the Duke of York openly acknowledged their mistresses of gentle birth and title and made no bones about sleeping with strolling actresses and casual wenches. Surely George Villiers was the equal of any Stuart! Anyway, Bucks was too busy to worry about common fame and what it might say of him. He was forever plotting with his private cabal, improving his position, and, above all, entertaining the King.[9]

On Saturday, May 23, for example, the King and his retinue went to Lord Cornwallis's house (Culford, in Suffolk) after a great horse race at Newmarket. The next day (as Pepys heard later), "The Duke of Buckingham in the afternoon to please the King made a bawdy sermon to him out of Canticles, and . . . my Lord Cornwallis did endeavor to get the King a whore, and that must be a pretty girl, the daughter of the parson of the place, but . . . she did get away, and leaped off of some place and killed herself, which if true is very sad." The romantic fate of the parson's daughter strains credulity to the breaking point, but the bawdy sermon is likely enough. Bucks was one of those, said Clarendon, "whose wit consisted in abusing Scripture, and in repeating and acting what the preachers said in their sermons and turning it into ridicule." Perhaps the following mock sermon is not the one which amused the King on a Sunday afternoon in Suffolk, but it is a good sample of Buckingham's style.

Picture him in a great hall before a ribald group of courtiers, the King seated in their midst with a smile on his sensuous lips. Give the duke a black gown to hide his splendid clothing, and watch him imitate the nasal canting, eye-rolling, and sniffling of a Puritan preacher, one of those fiery fellows of whom he wrote, "At dinner they lay as fiercely about 'em as in the pulpit,"

Where close and home they to the matter fall,
And use and application make of all.[10]

With hands clasped and eyes turned up to heaven he announces his text: "A lewd woman is a sinful temptation, her eyes are the snares of Satan, and her flesh is the mousetrap of iniquity." Then he warms to his sermon:

"My text (beloved) I could divide into three and thirty parts, but for brevity's sake [I] shall confine myself to three only. First, a lewd woman is a sinful temptation, which is a positive truth. Secondly, her eyes are the snares of Satan, which is an undeniable certainty. Thirdly, her flesh is the mousetrap of iniquity, which trap (beloved) I fear you have all been caught in.

"I shall now explain at large what I mean by a lewd woman. I mean that unsanctified flesh which breaks through the confines of modesty and rambles through the brambles of impurity to graze on the loathsome commons of adultery and glut their insatiable appetites with the unsavory fodder of fornication till they've fired their tails like Samson's foxes to burn down the main-mast of that earthen vessel, man. . . .

"The conversation of a lewd woman is dangerous. She flatters with her tongue and charms with her tail till her pleasing dalliances, her languishing looks, and lecherous kisses [have] roused up the devil in the flesh. Then arises a hurly-burly in nature. He embraces the temptation in his arms, and casting her on a couch full of crackling infirmities, she tussles, he bustles, the couch shrieks out to discover the baseness they are acting. But, alas! it being in the tents of the wicked, nobody will hear till they have glut-

ted their souls with forbidden fruit and sowed their polluted seed amidst the thorns of abomination. . . .

"I shall now proceed to the second part of my text, viz.,
her eyes are the snares of Satan. That is (friends) they are
the deluding baits which first influence your frail natures
by their pinking and winking, their rambling and rolling,
their long and languishing motions. . . . [You become] so
enamored with this Satan's gimcrack that then 'tis 'oh! that
I could,' and 'Aw, that she should,' 'Yes, that I would!'
Thus are ye never satisfied till you are well pickled in the
abominable souse-drink of corrupt filthiness and come out
loathsome swine, fit for nothing but the company of that
polluted herd which the devil drove headlong down a steep
hill into the raging ocean, whether to wash them or to
drown them (beloved) I leave you to judge. . . . Therefore I say unto you, the eyes of a lewd woman are the
snares of Satan. They are the very allurements with which
he baits his mousetrap of iniquity; this is the ignis fatuus
that leads you into dark pits, stinking bottomless pools, and
filthy water-gaps of destruction. . . .

"So much for the first and second part of my text. I come
now to the third and last part, wherein I shall endeavour
to handle the mousetrap of iniquity, which I fear (beloved)
you have all been handling before me. . . . This trap of
Satan lies hid like a coney burrow in the warren of wickedness between the supporters of human frailty, covered over
with the fuzzes of iniquity which grow in the very cleft of
abomination. A lewd woman (beloved) I say is this warren
of wickedness; therefore let not her eyes entice you to be
fingering the fuzzes which grow in the cleft of abomination, lest Satan thrust you headlong into the mousetrap of

iniquity. Let not Satan with his cloven foot tread upon your tender consciences, but erect your actions upon the pedestal of piety, that Providence may put you in a posture of defense against the devil and all his accomplices.

"Thus shall I conclude all with my hearty wishes for the congregation here present: May Providence hedge you and ditch you with His mercy and send His dung-carts to fetch away the filthiness from among you. May your actions shine bright in the sunshine of piety, or else remain covered with the shadow of perfection that whatsoever you do may be much to your own praise and the glory of us double-refined Christians. Thus shall you live secure from the vile touch of the envious serpent, moated round about with the flowing tide of perpetual happiness. That you may bathe your sinful flesh in the streams of repentance! That you may enter undefiled into the congregation of the right-eous!"

To churchmen of all denominations this was blasphemy. To the King and his profane courtiers it was only a parody of the ranting style of a fanatic preacher—amusing and harmless, but not, of course, designed for the ears of ladies. To Bucks it was merely one of the many devices by which he sought to make himself indispensable to King Charles, a connoisseur of wickedness.

Bucks was well aware that, as a royal favorite, he stood in slippery ways. As he himself wrote, " 'Tis as dangerous to slip in a very smooth way as to stumble in a rough one." Since he was a minister supported by a very small faction, and without a coherent political party to head, his power came all from the King. Unlike a modern premier, he carried no ministry into office with him. He was only one of a number of ministers, each with his own axe to grind. None of them would have hesitated a moment to cut the duke's throat. He knew that he could remain in power only so long as he could amuse the King, frustrate his colleagues by fair means or foul, and persuade Parliament to grant funds. Above all, he could brook no rivals in the King's favor.[11]

All through 1668 he fought on several fronts at once. Partly for the prestige of a definite article—he wanted to be "the" something or other—and partly because his famous father had held the post, he negotiated with the Duke of Albemarle for his place as Master of the Horse. Technically the Master was only a head groom, in charge of the King's stables, horses, coaches, footmen, grooms, farriers, smiths, coachmen, and saddlers. Actually he was a Household official of great dignity, ranking with the Lord Steward (the Duke of Ormonde) and the Lord Chamberlain (the Earl of Manchester). He was ex officio a member of the Privy Council; he rode at the King's right hand in formal processions and accompanied him on all trips and "progresses" about the kingdom. (On one progress the agitated mayor of a small town addressed King Charles as "the father of his people." Behind his hand, Bucks whispered, "Of a good many of them!")

There was little connection between the importance of an office and the salary attached to it. The Chief Secretary of State was paid £1,850 a year (although Arlington had in addition a pension of £2,000 a year on the Excise). The Lord Steward was paid £100 a year ("and sixteen dishes each meal"); the Lord Treasurer received £4,000 a year, and the Master of the Horse £66/13s/4d, plus meals and lodgings at Whitehall. Of course, since the King spent thousands annually on his stable, some coins could stick to the fingers of a clever official, but Bucks was never very good at sleight of hand.[12]

Albemarle, tired and sickly, let it be known that his place was for sale. Buckingham's old enemy, Lord Ossory, coveted the post, but the duke outbid him. Late in May a deal was concluded at the enormous price of £20,000 (roughly $400,000 today), and on June 4 Bucks was sworn into office.

Now, with his numerous titles and places, Bucks could outrank anyone but the Duke of York. A test case came in September, when the King was "on progress" with a full train of grandees. At Bagshot, said Pepys, Buckingham "caused Prince Rupert's horses to be turned out of an inn [stable], and caused his own to be kept there, which the Prince complained of to the King, and the Duke of York seconded the complaint; but the King did overrule it for Buckingham." The King was right, of course: by long-standing precedent the Master of the Horse had first choice of stabling. Yet Bucks enjoyed humbling his enemies, of whom crusty old Prince Rupert was not the least. To Pepys, a typical man in the streets, it seemed that truly Buckingham did now "rule all." [13]

Pepys and his kind—the little men of government—had only glimpses of the battles raging about the throne. To become all-powerful, Bucks had to get his enemies out of office and his friends in. Since Arlington, Lord Ashley, and the Duke of York were also fighting to get or keep their friends in office, the ministry was constantly in a state of civil war, with the lines of alliance blurring and shifting week by week. No weapon was outlawed, and no quarter was given to a beaten foe.

Above everything else, Bucks, Arlington, and Ashley feared that old Clarendon, now eating the bitter bread of exile, might return to power. If he did so, they would be lucky to escape with their lives. Thus they found it expedient to join in opposition to the Clarendonians (or Yorkists), who were headed by the Duke of York and strongly supported by Ormonde, the powerful Lord Lieutenant of Ireland. It was a very uneasy alliance; for example, Bucks and Ashley wanted to oust Ormonde from his lord lieutenancy, while Arlington, a shifty customer, professed friendship for the Irish duke, and tried to play the canny neutral.

Warned that he was a prime target, Ormonde came to London in May to fight his enemies face to face. Buckingham "made him a visit upon his coming to town, and made solemn protestations that he had no will or intention of doing him hurt." Actually, he was eager to make an ally of the grave, dignified old duke, but between the reactionary Anglican and the liberal deist there could be no compromise. With their overtures rebuffed, Bucks and his allies discussed impeaching Ormonde, investigated his finances, cooked up a list of charges, and had to drop them for lack of proof. Sir Robert Howard offered large rewards to Lord Orrery, President of Munster, to bear witness against Ormonde, but Orrery was more timid than tempted. The honest old duke was a tough nut to crack.

What with one thing and another, the summer passed, and Ormonde was still unshaken. Matters might have gone harder for him had it not been that two of his foes had troubles of their own. Lord Ashley almost succumbed to a suppurating ulcer in his side, and Sir Robert Howard came alarmingly close to a charge of treason. Sir Robert (the "Sir Positive At-all" of Shadwell's *The Sullen Lovers*) was a dogmatic, talkative, quarrelsome fellow, with the tact of an elephant. He had recently published a windy epic poem, *The Duel of the Stags*, which, he insisted, was the result of some faithful nature studies in Windsor Forest. However, he had dedicated the poem to Buckingham in terms which smacked more of politics than poesy. The town identified the warring stags—one the "monarch of the herd," and the other a subject "that showed least fear and counterfeited love"—with King Charles and Buckingham. Vigorously Howard denied any "allegorical" intention at all. His annoyance was not diminished when two of his flippant friends, Lord Buckhurst and Henry Savile, circulated a parody called "The Duel of the Crabs," in which the mighty stags (*Cervus elaphus*) were reduced to two crab lice (*Phthirius pubis*), and their sylvan battlefield became the pilose anatomy of a prostitute. Sir Robert was fair game, even to his friends.[14]

Although Bucks and Arlington seemed to be partners in a deadly game of cards, each was actually trying to strengthen his own hand at the expense of the other. Earlier in the year, Bucks had blocked the appointment of two Arlington supporters to the Privy Council. In September, Arlington managed to substitute one of his friends, Sir John Trevor, for Sir William Morice (a Clarendonian) as the other Secretary of State. Trevor paid £8,000 for the post. In October, Bucks and Arlington joined forces to oust Lord Anglesey (a Yorkist) as Treasurer of the Navy and replace him with a commission of two: Sir Thomas Little-ton, Arlington's man, and Sir Thomas Osborne, Bucking-ham's protégé. So far the two ministers were fairly even, since Bucks managed that autumn to get his good friend Dr. John Wilkins, a liberal divine, appointed Bishop of Chester. But while Bucks wasted his time with clergymen, Arlington cultivated clever scoundrels. His candidate for Ambassador to France, Ralph Montagu, finessed Bucks into recommending him to the King, got the post, and for two years kept the duke happily ignorant that he had boosted an Arlington man! [15]

Preferment to the King's bed came also within the ministerial function. Here Arlington was at a distinct disadvantage. Bucks had his two protégées, Moll Davis and Nell Gwyn, whose success had already given My Lady Castlemaine a pair of black eyes. The great lady, angered at Bucks' "greatness and his ill usage of her," allied herself with the Duke of York's party. Other ministers sought to "manage" mistresses with indifferent success. Lord Ashley brought pretty Jane Roberts (said to be the daughter of a clergyman) to the King's attention. She was his mistress for a short time, but the competition was too keen, and "she was never easy in an ill course." In 1668, the Royal Keeper had at least five doxies in play at one time. The fifth was Lady Castlemaine's waiting woman, Wilson, whose great beauty the King discovered all by himself. Conceiving it her duty not to stand out against His Majesty's desires, Wilson found that conception was not always a blessing. Some months later, when her condition became obvious, her mistress was "so vexed that she turned her into the street at midnight." [16]

Usually Buckingham got his way with the King after "merry entertainments" of wine, wit, and ribaldry. Some of those evenings were mildly scandalous, especially when the duke had his friends Buckhurst, Sedley, and Baptist May, the Keeper of the Privy Purse, as his assistants. There was one October night at Bury St. Edmunds when the King was so drunk that he was unwilling, or unable, to give Lord Arlington an audience. A few nights later, at a drinking bout in Thetford, the King and his friends "did make the fiddlers of Thetford to sing them all the bawdy songs they could think of." Their repertory was quite extensive. At the end of such an evening, when the King was mellow and malleable, Bucks and his cohorts would coax him to appoint this man or dismiss that one, or try to drill into his head some "lesson of the ruling art," as they conceived it.

Even if His Majesty did not always grant his friends' requests, he enjoyed their company and took good care of them. When plump Lord Buckhurst and little Sir Charles Sedley were arrested by the watch one October night for "running up and down all night with their arses bare, in the streets," the King had the constables laid by the heels for interfering with the amusements of gentlemen.[17]

But against the influence of the Duke of Ormonde, not even wine and bawdy songs could prevail so long as Arlington refused to join the cabal opposing him. The Secretary was willing enough to join forces against a lesser target of the Buckingham faction: Sir William Coventry, Commissioner of the Treasury, who had shifted sides and was now a Yorkist. Arlington wanted to get rid of the Treasury Commission and become Lord Treasurer, drawing a fat salary with huge commissions. Bucks considered a horse trade but decided against it. He distrusted Arlington because he was now quite sure that the Secretary had plotted "to hang him at that time when he was proclaimed against" the year before, and Arlington feared Bucks because he knew that the duke knew the truth about that episode.

Conservatives looked hopefully to the time when Bucks and Arlington would come to open war. Meanwhile, seeing the duke's growing power, they feared the worst. One was sure that Bucks planned to bring about such a state of confusion that if the King died without legitimate issue, the nation would "break into pieces again," and fall into the chaos of a commonwealth. Another (remembering the canard about Bucks and Heydon, the astrologer) suspected him of plotting a *coup d'état* "to overthrow all the kingdom and bring in a commonwealth, wherein he may think to be general of their army, or to make himself king, which . . . he may be led to by some advice he hath had with conjurers, which he do effect." [18]

These were all groundless rumors. When Buckingham's interest was thoroughly engaged, his energy was frightening to the slothful. But he was neither a dictator in embryo nor a social reformer. True, he distrusted kings and railed against monarchy, but he distrusted "the people" just as much. On the one hand he could write, "Only the two weakest times of Rome were governed by kings: her childhood and old age," and on the other, "The breath of the people is like the wind: it blows only where it lists." His only real link with the Nonconformist republicans was his concern for liberty of conscience. Whether the right to govern came from above, as the divine rightists asserted, or from below, as the radical Left argued, he neither knew nor cared. He was a politician, not a philosopher. "The coming in of original power," he wrote, "is as obscure as that of original sin." Bucks wanted power, no matter where it came from. Therefore, with one side of his personality he courted the King, and with another side he sought to please the people—all for his own advancement.[19]

In the autumn of 1668 he turned again to his dream of an alliance with France. Through his former love, Princess Henrietta, now Duchess of Orleans and King Louis' sister-in-law, he offered France the prospect of a union with England in a war against Holland. His emissary to the duchess was his confidant, Sir Ellis Leighton, a sharp, grasping, and wholly untrustworthy man, who had so charmed his patron by his wit that no one dared say a word against him.

Buckingham's policy, said Leighton, was to advance always "in the good graces of the King by hunting parties, entertainments, and pleasures, [and] to make him understand how useful this alliance would be to his subjects by increasing their commerce, and how glorious for himself by giving him the means to some day defeat the Dutch and raise up the reputation of England, which the last insult of the Dutch [in the Medway] had sullied." Moreover, since it was important to please the kingdom as well as the King, Bucks claimed that by means of his party in Parliament he could get general approval for the treaty. It would, of course, take time to prepare the ground, perhaps a year. As Bucks wrote to the Duchess of Orleans, "For the love of God, don't be impatient; and consider that in a place where every measure must be taken to gain the good will of the people, one cannot act with so much dispatch as might be wished." [20]

In the chilly grandeur of Versailles, Louis XIV sat like a beady-eyed spider, spinning webs of diplomacy and baiting them with gold. No fly was too small for his net, and its threads were woven through every court of Europe. Buckingham's project was tempting, but Louis was too wary to pounce on it at once. Distrusting the duke's republican leanings and his power to deliver according to promise, he bought the dubious loyalty of Leighton for four hundred pistoles and a small pension, and sought to bribe Arlington and *his* personal emissary to France, Joseph Williamson. Meanwhile he ordered the Duchess of Orleans to encourage the project and cajole the projector. [21]

Pleased by the Duchess's flattering letters, Buckingham, who could juggle a dozen intrigues at once, kept the glittering bauble of an alliance dancing. He saw himself the general of an English army, with the hated Dutch prostrate before his banners, suing for terms. He saw Englishmen— his merchant friends in the City—engrossing the trade of Europe. With trade would come ships, seamen, naval power, and the expansion of Protestant England throughout the seven seas. He, of course, would be the engineer of all this glory. It was a beautiful dream. Bucks had no suspicion of the dark schemes even then brewing in the mind of the man whom he called in contempt "the Prince d'Amour."

VII

THE PLOT WITHIN THE PLOT
1669–1670

CHRISTMAS CAME with wassail and holly, and the new year dawned in peace. All was quiet on the continent, where Louis XIV drilled his armies and prepared for new conquests as soon as he could break up the Triple Alliance—England, Holland, and Sweden. Since the English Parliament was prorogued from August, 1668, to October, 1669, all was reasonably quiet in London, too. Arlington was not anxious to deal with the unruly Commons until the King's need for money made a session imperative. Buckingham, unlucky with legislators of late, wanted a dissolution and a new election, hoping for more republicans in the House of Commons.

The London quiet was only relative. The war between the rival ministers went on at its usual pace, with forays, reprisals, and occasional truces while recruits and ammunition were brought into the lines. In one such truce Roger Boyle, Earl of Orrery, joined the Buckingham faction, and

in the next few engagements did notable service. But behind all the petty intriguing of politicians a plot of immense
importance was rapidly taking shape.

On January 29, 1669, King Charles called a secret meeting in his brother's apartments in St. James's Palace. There,
to the Duke of York, Lord Arlington, Sir Thomas Clifford
(Treasurer of the Household), and Lord Arundel of Wardour (Queen Henrietta-Maria's Master of Horse), he declared himself a Roman Catholic and proposed an alliance
with France in a "Grand Design" to bring England back
to the Mother Church. Arundel was a professed Catholic;
York was a secret convert; Clifford was about to become
one; and Arlington—ostensibly a Protestant—never let religion interfere with politics. Eventually he found Catholicism a good religion to die in.

Although the King may have been sincere in his own
profession of faith, it is unlikely that he really believed
it possible to convert England. He knew how deeply the
fears of popery were burned into the minds of his subjects
by the fires of Smithfield in the days of Bloody Mary;
how conditioned they were by the St. Bartholomew Massa-
cre, the Gunpowder Plot, the Irish Rebellion of 1641, and,
most recently, the Great Fire of London. That holocaust
was attributed in all seriousness to "the treachery and malice
of the Popish faction, in order to the effecting their horrid
plot for the extirpating the Protestant religion and English
liberties, and to introduce popery and heresy."

Charles had in mind a package deal with Louis XIV,
"His Most Christian Majesty," who fancied himself not
only as the conqueror of Europe but as the grand champion
of Catholicism. Charles proposed to offer Louis a free hand

on the continent, sea power to aid in the destruction of Holland, and the glory of converting heretical England. In return he would demand subsidies to pay the costs of war and certain territories on the continent and in the Americas—crumbs dropped from the tables of France but to England the beginnings of a vast and spreading empire. Finally, if by some miracle the project to Catholicize England should work out, he would become an absolute monarch, forever free from the House of Commons with its power of the purse. Truly it was a "Grand Design," and three of the little cabal at St. James's Palace hailed it with enthusiasm. Only the cautious Arlington had his doubts.[1]

Negotiations with France were started at once. A plot of such grandiose scope had to be handled with the utmost secrecy. All through the winter and spring, messengers— Lord Arundel, the Earl of St. Albans, Sir Richard Bellings, and an Italian astrologer, Abbé Pregnani—journeyed back and forth across the channel bearing coded messages between King Charles, King Louis, and the Duchess of Orleans. The French and English ambassadors were ignorant of the plot, and the only English ministers in the secret were York, Clifford, and Arlington. The other ministers, Buckingham, Ashley, and Lauderdale, stout Protestants all, were the King's stalking-horses. They could be, and eventually were, admitted to the negotiations for a military alliance with France against Holland, but never into the religious part of the plot. Charles was playing a dangerous game, but so long as his ministry was dominated by Protestants—two of whom, Bucks and Ashley, had strong republican sympathies—no one was likely to suspect his hidden purposes.

To one who knew the secret of the Grand Design, Bucks and his friends must have looked like pawns, moved by the King's unseen fingers. For example, on the night of February 11, the duke won what seemed to be a glorious victory. At a merry entertainment he persuaded the King "to promise absolutely" to take away Ormonde's commission as Lord Lieutenant of Ireland. Three days later, the King announced the removal, and soon afterward he appointed Lord Robartes, a sullen, morose Presbyterian, as Ormonde's successor. For Lord Orrery, who wanted to be Lord Lieutenant himself, this was a hollow victory, but Buckingham, sure that the time was coming when he could make or unmake lord lieutenants at will, was undisturbed. He contented himself for the nonce by securing the post of Prebendary of Westminster Abbey for his chaplain, Dr. Sprat, and went on happily with his intrigues.[2]

Of course, the fact of the matter was that Ormonde's removal fitted in with the King's secret plans. Ireland must be governed by a weaker man, one likely to accept the Grand Design. Lord Robartes was appointed only until the King could find a safe man, with Catholic sympathies.

Ormonde, a truly loyal servant, blamed his fall on Buckingham and accepted it without a word of complaint to the King. Still Lord Steward of the Household, he continued to discharge his duties faithfully, a lonely old man neglected by King and Court. To his son, Lord Ossory, he was bitterly vocal about "that vile man" Buckingham and his allies. "As for the Duke of Bucks," he wrote, "I am confident he not only undervalues, but hates the King's person and his brother's, and has designs apart, if not aimed at the ruin of them both." Ormonde was partly right; Bucks certainly undervalued the King and hated the bigoted, narrow-minded James, Duke of York. One of Buckingham's epigrams expressed perfectly his estimate of the royal brothers: "The King could see things if he would; the Duke would see things if he could." Bucks would have been most happy to ruin the Duke of York, heir presumptive to the throne.[3]

Jubilant over Ormonde's fall, Buckingham set out to destroy another Yorkist, Sir William Coventry. Following his custom of negotiations before making war, he offered to make Coventry "chief minister of state," and declared that "of all men in England he would have chosen W. Coventry to have joined entire with." Coventry's refusal to accept an alliance sealed his doom.

Sir William was an able public servant, but something of a solemn prig and totally without humor. He was very proud of a round table in his office, so constructed that he could sit in the center and turn to all points of the compass. To Buckingham, the master of burlesque, this rather silly device was irresistible. In collaboration with Sir Robert Howard, Bucks set to work on a comedy designed for production at the King's Theatre. The high point of the play was to be a scene with two tables, "like that which [Coventry] hath made . . . with a round table in the middle," said Pepys, "to turn himself in." As a satire on Coventry's methodical habits, the playwrights planned to have drawers in the tables, labeled "Affairs of Spain," "Affairs of Holland," and the like. Actors personating Coventry "as master," and Sir John Duncomb, a fellow Commissioner of the Treasury "as his man or imitator," were to sit at the tables, "and their discourse in those tables, about the disposing of their books and papers, very foolish," said Pepys.

Hearing of the work-in-progress, Coventry complained to the King, who sent for the comedy, read it, and found nothing offensive. (The authors had cut out the pertinent scene for the occasion!) Coventry was not fooled. Brutally he warned the actors of the King's Theatre that "if any of them did offer at anything like representing him . . . he would cause his nose to be cut." To make assurance doubly sure, he sent his nephew, Henry Savile, to the Duke of Buckingham with a challenge.

Now the duke was in a quandary. If he refused to fight he was a coward in the world's eyes; if he fought with Coventry and had the bad luck to kill him, he could hardly hope for the King's pardon again. Colbert, the French Ambassador, urged him "not to hazard his valuable life in such an affair; an action, too, singularly unnecessary after the proofs of courage he had so lately given"—in the duel with Shrewsbury. Fortunately, while Buckingham hesitated, Sir Robert Holmes, his second in the earlier duel and "his champion ever since," told the King about the challenge. This time His Majesty acted promptly and prevented the meeting.

Two days later, at a meeting of the Privy Council, the King asked Buckingham to say "upon his honor, whether he had received any challenge from W. Coventry." The duke was forced to admit that he had. Asked then if he had sent a challenge, Coventry refused to answer on the ground that he should not be compelled to testify against himself. This plea the King took as a confession; he dismissed Coventry from the Privy Council and sent him to the Tower. Then he set off for Newmarket, leaving Sir William to cool his heels "during pleasure."

This was very severe punishment for merely sending a challenge. The real reason for it, of course, was the Grand Design. On March 7 the King wrote to his sister in France, "I am not sorry that Sir William Coventry has given me this good occasion, by sending my Lord of Buckingham a challenge, to turn him out of the Council. I do intend to turn him also out of the Treasury. The truth of it is, he has been a troublesome man in both places, and I am well rid of him." Coventry, too, was a sturdy Protestant, a man of integrity, and one not easily fooled.[4]

The Yorkists and Clarendonians—all old cavaliers—rallied around Coventry, and during the fortnight he spent in prison hardly a day went by without its quota of visitors. They came to condole with Sir William and to denounce Buckingham. One day Pepys found himself with a group of cavaliers, among whom there was "one that was very plain in cursing the Duke of Buckingham, and discoursing of his designs to ruin us, and that ruin must follow his counsels, and that we are an undone people." Every time Bucks defeated an enemy, two sprang up to replace him.

Where would he strike next? On March 29, Ormonde wrote bitterly to his son, "It is confidently affirmed the Duke of Bucks came to town when the King came [from Newmarket on March 20], but he has not appeared unless to the widow of his own making, or to his more private friends and advisers. Yet when he shall think fit to break forth he will, or will seem, to carry all before him."[5]

Not this time. For two weeks Buckingham disappeared, to the tune of the usual rumor that he was "with his wenches." He had gone to visit the Duke of Albemarle at his country estate, Newhall, with a daring proposition. If Albemarle would join in forcing the election of a new Parliament, Bucks would see to it that he replaced the Duke of York as Lord High Admiral—a lucrative and important ministerial post. In happier days the tough old warrior, who loved money mightily, would have been tempted, but he was too old, too sick, and too fearful of what his former friends, the Nonconformists, might do to him if they got in power. This was Buckingham's first attempt to strike at the Duke of York, but it was by no means his last.[6]

At Newhall, Bucks fell ill of a fever, and it was not until some time after his return to town in April that he fully recovered. If he took stock of his achievements to date, he had little reason to feel content. Clarendon, Ormonde, and Coventry were out, but Arlington, his ally for the moment, was still his rival, and York, powerful as ever, was his bitter enemy. Whatever the man in the street thought, Buckingham was still far from his goal as chief minister. He was only one of the Cabal which, together with the King and the Duke of York, constituted the Committee for Foreign Affairs—it came to acquire its capital C because the initials of five great men formed the word: Clifford, Arlington, Buckingham, Ashley, and Lauderdale. The Cabal had neither head nor body; it was merely an alphabetical accident.

After his recovery, Bucks sent a message to the Duke of York, offering his friendship and services. Scornfully, York refused the offer. Thereafter for some weeks the giddy Duke of Bucks, pretending that "His Royal Highness had a design to have him murdered," armed his lackeys "with pistol and knife," and whenever he went out of town "had always two musketoons in his coach and many horsemen well armed to attend him." The King, who had little love for his brother, was greatly amused.[7]

Posterity has cause to thank Buckingham for one good deed that spring: the appointment of little Christopher Wren, astronomer, architect, and wit, to succeed Sir John Denham as Surveyor of the King's Works. Although Wren was Buckingham's friend, his appointment was dictated by neither friendship nor politics. The leading contender for the post, Hugh May, Assistant Surveyor, was also Buckingham's friend. In fact, he had been the duke's follower, "for twenty years together, in all his wants and dangers," and had every reason to expect preferment. But the duke recognized Wren's superior genius as an architect, and the landscape of modern London bears out his judgment. Nevertheless, after Wren had built in Fish Street Hill a top-heavy Doric column (202 feet high) to commemorate the Great Fire of London, Bucks poked fun at it with a characteristic squib:

> *Here stand I,*
> *The Lord knows why,*
> *But if I fall,*
> *Have at you all!* [8]

All this time negotiations for the Grand Design were moving forward, slowly but steadily. Buckingham, as the leader of the "fanatic" party, was the most dangerous of the Protestant ministers, and the King went to great lengths to keep him well deceived. On March 22, for example, he wrote to the Duchess of Orleans in cipher, "[Buckingham] knows nothing of [Charles II's] intentions toward [the Catholic religion] nor of the person [Charles II] sends to [the King of France]." On April 25 he wrote, "It will be good that you write sometimes to [Buckingham] in general terms, that he may not suspect that there are further negotiations than what he knows of. But pray have a care you do not say anything to him which may make him think that I have employed anybody to [Louis XIV], which he is to know nothing of, because by the messenger he may suspect that there is something of [the Catholic religion's] interest in the case, which is a matter he must not be acquainted with." Again, on June 6, "I have sent your letter to [Buckingham] and what you write to him is as it ought to be. He shall be brought into all the business before he can suspect anything, except that which concerns [religion], which he must not be trusted with. You will do well to write but seldom to him, for fear something may slip from your pen which may make him jealous that there is something more than what he knows of."[9]

One can only conjecture what Bucks might have done had he discovered that Charles planned to convert England to Catholicism, with the aid of French arms and gold. In his passion he might well have stirred up a tempest of riot and rebellion capable of whirling Charles from the throne. But the secret of the Grand Design was well kept. Years later, like many others, Bucks had strong suspicions, but it is doubtful whether he ever learned the full truth.

There had been times that spring when Bucks suspected that others were trying to cut the ground from under his feet, negotiate a simple treaty of alliance, and get all the credit. In January, for example, Abbé Pregnani, astrologer and chemist, had suddenly appeared at Whitehall on very mysterious business. Not long afterward, the Duchess of Orleans' enthusiasm for the alliance seemed to be waning. Then, from Mary, Duchess of Richmond, in France, came a warning that Bucks was being bypassed in the negotiations. The angry duke protested in strong terms to the French Ambassador (who as yet knew nothing about the Grand Design), wrote a sharp letter to the Duchess of Orleans, and refused to be pacified until she sent him a soothing and tactful answer. Pregnani, who had accompanied the Court to Newmarket, and "had the ill luck to foretell [the results of races] three times wrong together," went back to France as secretly as he had come.[10]

Bucks continued to intrigue for an alliance, but he was growing discouraged. King Louis was overcautious and full of doubts; King Charles appeared to be only mildly interested. Charles talked about Parliament, the Triple Alliance with Holland and Sweden, and his own need for money. Before there could be a military alliance with France there must be a commercial treaty. He set Bucks to working one out with Ambassador Colbert, and the dashing duke found it all very dull.

Like most brilliant men, Buckingham saw by flashes of intuition what had to be done, and was all for doing it at once. The caution, or inertia, of slower (and sometimes more cunning) minds enraged him. When he could not get his way by persuasion or stronger measures, he lost interest, and turned to another of his diverse activities. Perhaps one reason why he failed to penetrate the Grand Design was that he was always busy with a multiplicity of affairs (it was a part of Arlington's duty to keep him occupied!). Something was always happening to distract him. In May, for instance, there was the affair of Harry Killigrew and Lady Shrewsbury again.

In France, something over a year ago, Killigrew had got into a truly desperate scrape. "The pleasant story" of the episode, as it came to English ears, was that Killigrew, bent on seducing a young woman whose mother guarded her too closely, had "opiated the mother and daughter, and then ravished the daughter." He was captured, convicted, and sentenced to hang, but "by the great mediation of the Queen Mother and Madame"—the Duchess of Orleans— he was reprieved and banished. It was unthinkable that an English gentleman should hang for a mere rape.

Late in March, 1668, he returned to England. Still in disgrace at Court, he haunted the London underworld as one of "the Ballers," a company of wild blades who made their headquarters at the brothel kept by a famous bawd, "Lady" Bennet, where gay damsels danced naked for the pleasure of the patrons. Pepys met Killigrew and some of the other "Ballers" one night at Vauxhall, and was fascinated by their "mad, bawdy talk." [11]

Evidently Killigrew continued his bawdy talk about Lady Shrewsbury also, boasting, as before, that "she had denied him no favor." In the course of time, his brags came to Lady Shrewsbury's ears. Quite rightly, Anna-Maria blamed all her troubles, her husband's death, and her present anomalous situation on Killigrew. But for the scandal stirred up by his malicious tongue, she might still be an honored wife—seeing her lover, of course, at frequent and exciting assignations. Now the cad was back again, repeating his lies and reviving all the old scandal. This time she decided to take matters in her own hands and teach him a thorough lesson.

She laid her plans with care, noting Killigrew's habits and the route he always took late at night to his home at Turnham Green, near Hammersmith. On the night of May 18, a black mourning coach drawn by six horses and attended by four footmen armed with knives and cudgels halted in the shadows beside the highway to Hammersmith. After a while a hackney coach came creaking along the white ribbon of road in the moonlight. As it draw abreast, the footmen leaped out of ambush. One jerked the hackney to a halt; the others flung open the coach door and dragged out the startled passenger. Cudgels rose and fell. From the mourning coach a woman's voice screamed, "Kill the villain!" Killigrew struggled to his feet and reached for his sword. Then came the flicker and rasp of steel, oaths, and cries of anger. In a moment the deed was done; the mourning coach pulled away with a clatter and roar, the footmen hanging on to the carriage straps. The dazed hackney coachman was left to take care of his passenger, who lay senseless in the dust, bleeding from nine wounds.

The next day all London was a-buzz with the news. The combination of clues—the mourning coach, the clear evidence of feminine vengeance, and the long history of bitterness between Killigrew and Lady Shrewsbury—all pointed to Buckingham's mistress as the instigator of the attack. (It was even said that she had her children with her in the coach!) That afternoon, in the Queen's bedchamber, the worried Duke of Buckingham ("still passionately in love with this virago," said Ambassador Colbert) came to her defense, declaring that he had spoken "with somebody that was by (which all the world must know that it must be his whore, my Lady Shrewsbury), who says that they did not mean to hurt, but beat him, and that he did run first at them with his sword." The Duke of York was exultant at this apparent evidence of conspiracy, hoping that it might cost Bucks "his life in the House of Lords."

Lady Shrewsbury went into hiding. Killigrew swore "informations," and the Lord Chief Justice set inquiries afoot. Had Killigrew died it might have gone hard with Anna-Maria. (Pepys declared that Killigrew's servant was slain, but he seems to have been mistaken.) Three days later the word went around that "H. Killigrew is better this morn, so as the countess (if he continue thus) may leave her retreat and appear again." He continued to improve, and with returning health deemed it prudent not to press charges. The Lord Chief Justice looked the other way, and Anna-Maria returned to the arms of her anxious lover.[12]

Buckingham's other distractions were less worrisome. Cosmo de' Medici, Prince of Tuscany, came to England in the spring of 1669, and the dignitaries of the realm took turns entertaining him. Early in June, Bucks invited him to a "sumptuous dinner" at Wallingford House, and arranged for the King and the Duke of York to appear as if by accident. It was a very ceremonious meal, even though the King, laying aside protocol, permitted the others to sit at table with him. "The table," wrote Medici's secretary, "was served in a splendid style, suitable to the rank of the guests and the munificence of the host." The King pledged the

Prince in cup after cup of wine, and the Italian's toast to the King and the royal family was greeted by three rousing cheers "from all present." Charles and Cosmo engaged in a gallant contest over which should have the privilege of kissing the other's hand. Cosmo won, kissed the King's hand, and in return received a kiss "on the face." It was all very fine—and expensive—but not much fun for the host.[13]

Buckingham enjoyed himself most at small dinners with a few witty friends. A day or two after the feast for the Prince of Tuscany, he traveled with a small party to Denham—the late Sir John Denham's country house—"with a design to buy it." He needed a country house near London, where he could entertain as befitted his rank and station. On the homeward journey (said Sir John Clayton, a City merchant), "we dined at Uxbridge, and never in all my life did I pass my day with such gusto, our company being his grace, Mr. Waller [the poet], Mr. Surveyor [Christopher] Wren, and myself; nothing but quintessence of wit and most excellent discourse." [14]

This was more like it. Buckingham was aptly described as "the merriest man alive," and wit was always the lure to draw him from politics. As a fellow wit wrote of him,

> *Let him at business ne'er so earnest sit,*
> *Show him but mirth, and bait that mirth with wit,*
> *That shadow of a jest shall be enjoyed,*
> *Though he left all mankind to be destroyed.*[15]

He was not only a wit himself but the judge of wit in other men. He professed himself a Jonsonian classicist, despising the fustian of modern poetry, and the silly rant of "heroic" plays. Like his friend Cowley, he believed that true wit meant completeness and perfection in any artistic effort, and that it was not merely jests, "florid talk," poetical adornments, puns, obscenity, bombast, or an "odd similitude." When Edward Howard (Sir Robert's brother) published early in the summer a foolish heroic poem, *The British Princes*, Bucks led a pack of baying wits in savage onslaught against it.

The result was a sheaf of eight satiric poems, so alike in theme and tone that it seems certain they must have been produced during the course of a merry evening at Wallingford House. The writers were the duke; three of his noble friends, Lords Buckhurst, Rochester, and Vaughan; his secretary, Martin Clifford; his chaplain, Thomas Sprat; plus Thomas Shadwell, a rising young playwright; and learned Samuel Butler, the author of *Hudibras*.

One pictures them sitting about the table after dinner, the debonair duke at the head in the full splendor of silks, laces, blond periwig, and plumed hat, his handsome face flushed and animated. Healths are proposed and drunk. The conversation flows rapidly—affairs of the day, the latest scandal at Whitehall, the new play at the King's House, politics, a bawdy story or two. (Sample of the Restoration genre: "A seaman returning home said to his wife, 'Are you turned bawd [procuress] yet?' 'No, John,' said the woman, 'I am a whore still, and I hope God will keep me so.'") [16]

Someone mentions Howard's poem. There is general laughter and a hail of witticisms. Someone else—perhaps the duke, who was a leader in such matters—proposes a competition to see who can write the sharpest set of verses against

Howard. The servants bring pens, ink, and paper, and refill the glasses. Everybody sets to work.

Buckingham's poem, "On Two Verses of the Same," was not the least or poorest of the lot. He chose to play with two of Howard's silliest lines:

> *But Fame had sent forth all her nimble spies*
> *To blaze this match, and lend to Fate some eyes.*

"Lend to Fate some eyes!" What balderdash! Gravely, Bucks pretended to be writing in defense of Howard and his remarkable image:

> *"But wherefore all this pother about Fame,*
> *A man might say," says one. "The very same*
> *Demand might well be made," another cries,*
> *"Of Fate, and how it got from Fame such eyes."*
> *'Tis well; you're witty persons both, say I;*
> *Yet to your wit thus boldly I'll reply:*
> *Fate is the twin of Chance, by which you find*
> *Fate must needs see, except that Chance were blind;*
> *For among friends 'twere inequality*
> *To think one should be blind and 't'other see.*
> *Now tell me, critics, do not all the wise*
> *Profess that which they see, they see with eyes?*
> *And the same figure do not I advance*
> *When I protest I saw a thing—by chance?*
> *Since then so various things by Chance we see,*
> *Fate might have eyes to multiplicity;*
> *But our mild author says it has but some.*
> *Thus, critic vile, thus have I struck thee dumb,*
> *And thus subscribe myself, with heart and hand,*
> *The author's friend, most humble servant, and Buck-*
> *ingham.*[17]

Ned Howard, crushed to earth, soon rose again, and re-turned to attack his critics. A merry little war ensued, last-ing for several months, but Buckingham took no part in it. Criticism was only one of his many diversions.

By September Harry Killigrew had regained both his health and his senses. After making abject apologies to Bucks and Lady Shrewsbury for his past conduct, he was forgiven all around, and the King gave him leave to return to Court. If Anna-Maria apologized for the misconduct of her footmen the fact is not recorded.

The lovers continued their usual life, still deeply—but not peacefully—in love. Both were quick, passionate, and proud; there must have been quarrels. Some of Bucks' little epigrams sound remarkably personal, as if they were writ-ten in moments of anger: "Mahomet makes that our happi-ness in Heaven which is our greatest punishment on earth, handsome women." "Their power is so absolute that I think the devil's promise was made good to women, when he said, 'Ye shall be like gods.'" "'Twas well for man that woman was made, for else *he* had been the vainest thing of the Creation."

But no clash of personalities could break the strong bonds that held them in their illicit union. They lived hectically, without thought of the future. They were constantly on the go, driving, dancing, dining, drinking, and talking until all hours of the morning. Once the old poet Edmund Waller wrote to his wife from his lodgings in St. James's Street, "The Duke of Buckingham with the Lady Shrews-bury came hither last night at this time and carried me to the usual place to supper, from whence I returned home at four o'clock this morning, having been earnestly entreated to sup with them again tonight, but such hours cannot be always kept." The energetic duke had found a worthy mate.[18]

In the autumn open warfare broke out between Buckingham and Arlington. The immediate cause of the quarrel was the fact that Arlington "made up with the Duke of York," and so aligned himself temporarily with the Ormonde faction. There were rumors that Arlington "should out," and delighted news writers reported every skirmish: "Bucks and Arlington cannot set their horses together." "Arlington sits fast." "Bucks and Arlington are still pecking one at the other." Weeks went by, and at last the King commanded a reconciliation. Arlington paid the duke a visit at Wallingford House, "where they mutually unfolded their grievances." Arlington protested that Bucks encouraged "his mortal enemy, the Earl of Orrery." Bucks complained that Arlington mistreated his friends, particularly Sir Thomas Osborne and Sir Ellis Leighton, "and that he was an encourager of his enemies." The net result of the conference was an armed truce, agreed to on November 6. But ten days later a news writer reported cheerfully, "Bucks and Arlington are broke out again."[19]

Parliament had convened on October 18, but what with the enmity of the two ministers, the continued jurisdictional quarrel between the two Houses about the case of Skinner vs. the East India Company, and the factionalism and discontent of the Commons, it accomplished nothing. The King, rapidly nearing bankruptcy, was in desperate need of money, but his ministers spent more time and energy in fighting one another than in working for a bill of supplies. Privately Bucks resorted to his favorite weapon, ridicule, burlesquing Arlington before the King. Publicly he attacked one of the weakest of the Secretary's friends, Sir George Carteret, Treasurer of the Navy during the Dutch War. A sweeping investigation of his books showed nothing to shout about, but the Buckingham faction spread the rumor that Carteret was short some £800,000 in his accounts, a good part of which, they said, had been spent by the King "for his pleasure." In reprisal, Arlington and Ormonde brought in a bill to impeach Buckingham's friend, Lord Orrery, of high treason. The King prorogued Parliament on December 11, barely in time to prevent the submission of bills impeaching Ormonde, Buckingham, "and many others." A politician's life was not a happy one. Behind every minister hovered always the dread spectre of the Earl of Strafford, impeached by Commons in the time of Charles I, convicted of high treason, and beheaded on Tower Hill. It could happen to anyone.

In all this excitement, Buckingham lost sight of his projected treaty with France. But the Grand Design was moving along. Charles had named his price to Louis: a million pounds with which to set out his Fleet and two hundred thousand for announcing his own conversion to Catholicism. While Louis haggled, Charles consolidated his position at home, strengthening his small army and placing loyal officers in command of forts and arsenals. Ambassador Colbert was now admitted into the full secret and proved very useful at keeping the wool pulled over Buckingham's eyes. Charles told Colbert that he was sure of the duke's affection and loyalty and of his desire for an alliance with France. Colbert's rôle was to encourage him and lead him on; meanwhile the King "would work things in such a way that the duke would think himself to be the principal promoter of the league." [20]

But when Parliament met again on February 14, 1670, Bucks forgot all about foreign alliances in his eagerness to pursue the most daring project of his political career, a plan to divorce the King from his barren wife, marry him to a princess more likely to produce an heir to the throne, and thus ruin the Duke of York, the present heir presumptive. The Roos divorce case was to set the precedent, and into the prosecution of that famous affair Bucks threw all his tempestuous energies.

VIII

INTRIGUES AND FARCE
1670–1671

O N JANUARY 3, 1670, the old Duke of Albemarle died at his lodgings in the Cockpit, a part of Whitehall Palace across King Street, opposite the Privy Garden. By virtue of his office as Master of the Horse, Buckingham succeeded to Albemarle's lodgings when he chose to use them, but it was some time before he was able to take even token possession. A severe illness kept him in bed all through the holiday season, and his absence from important events during January and February argues that his convalescence was slow. Although Parliament convened on February 14, he failed to appear in the House of Lords until March 5—significantly at the first reading of a bill entitled, "An Act for John Manners, called Lord Roos, to marry again, living his wife, from whom he is divorced." The tentative use of Lord Roos's courtesy title was designed to disarm Buckingham, in case the duke wished to make trouble again. But this time Bucks was one of the strongest supporters of the bill.

Although Lord Roos had divorced his wife "from bed and board" and illegitimized her children, she was still technically his wife, and he could not marry another so long as she lived. Now he asked the House of Lords to dissolve his marriage completely and give him leave to remarry. Thus he would be saved from the sin of "wenching" and could get legitimate heirs for his titles and estates. Because there was no precedent for his bill, the Lords Spiritual and Temporal debated it long and furiously, citing Scripture and civil and ecclesiastical law and wrangling over terms until the original issue was almost forgotten.

The Duke of York's party, fearing that the precedent set by the bill might encourage King Charles to divorce his own wife and remarry, fought furiously against it. Buckingham's faction promoted it with equal ardor. The French Ambassador thought Bucks was merely trying to mess up the affairs of Parliament and drive a wedge between the King and his brother, but wiser men argued that he wanted to help the King get a new wife and so disinherit York. Bucks may have had a more personal reason as well. The King had been heard to say that "he knew not why a woman might not be divorced for barrenness, as a man for impotency." Buckingham, too, had a barren wife.[1]

At each successive reading, the debate over the bill waxed hotter. Buckingham spoke only once, quoting Bellarmine to show his learning. He suggested the passage of a more general law permitting divorce on the grounds of "the adultery of the man as of the woman." Such a law might have excellent moral results, he said, since it would "oblige

men as well as women to live more virtuously." The listening members forebore the obvious comment.

Buckingham's interest in the Roos bill is shown by the
fact that he appeared in the House only when it was sched-
uled for debate, and accepted appointment during the
session to only one committee: that for the consideration
of the bill. But his most effective work was done behind
the scenes. It is quite possible, for example, that he was the
"chief officer of state" who drove to Chalfont St. Giles to
consult with the blind old poet, John Milton, "as being the
prime person that was knowing" on the subject of divorce.[2]

King Charles was so interested in the argument that on
March 21 he appeared unexpectedly in the House of Lords,
to the great confusion of the members. Claiming that he
was only resuming a right of his ancestors, he came back
again and again, standing usually near the fireplace, chatting
with the lords who crowded about him, or listening to the
debates. He declared that it was "better than going to a
play."

On March 28, after a debate which went on "from
eleven in the morning until past six at night," the Roos bill
passed by a narrow margin. The Buckingham party immediately set to work on a bill of divorcement for the King.
But Charles, who had dallied with the idea, suddenly
changed his mind and refused to let the bill be presented.
The party brought every kind of pressure to bear. For example, Dr. Gilbert Burnet, a bitter anti-Yorkist, worked
out elaborate arguments in favor of divorce for barrenness,
and suggested that if His Majesty refused a divorce, Parliament might legalize the practice of polygamy for the King
only. "I see nothing," he wrote, "so strong against polyg-

amy as to balance the great and visible imminent hazards that hang over so many thousands, if it be not allowed." But the King had too much affection for poor, homely, little Catherine to make her miserable (as he said), "only because she was his wife and had no children by him, which was no fault of hers." Buckingham was sorely disappointed at the failure of his plot.

Burnet is the authority for the statement that, in desperation, Buckingham proposed to steal Catherine away and send her to a plantation, so that the King could get a divorce "upon the pretense of a wilful desertion." But Burnet had not the slightest sense of humor. As one of his contemporaries wrote, "If this story can be true, none but such an extravagant man as the Duke of Buckingham was capable of saying so ridiculous a thing in jest; and none but such a historian as Dr. Burnet to tell it again in earnest."

As for Lord Roos, it is pleasant to record that life was kinder to him thereafter. True, his second wife, Anne Shirley, died in childbed in 1672, but in the seventeenth century the death of a wife in childbed was a common theme for sorrow. Roos's third wife, Catherine Noel, lived with him happily for many years and helped him found the ducal house of Rutland. Anne, the first Lady Roos, pursued her wicked ways and finally vanished in the mists and bogs of Ireland.[3]

Parliament adjourned on April 11, after passing a number of private bills, a vicious Conventicle Act aimed at Nonconformists, and an act taxing wines and spirits for seven years, designed to increase the King's income some £300,-000 a year. Since even this was too little to pay the costs of government and clear up his debts, Charles was forced to stake everything on the Grand Design. After some months of dickering, he had allowed King Louis to beat down his original prices. Now the figures were fixed at £225,000 a year (about $4,500,000) for the costs of the war with Holland and £150,000 (about $3,000,000) as the price of announcing his conversion to Catholicism. Late in April the secret treaty was ready for signing. On May 16 the Duchess of Orleans arrived at Dover, ostensibly to visit her brothers but armed with full instructions for the working out of last minute details. The King and his Court went to meet her in full force.

For two weeks there was high festivity in the crowded little town and at nearby Canterbury, with dinners, dances, and comedies. On May 22 the secret Treaty of Dover was signed by Arlington, Arundel, Bellings, and Clifford for England, and by Colbert for France. It was left to Charles to find a convenient time for publicly declaring his conversion (he never found one), and King Louis was to choose the moment for starting the war with Holland *after* Charles had declared his Catholicism. The flow of French gold was to begin within six months of the date of the signing.

Of course the Duke of Buckingham went to Dover to dance attendance upon his romantic idol, Henrietta, Duchess of Orleans. (One suspects that Lady Shrewsbury stayed at home.) Lost in glamor and gallantry, Bucks failed to suspect the intrigue going on under his aristocratic nose. For him the only result of the duchess's visit was a reconciliation (a "peace making") with Arlington, brought about by Henrietta's gentle insistence. After the merry-making was all over, Bucks wrote to Leighton (in Ireland), "I suppose you have heard of the peace making at Dover.

Since that I know not anything has happened but the usual entertainments of the day, that is, eating, drinking, and so forth. All things [relating to a treaty with France] are put as they were, and I believe will be till either Madame [the duchess] comes over again hither, or somebody else goes thither."

Henrietta was destined never to see England again. Her mission accomplished, she sailed for France on June 2. Three weeks later she was dead.[4]

With the news of her death came rumors that she had been poisoned by her husband, Philippe, Duke of Orleans, an effeminate, petty-minded tyrant with homosexual tendencies. King Charles was prostrated with grief and anger; a mob attacked the French Embassy in London; and Buckingham flew into a furious passion, vowing dire revenge. Even after the official post mortem showed that the duchess died of "cholera morbus" (actually it was a perforated duodenal ulcer), Buckingham remained bitter and inconsolable. Ambassador Colbert reported that he was pretending grief "because he thinks to make himself more agreeable to the people." But Colbert had the soul of a peasant. What could he know of romance and chivalry? One broken phrase in Buckingham's Commonplace Book suggests the reality of his grief: "Where she lives now as happily in Heaven as I should have done on earth had she stayed here."[5]

However, Bucks was not so heartbroken as to neglect his political career. Protocol demanded that an envoy be sent to France to thank King Louis for his message of condolence and to represent King Charles at his sister's funeral. If Bucks went as the envoy, he would have an opportunity to talk to King Louis about the treaty of alliance he had worked for so long. To Bucks that treaty had become an obsession. He saw it as his surest way to supreme power in England and his protection against his enemies. When his friend and confidant, Sir Thomas Osborne, tried to talk him out of his plan and said "it would be his ruin," Bucks replied that he must go on with it, "for it might save him a few years, while if he refused, the Duke [of York] and Arlington would ruin him in three months." [6]

To Buckingham's delight, King Charles accepted his proposition almost eagerly. In fact, it fitted the King's private plans to perfection. To cover the secret Treaty of Dover and deceive the English Protestant ministers, there must be some kind of sham treaty which could be made public if necessary. Now here was the unsuspecting Buckingham, offering to negotiate such a treaty all by himself! Messages flew across the channel to alert King Louis and his ministers. Knowing that opposition only made Bucks determined, York, Clifford, and Arlington pretended to be dead set against his project. Even Lady Shrewsbury—"a nymph with a still seductive face"—opposed Buckingham's journey, but she had a very good reason for wanting her lover at her side: she was pregnant.

Buckingham's friend, the Count de Grammont (who knew nothing about the Treaty of Dover), was in England at the time. Now, to add to the farce, King Charles asked Grammont to go to France with the duke as his "gouverneur," and help him make a treaty. Charles knew that with the vain, talkative count at his side Bucks would never learn anything about the Grand Design. Grammont, convinced that he was a great diplomat, accepted the duty with enthusiasm and left England well in advance of his friend to make sure that Bucks would get a rousing welcome in France.[7]

Late in July Buckingham, armed with all sorts of instructions from the King and the Protestant ministers, Ashley and Lauderdale, set out for Paris by way of Deal and Dieppe. With him went Lord Buckhurst, Sir Charles Sedley, and several other wits well qualified to "lead the Muses and the Graces such a dance as may instruct and civilize fair France." Another party containing Samuel Butler, Dr. Sprat, and the famous comedian, Jo Haines, followed hard on their heels. Although he expected to be gone for only a fortnight, Buckingham was prepared for anything.[8]

Meanwhile, King Louis was setting the stage for the farce. He ordered the Duchess of Orleans' splendid apartment in the palace of St. Germain swept and garnished, staffed it with servants, and stuffed it with delicacies, planning to pay all of Buckingham's expenses and supply him "with every luxury that can be desired." He even set aside one of his own coaches for the duke's use, with eight nimble footmen attached.

Delayed by contrary winds and stormy seas, the travelers made a very slow trip. They arrived in Paris on August 8 and went first to Ambassador Montagu's house, where they stayed while a tailor fitted Buckingham with raiment appropriate to his splendor as Envoy Extraordinary. Grammont hastened to greet the duke with Louis XIV's compliments, and thereafter remained as close as possible to his protégé during the ensuing month of entertainments. King Louis received Bucks with flattering unction, installed him at St. Germain, dined, talked, hunted, walked, and drove with him, and turned Paris inside out to keep him amused.

The entertainments were of such diverse kinds as a grand review of troops, the solemn burial of the Duchess of Orleans at Saint Denis (nearly three months after her death), a mock naval battle, "a public feast on St. Louis' Day," and sumptuous banquets nearly every night, with the greatest nobility of France as hosts. The sham battle of August 23 was the high point of the festivities. King Louis had recently completed his magnificent canal in the park at Versailles. His mimic sea battle consisted of an attack on "a great ship" by dozens of small boats, decorated with streamers and flowers, and manned by the King, the Queen, and all the beauties of the Court in brilliant costumes. There were trumpets and kettledrums, but no shooting lest the ladies be discomposed. The whole affair was a symphony of sound and color—violins, gay voices, the splashing oars, the clipped green trees of the park, and the amber and gold of Versailles, drenched in sunlight. Later in the evening there was more music, a collation of fruits, sweetmeats, and fish, and the outdoor performance of a "Pastorale." It was all done in the true spirit of a baroque age. Buckingham spoiled the grand effect by eating too much fruit. He was unwell for several days.

Side by side with the month-long carnival, the business of the sham treaty went forward, seriously on the English side, and with well controlled mockery on the French. On August 15 Bucks wrote to Arlington, "I have had more honors done me than ever were given to any subject. . . . Nothing but our being mealy-mouthed can hinder us from finding our accounts in this matter, for you may almost ask what you please." Two days later he wrote, "I am every day convinced of the happy conjunction we have at present in our hand, of any conditions from this Court that we can in reason demand. The King of France is so mightily taken with the discourse I make to him of his greatness by land that he talks to me twenty times a day. All the courtiers here wonder at it, and I am very glad of it." Arlington chuckled and filed the letters away.[9]

The farce moved on apace, and Bucks was fooled to the top of his bent. Every day King Louis gave him new "demonstrations of esteem and confidence." He agreed to all of Buckingham's proposals and promised him honors and rewards—particularly the command of an English army in Flanders. How the King and his ministers laughed at the duke's "étourderie" (giddiness) behind his back! He suspected nothing, of course; he thought King Louis was an honest gentleman and credited his success to his own persuasive tongue.

In England, King Charles was offhand and flippant about Buckingham's mission. He told Ambassador Colbert that he had given Bucks leave to return "whenever he pleased." He added, however, that "if the ladies of France kept the duke much longer, he would not be responsible for the anger of the ladies of England"—the Duchess of Buckingham and the Countess of Shrewsbury—"who awaited him with great impatience."[10]

Long ago Mary Villiers had made her decision: half a husband was better than none. United by their common love, the duchess and the countess had become fast friends. Before Bucks left for France he consigned his pregnant mistress to his wife's care, and the duchess, concealing her own grief and envy, accepted the responsibility "to please her husband."

Since Mary Villiers hated the sea, it was probably Anna-Maria who conceived the foolish project of traveling to Calais to meet the duke on his homeward journey. Even though the two ladies had dozens of servants to protect them, traveling was difficult and dangerous. There were highwaymen and thieves along the ways; the inns were small, rough, and infested with fleas, while the little yachts which plied the channel were called "pleasure boats" only by courtesy. Nevertheless, the good-natured duchess agreed to make the trip, and a week after Buckingham's departure for London, his wife, his mistress, and their servants took ship for Calais.

Few knew where they had gone. Lord Fairfax, informed by a friend that his daughter could not come to Nun Appleton to see him that summer because she was on her way to Calais, was mystified by her "sudden resolution." Had he known about Anna-Maria's interesting condition he would have understood; the longings of a pregnant woman must be satisfied lest her child be injured, and Anna-Maria was wailing for her ducal lover. Unfortunately, contrary winds blew the pilgrims into Margate on August 2. Thence, when the seas abated, they returned to Dover, gave up the journey to Calais, and settled down to await the duke's return.[11]

They had a long wait. What with treaties and entertainments, Bucks found it difficult to tear himself away. On August 30 he began the round of visits which constituted a formal leave-taking. That night, while he was dining with one of King Louis' favorites, Antoine, Count de Lauzun, a richly dressed cavalier (the King) and two ladies entered;

all three were masqued. While music played and the guests watched, the trio went into a stately dance in which the ladies seemed to be begging the cavalier to give up the glittering sword at his side. The dance ended, the ladies disarmed the Duke of Bucks; the cavalier handed them the precious sword, and they belted it about the duke's waist.

The sword, "beset with diamonds," was valued at twenty thousand crowns (about £1,500). The story goes that in the next few days a number of courtiers visited Buckingham to inspect the marvelous weapon, and that some nimble-fingered gentleman managed to pick out two or three diamonds. The duke had to have them replaced at his own expense.[12]

Protocol and preparations took a full week. One preparation was rather troublesome. During the Duchess of Orleans' visit to Dover, King Charles had been deeply smitten by a little Breton Maid of Honor, Louise de Keroualle. After the Duchess's death, Buckingham told Charles that it would be "a decent piece of tenderness for his sister to take care of some of her servants." The King understood, and eagerly offered to invite Louise to England, in the rôle of Maid of Honor to the Queen. To King Louis the duke told another tale, "that he [Louis] could never reckon himself sure of the King but by giving him a mistress that should be true to his [Louis'] interests."

Blond Louise de Keroualle, a clever, calculating young woman of distinguished manners and no morals to speak of, was easily persuaded to become Ambassadress to the British Bedchamber. She was extremely ambitious; her current lover, the Count de Sault, could do nothing to advance her interests; and she had grown tired of waiting for King

Louis to toss her his pocket handkerchief—his regal way of inviting a beauty to share his bed.

Buckingham's problem was how to get Louise to England. He was impatient to get home and disliked the idea of suiting his usual headlong gait to the whims and fancies of a French lady of quality, accustomed to slow and stately travel and all kinds of formal courtesies. Besides, he might find it difficult to explain her presence to Lady Shrewsbury, who was pacing the English strand, longing for his return. Perhaps the yacht which had brought him to Dieppe was still in port; if not, he could send one over for Louise after he reached England.

Early on the morning of September 6 (after he had spent a convivial night with the Count de Sault) Buckingham set out for Calais with Mademoiselle de Kéroualle and her maid in a traveling coach. Outside Paris the party split; some of Buckingham's servants headed for Dieppe, convoying the new Maid of Honor, while the eager duke galloped apace for Calais. At Boulogne he found a ship ready to sail, and on September 10 he was safe in the arms of his beloved. In all the excitement of home-coming, Bucks forgot about Louise, who remained fuming in Dieppe for at least a fortnight. However, Ambassador Montagu heard about her plight and wrote to Lord Arlington, who sent a yacht for her. She was furious with Buckingham.[13]

No matter; soon after her arrival in London, Bucks coaxed her into a good humor again. He himself was in fine fettle. His trip had been highly successful, socially and politically. Of course it had been expensive as sin. Before he left England, Bucks drew £2,000 from the Treasury to pay for his trip; yet when he was ready to leave Paris,

Ambassador Montagu had to provide him with cash for his return journey. Eventually the Treasury paid out an additional sum of £3,210 for full payment of all his charges. But these were only official expenses. As befitted a great duke, he had to spend his own money lavishly for all sorts of items—clothing, jewels, gifts to hosts, and largess to lackeys. As Brian Fairfax said, "His embassies into France and Holland cost him much more than a diamond picture or a sword [King Louis' usual gifts] could recompense." [14]

To Buckingham's mind it was money well spent. Now, in the autumn of 1670, his prestige was at its peak; his cherished treaty was working slowly toward completion; and on the horizon of his future blazed the pride, pomp, and circumstance of glorious war. Best of all, after thirteen years of longing, he was about to become a father. True, the child would be a bastard, incapable of inheriting estates and titles, but King Charles had shown that it was possible to recognize his royal bastards—the Duke of Monmouth, the Earls of Plymouth and Southampton, and others still to come—ennoble them, and provide them with fair demesnes. If the King could do it, so could the great Duke of Buckingham.

Of course the polite world on both sides of the Channel knew all about Buckingham's affair with Anna-Maria and accepted that affair without criticism. Lord Arlington suggested to Ambassador Colbert that if the French wished to keep Bucks tied to their interest, they should give Lady Shrewsbury a pension. King Louis settled ten thousand livres a year on her (about £800), and both the duke and his mistress were properly grateful. Bucks rejected with scorn every bribe he was offered, but it was quite all right for a lady to take money from a king—foreign or domestic. Kings were the visible symbols of Providence.[15]

The polite world knew all about Anna-Maria's pregnancy, too, and talked about it with typical Restoration frankness. In mid-October a courtier wrote to a friend in the country, "The Countess of Shrewsbury's belly begins to swell, and she gives us a fair probability of a hopeful issue." The Duke of York is authority for the statement that at about this time Bucks went through a form of marriage with Lady Shrewsbury, with his chaplain, Dr. Sprat, officiating, and that thereafter "the true duchess was called in raillery 'the dowager duchess.' " It may be so. The horseplay of the wits was not notable for delicacy.[16]

While awaiting the "hopeful issue," Buckingham occupied himself with his usual diversity of affairs, concentrating on the treaty with France. King Charles appointed the five members of the Cabal as commissioners, and told them to go ahead. To maintain the farce and keep Buckingham stirred up by opposition, Colbert dragged his feet, and Arlington pretended to oppose the whole business. Bucks suspected bribery. He told Colbert that the Dutch and Spanish Ambassadors had offered him £200,000 to change sides. He had rejected the bribe, of course, but had Arlington been equally virtuous? Perhaps the Secretary's opposition was caused by jealousy of Buckingham; perhaps he was ruled by his Dutch wife—who could tell? Deeply concerned over the delays, Bucks wrote indignant and excited letters to King Louis and received a soothing reply. With delicate flattery Louis addressed him as "Mon cousin."

King Charles was the real cause of the delay. The original plan had been to declare war against Holland in the spring of 1671, but Charles was far from ready. Parliament was in session through the fall and winter, and he was asking for large supplies—to maintain the Triple Alliance, he said! Cleverly he played on Louis' fears by insisting that before engaging in the war he must declare himself a Catholic, even if England flamed with revolution. But Louis needed the English sea power for the destruction of Holland; the Grand Design could be put off, indefinitely if need be. With pretended reluctance Charles agreed, but still insisted on having the money promised for his declaration of Catholicism. He got it.

Behind the scenes, Arlington shaped the sham treaty to agree in all major provisions with the secret Treaty of Dover—except, of course, that there was no mention of Catholicism. The subsidy for the Grand Design was added to the subsidy for carrying on the war, and the date for declaring war was set for the spring of 1672. The whole business was a masterpiece of double-dealing by which Charles succeeded in cheating Louis XIV, his own Protestant ministers, and his Parliament. The sham treaty—the Treaty of London—was signed on December 21, 1670. Only the two kings, their ministers, and their ambassadors knew of its existence.[17]

The versatile Duke of Buckingham rarely confined himself to one intrigue at a time. Treaties and foreign affairs were not enough to occupy his restless mind; he must also carry on his domestic wars. Thanks to his plotting, some time in the winter of 1670–71 another of his enemies, Barbara, Countess of Castlemaine, bit the dust.

In August, 1670, the King, appreciating Barbara's many virtues, had raised her to the title of Duchess of Cleveland, giving her the estates and income to support that exalted rank. Nevertheless, her power over the King was waning. Moll Davis, happily installed in a fine house in Suffolk Street, and Nell Gwyn, living in Pall Mall with her infant son by the King, had driven the great lady from the royal bed. She consoled herself with a succession of lovers: Henry Jermyn, Charles Hart, a handsome actor, and Jacob Hall, a well muscled rope-dancer. In a general way the King was aware of her infidelities, but so long as she caused no open scandal he was content to leave well enough alone.[18]

Aware of his cousin's vindictive temper, Buckingham was not so easily satisfied. As he once confided to his Commonplace Book, "I prepare myself against fortune and strike first; for in probability of a war 'tis best to begin." The duchess must be soundly defeated to make way for the new pretender, Louise de Keroualle, whom Bucks planned to manage for his own interest as well as that of France. His previous ventures in mistress-management had proved rather disappointing. Moll Davis, a feather-brain, was an interesting bedfellow, but she never touched the King's heart, and Nell Gwyn, a pretty entertainer with a lusty wit, amused his Majesty but rarely influenced him. De Keroualle looked very promising, even though she had a "baby face, melancholy eyes, and languid walk." Hers was not the type of beauty to appeal to Buckingham, but she had bewitched the King ever since her arrival in early October. Charles gave her lodgings in Whitehall and visited her daily, panting with passion, while she played the coy ingénue. The Duchess of Cleveland was working to thwart this new intrigue—not because she loved the King but because she wanted no other hand but hers in the King's pocket.[19]

Buckingham's plan was simple enough: to arrange matters so that the King would catch the duchess *in flagrante* with her lover of the moment. Working out all the details was not so easy. After ferreting out the duchess's intrigues and setting his trap, Bucks had to persuade the lazy King that his honor was involved, that there was danger of open scandal, and that he should take steps. Charles disliked trouble, and the rôle of an outraged keeper was new to him. But Buckingham was not to be denied.

There are half a dozen versions of what finally happened. The most concise is Bishop Burnet's laconic statement: "The Duchess of Cleveland, finding that she had lost the King, abandoned herself to great disorders, one of which, by the artifice of the Duke of Buckingham, was discovered by the King in person, the party concerned leaping out of the window." According to the story told by a later French Ambassador (Barillon, in 1677), Bucks gave a hundred guineas to one of the duchess's waiting women for information. Acting on her tip, he brought the reluctant King to Her Grace's bedroom at a critical moment. However, the duchess was warned in time to thrust her lover, Jack Churchill (the future great Duke of Marlborough), into a cupboard and lock him in. The King prowled about the room, spied the locked door, and ordered it opened. The cowering lover was discovered, and ignominiously hauled out. Charles is supposed to have said to him, "Go. You are a rascal, but I forgive you because you do it to get your bread." [20]

The most elaborate version of the episode appeared in

1676 as a French novel, *Hattigé, ou les Amours du Roi de Tameran*, by Sebastien Brémond. Tameran (England) is a kingdom where love reigns absolute, "and the young people, encouraged by their fathers' examples, get themselves mistresses before they get rid of the rod of their schoolmaster." The story of Osman, the King's chief minister; Hattigé, the King's mistress; and Rajep, her handsome young lover, is a highly colored romance built on what was obviously a well known bit of scandal. Shortly after the appearance of *Tameran* a "key" was published; Osman was identified as Buckingham, Hattigé as the Duchess of Cleveland, and Rajep as Jack Churchill.[21]

In spite of attempts by Churchill's most illustrious descendant to cast doubt on the episode, there is every reason to believe that the young soldier was the duchess's lover at this time, that Buckingham intercepted some of her letters to him, and that he either was found in bed with her or escaped by leaping out a window—or (as another story has it) was captured by Buckingham while attempting to escape "out of the back door." Churchill, a handsome but poverty-stricken ensign in the Guards, probably became the duchess's lover early in 1670. From June through October he was with Sir Thomas Allin aboard the *Resolution* in the Mediterranean. On his return to London in November he resumed the old relationship, with the farcical but not particularly serious results we have just seen.[22]

The King, we are told, banished the lover from Court. However, he could not banish him from the affections of the duchess, who refused to give him up. After a lengthy argument, the King washed his hands of her with what dignity he could muster. Years later, when the duchess was in a scrape again, she reminded his Majesty, "And I hope you will be just to what you said to me, which was at my house when you told me you had letters of mine; you said, 'Madam, all that I ask of you for your own sake is, live so for the future as to make the least noise you can, and I care not who you love.'" Churchill remained her lover for more than a year, fathered a daughter upon her, and founded his fortunes by wisely investing the £5,000 which gratitude moved her to bestow upon him.[23]

At any rate, Buckingham's scheme succeeded, and the way was cleared for his protégée, Louise de Keroualle. Everything was going splendidly for the duke. Arlington, too, was losing his power (or so Bucks thought). The treaty with France was about to go into effect, with a provision giving the duke command of an English army in Flanders, and visions of martial glory danced through his head. He could claim with reason that what he had done was for the good of England, but the canny politician always cuts himself a slice of the pie.

Bucks enjoyed the highest possible favor at Court. When William, Prince of Orange, came to visit his uncle, King Charles, Bucks plied him with wine so vigorously one November night that the morose young prince forgot decorum and dignity and had to be forcibly restrained from breaking into the apartments of the Maids of Honor. When the Duke of Ormonde was assaulted in St. James's Street and abducted by a band of outlaws, barely escaping with his life, the Ormonde-York faction tried to blame the assault on Buckingham. It is highly unlikely that he had anything to do with the affair; anyway, nothing could diminish his favor with the King. When the ladies of the Court prepared a "grand ballet" early in the winter of 1671, Buckingham, very richly dressed, was given a prominent part in the dancing.

Late in February, 1671, Buckingham's joys were crowned when Lady Shrewsbury gave birth to a son. Since an illegitimate child had no family name, Bucks had every right to give it his own and have it christened George Villiers. He had no legal right to hail it as Earl of Coventry (his own title at birth), but since the King himself stood godfather to the child it may be presumed that His Majesty had promised to confirm the title in due course. In his ecstasy Buckingham grew young again. At long last he had a son.

A few days after the christening George Villiers III was dead.[24]

IX

THE GAUDY STAGE
1671

O N MARCH 12 Buckingham buried his son in Westminster Abbey, "by the title of Earl of Coventry,
with all the solemnities, rites, and formalities of
such an interment." The discreet Abbey recorder merely
noted the fact that "a young male child was laid in the
Duke of Buckingham's vault, being related to that family."
A few days after the funeral, Bucks retired to the country,
where for some weeks he remained "inconsolable." Lady
Shrewsbury's emotions are not recorded, unless, perhaps,
one of the duke's epigrams describes her at this time:
"Affliction can no more take away her lustre than showers
of rain can quench the sun." [1]

The pomp and ceremony of the funeral surprised even
Bucks' friends and offended everybody else. It was right
and proper for a gentleman to provide for his by-blows,
see to their upbringing and education, and encourage their
careers. But the duke's almost royal acknowledgment of

his illegitimate son went too far, and his assumption of the right to name him Earl of Coventry struck at the very roots of the peerage. It was bad enough for King Charles to ennoble his own bastards; it was outrageous for Buckingham to try to imitate him.

In the depths of his grief, Buckingham paid no attention to gossip and black looks. Fate had stricken him. "My happiness," he wrote, "is like a winter's sun, that rises late and sets, alas, betimes." Anna-Maria had been his mistress for more than four years, and the poor infant who now lay beneath the stones of the Abbey was the sole result of their labors. Could he ever hope to father another child?

At forty-three, Bucks was growing old (Anna-Maria was almost twenty-nine). He was putting on flesh, blurring the strong outlines of his still handsome face, and his teeth were going one by one. True, he was more vigorous than most men of his age, but time and dissipation were taking their usual toll. Probably, too, like most of his libertine friends, he suffered from the disease of the century, gonorrhea, and was only occasionally fecund. No wonder that he was "inconsolable." No wonder that he wrote, as if to a friend who had scolded him for the "prodigality" of his grief, "Alas, how you're mistaken in the measures of my vast grief! It is not prodigality for rivers to bestow upon the sea such constant bounties, since they have at home a source forever to supply the expense."

Yet, even without good cause, it was natural enough for Buckingham to give way to passion. He was an actor in the world's great theatre—ordinarily cheerful, gay, witty, and graceful, attracting every eye and loving the center of the stage. His enthusiasm was quick, his friendship ready, his wit effervescent. But he responded to events like a weather vane to the winds, and his passions—love, joy, anger, or sorrow—were always extravagant.

The truth is that beneath his self-confidence lay always doubt; opposed to his positivism was always denial. He sought fame knowing how worthless it was, for "A man's fame and hair grow most after death, and are both equally useless." He courted popularity well aware that "The people like a common vice better than an extraordinary virtue," and "are so base that if a man has a good name he is half hanged already." Although he wanted to be great in the world's eyes, he could write, " 'Tis only the base yielding of some makes others great, as the sinking in of the waters made the hills," and, bitterly, "Great men cheat by gross, and are cheated by retail." He was a man of action, living in a constant bustle and stir of affairs, yet once in a clear-sighted moment he tossed off an ironic couplet,

> *Methinks I see the wanton hours flee,*
> *And as they pass, turn back and laugh at me.*

Bucks was the embodiment of paradox.[2]

Sorrow always wears out with time, and the duke had too many affairs in hand to spend all his days in self-pity. He returned to London on April 7 and plunged into politics again. Parliament had been continually in session since the previous October, and the King's ministers had their hands full. To add to Buckingham's troubles was the nagging worry that Commons would not accept an alliance with France. Rumors of a secret treaty with France had wakened all the old English fears of Catholicism and had brought forth in Parliament some violent anti-French

speeches. Bucks and Ashley, ministers caught halfway between the old notion that they were the King's servants
only and the new idea that they served Parliament as well,
began to hedge their bets. To spread responsibility, they
had let Prince Rupert and the Duke of Ormonde in on the
secret of the Treaty of London, while declaring in public
that they were opposed to an alliance with France and
all for maintaining the Triple Alliance with Holland and
Sweden. Arlington and Clifford, they charged, were the
pro-French ministers. Piously those worthies denied the
charge and accused Bucks and Ashley. Meanwhile, secret
preparations for war went on, to the accompaniment of a
rising whisper that something else was in the wind, something involving popery—a word of dreadful omen. In the
next few years that whisper was to rise to the roar of an
outraged nation.[3]

By now the Cabal was hopelessly split. When sputtering,
red-faced Lauderdale was in town—his duties took him
often to Scotland—he sided with Bucks and Ashley. York
was always on the side of Clifford and Arlington. Sir
Thomas Clifford, a fiery convert to Catholicism who
wanted above all things to bring the Grand Design to frui-
tion, now emerged as the real chief minister. His bold spirit
and bulldog resolution appealed to the King even more
than Buckingham's brilliance or Arlington's cautious cunning.

To Bucks, however, Arlington was still the great enemy
who must be fought at every turn. One by one he had defeated everyone else who stood in his path to power. Old
Clarendon, still an exile in France, was getting his revenge
by writing his memoirs; Sir William Coventry was an hon-

ored but inactive member of Parliament; the Duchess of Cleveland, withdrawn from politics, amused herself with an endless procession of lovers; Ormonde, ousted as viceroy of Ireland but still Lord Steward of the Household, was usually ignored by everybody at Court, including the embarrassed King, who tried not to see his former favorite when the two met in the galleries of Whitehall. On one such occasion, the irrepressible Buckingham whispered in the King's ear, "I wish Your Majesty would resolve me one question, whether it be the Duke of Ormonde that is out of favor with Your Majesty, or Your Majesty that is out of favor with the Duke of Ormonde? For of the two, you really look the more out of countenance." But no one could put Arlington out of countenance. His plump, smug face and black-patched nose appeared at every council board.[4]

When Bucks returned to London he found himself already committed to one side in an argument between the two Houses of Parliament. Commons had sent the Lords a new tax bill, with duties on a long list of imported commodities. A majority of the Lords, among them Ashley and others of the Buckingham faction, objected to the tax on white sugar (favorable to English refiners but ruinous to colonial producers) and sought to reduce it slightly. Commons protested that the peers had no right to alter tax bills. The Lords stood their ground. Buckingham "stood up highly for the privilege of the House of Peers" and made matters worse. The resultant battle between the Houses ended with the loss of the bill and a prorogation on April 22.

Arlington and Clifford, leaders of the "Court Party"

(which some years later became known as the Tory Party), laid all the blame on Bucks and Ashley, as leaders of the "Country Party," that loose coalition of disgruntled cavaliers, Presbyterians, and republicans that later became the Whig Party. Arlington insisted that the loss of the bill had cost the needy King "a million of money." His Majesty was properly incensed, and for a short time Bucks was out of favor at Court. Score one for Arlington.[5]

The duke countered with a blow to Arlington's pride. In the spring of 1671, while the King and his Court were at Newmarket, a deputation of pompous Cambridge scholars came to see His Majesty. Buckingham made fun of them in quite audible tones. A bystander, remembering that the first Duke of Buckingham had been Chancellor of Cambridge, remarked that Bucks' father had had "a kindness for the place." "By God," said Bucks, "if they would choose me Chancellor, so would I too." On May 5 the death of the incumbent, Edward, Earl of Manchester, gave the university its chance to win grace.

Although the post was purely honorary and paid no salary, it had a high prestige value, and Arlington, too, sought it avidly. But Buckingham got the jump on his rival "with a whole packet of letters" recommending him to the scholars—letters from peers, poets, bishops, and men of learning. The fact that he was a Cantabrigian while his rival was an Oxford man gave Bucks an additional edge. He and his agents handled the business so quickly and decisively that when Arlington's agents arrived in Cambridge they found every voting member of the faculty already pledged to Buckingham. On May 11 the duke was unanimously elected Chancellor. Score one for Buckingham.[6]

He was not in England at the time of the election. King Louis had come to Dunkirk with "a great army of 28,000 men," and on May 9 Bucks crossed the Channel "to view the French Court and camp there" and to chat with Louis about preparations for the war with Holland. Bucks returned a week later, just in time to receive the university's letter notifying him of his election. He rewarded the bearer "nobly" and set June 7 as the date for the installation.

Although he was eager to take over his new post, he was far too busy at the moment. He had just been appointed a member of the new Council for Trade and Plantations, and the first meeting was set for May 26. Three days after that the Duke Elector of Saxony was to be installed as a Knight of the Garter at Windsor, with Bucks and Ormonde as his sponsors. In addition, Bucks had a great deal of entertaining to do that month. Because the French Court was so close to England, "a vast number of gentlemen and cadets, in fantastical habits, came flocking over to see our Court and compliment His Majesty." Among them were many of Buckingham's friends, and, of course, he had to return the hospitality which he had enjoyed on his own visits to France. Thus, for example, on May 25 "the Count de Roux and the rest of the French nobility that remain here were nobly entertained at dinner by his grace the Duke of Buckingham at Wallingford House, where great preparations were made accordingly." *Noblesse oblige*, whatever the cost.[7]

The colorful installation ceremony on June 7 cost Bucks a pretty penny, too. The expenses of his academic guests— a hundred or so in number—were paid by the university; every doctor received forty shillings and every bachelor and master twenty "towards the charges of his journey." To provide the proper setting for his magnificence, Bucks rented York House for the day from its tenant, the French Ambassador. There the first Duke of Buckingham had been installed as Chancellor, forty years earlier.

At three o'clock on Wednesday afternoon the academic procession formed at Exeter House in the Strand and wound through lanes of admiring citizens to York House. The Junior Bedell (marshal of the academic parade) led the way in his bedell's gown, velvet cap, gold hat band, and regent's hood, "holding his staff the round way upward." After him came the Regents, two by two, "in their gowns, caps, habits," and fur-trimmed hoods. Then came the taxers and proctors (disciplinary officers), and two more bedells, followed by the Vice Chancellor (the administrative head of the university), "in his scarlet gown, cope, and square cap." Next came five Cambridge bishops and a number of doctors of law and doctors of physic, "all in their scarlet gowns, copes, and square caps." Last came a rabble of divines from London and Westminster, graduates of Cambridge but, alas, dressed only in "black gowns, not in scarlet." As a news reporter said, the whole affair "was observed to be remarkable for the great respect showed by the university in the number that appeared, and the extraordinary kindness of the duke, both in the grandeur of his treat and the obligingness of his expressions and deportment." [8]

Buckingham greeted the procession inside York House, at the foot of the stairs leading to the Great Hall. He was "richly appareled," and with him were "divers of the nobility," also in their Sunday best. All marched together up to the Great Hall, where the Vice Chancellor delivered himself of a stately speech and gave Bucks his patent as Chancellor, "fairly written in parchment and adorned" and enclosed in a silver box engraved with the university's arms. Next the University Orator took over for an extended flight in sonorous Latin. Buckingham then took the oath of office and gave his inaugural address, "very handsomely and pertinently." Unfortunately his words were not preserved. Afterward the guests, hungry after so much oratory, flocked into the Great Dining Room to supper.

"His Grace sat in the middle of the upper table," and was most affable to the Vice Chancellor, at his left hand, and to the earls, bishops, barons, and doctors who sat at the high table. The guests gorged themselves on "a most noble supper, consisting of fish, fowl, and tart, and custard, and jellied, and banqueting stuff . . . sweetmeats and fruits of all sorts"—piled up in tiers on the tables. No doubt there were wines, too, although the timid university chronicler failed to mention them. Between eight and nine in the evening the dinner was over and the guests rolled home, convinced that their new Chancellor was a jolly good fellow indeed. To further show his "kindness" for Cambridge, Bucks sent the university £300 for the purchase of plate.[9]

He could ill afford it. For years Buckingham had been spending beyond his income, princely though it was. As he fell farther and farther into debt, he sold some properties and mortgaged others at high rates of interest. As mortgages came due he borrowed still more money on other properties to pay them off. The effect of this practice was cumulative. A schedule of his debts dated August 11, 1671, shows that he owed some twenty-five people a total of

£123,140 plus £9,097 accumulated interest—a grand total equal to about two and a half million dollars. The income from his estates was reduced from an estimated £25,000 a year or more (when the Civil War broke out) to £19,-181/18s/2d. He had also £1,000 a year as a Gentleman of the Bedchamber, and in January, 1671, he had made an arrangement with the King which probably netted him some loose change: he contracted to supply the royal stables at the set fee of £11,000 a year. His other sources of income were too trivial to list.[10]

Long habit had hardened the duke, and debt had lost its sting. He left the management of his finances in the hands of his friends, Lord Ashley, Sir Thomas Osborne, Major Wildman, the City merchant, Sir Robert Clayton, and Edward Seymour, Speaker of the House. When they warned him of his approaching ruin and pointed out ways to recoup his estate, he struck an attitude, professing to love poverty—and half believing his own words.

"Poverty and I are twins," he declaimed. "We have been both nursed and brought up together. It has been a friend and tutor to me. It has taught me wisely all the good I know, and helped me kindly in all the good I ha' done. I never quarreled yet, nor murmured at it; it never gave to me the least displeasure. So old, so good, so gentle a companion would you take from me at last? Oh, no! I'll carry it with me now sure to my grave!" Bucks was only a fair actor, but he was an excellent prophet.[11]

At any rate, his friends talked him into getting rid of York House. For years the great palace in the Strand had been a white elephant, expensive to maintain and difficult to rent. Architecturally it was outmoded, lacking the comfort and convenience of the elegant mansions that wealthy men were building around St. James's Square and westward along Piccadilly. On January 1, 1672, Bucks sold the property to a firm of builders, Higgs, Hill, Eddyn, and Green, for £30,000. In the next few years the firm demolished the palace with all its supporting buildings, leaving only the water gate, an arch of worn gray stone which still stands on the Embankment near Charing Cross Station. The builders cut up the grounds with streets and alleys, named them George Street, Villiers Street, Duke Street, Of Alley, and Buckingham Street, and erected a rookery of tenements. The naming of the streets—an act of filial, if whimsical, piety—gave Bucks' enemies a chance to accuse him of overweening vanity. But he was the *second* George Villiers, Duke of Buckingham; had he named the streets for himself there would have been at least a Second Alley! [12]

As fast as Buckingham lost money, Arlington gained. He knew to a nicety the art of cadging from a spendthrift monarch, and while he was by no means a miser he always got full value for the money he spent. Year after year the King gave him new leases or grants of money, and his income from the honest graft of his office as Secretary was enormous. He spent great sums beautifying Goring House, his town residence on the site of the present Buckingham Palace. (When Goring House burned down in September, 1674, the loss was estimated at forty to fifty thousand pounds.) Arlington's country house, Euston Hall, in Suffolk, was only fifteen miles from Newmarket, the little village on the open downs whither the Court went in spring and autumn for the races. Euston Hall was "a noble pile," said John Evelyn, "consisting of four pavilions after the

French [style], besides the body of a large house ... very magnificent and commodious. The staircase is very elegant, the gardens handsome, the canal beautiful." The mansion could easily accommodate two hundred guests and their servants.[13]

It was the lack of a similar country house somewhere near London that worried Buckingham. For several years he had been looking at every available property, usually taking friends along and making holidays of his little journeys. On August 19, 1671, for example, he went off in his coach with Lady Shrewsbury, Sir Charles Sedley, and James Porter to visit Holland House in Kensington, "which it is rumored that his grace is going to buy." [14]

But Holland House, too, failed to measure up to the duke's requirements. Eventually he gave up the search and bought a tract of land at Cliveden, five miles up the Thames above Windsor. There, on a hilltop overlooking the river and the surrounding countryside, he set about building a mansion that for sheer magnificence would surpass Windsor Castle itself. He spent years building it, and put into it all the money he could scrape together. John Evelyn visited Cliveden in 1679, when it was still unfinished, and reported to the anxious King Charles that, while it had a romantic setting and "buildings of extraordinary expense," it was by no means as beautiful as the royal residence at Windsor. At least it outshone Euston Hall.[15]

While Buckingham went house-hunting and rejoiced in his new dignity as Chancellor of Cambridge (Samuel Butler acted as his Secretary for Cambridge Affairs), his enemies conspired to hit him in a very tender spot. A provision of the Treaty of London (December 21, 1670)

called for an army of 6,000 English soldiers under Buckingham's command as an auxiliary force for King Louis'
campaign against Holland. Now Lord Arlington's brother-
in-law, the Earl of Ossory (Bucks' constant foe), put in his
bid to command this army, and the fact that it had been
formally promised to Buckingham meant nothing to Arlington. It was an excellent opportunity to oblige Ossory
and humiliate the duke.

He began his intrigue with his usual cunning, stirring up
the King's latent animosity toward Buckingham by remind-
ing him of the "million" he had lost in the last Parliament
because of the duke's stubbornness. Then he argued that
Bucks was not to be trusted with the command of an army
(he repeated his arguments to the French Ambassador,
pipeline to King Louis). Left to himself, said Arlington,
Bucks would fill up his army with "officers and soldiers
who had served Cromwell, and who, being still imbued
with the spirit of rebellion and republicanism, would be
better fitted to carry out the duke's evil designs than to
serve in the armies of King Louis." Since Charles himself
had his doubts about the duke's loyalty and intentions, this
argument was very effective.

Even more powerful was Arlington's next suggestion:
that by cutting down the size of the army and persuading
King Louis to shoulder its costs, Charles could save a siz-
able sum of money. As for Buckingham, surely he would
not wish to take the command of a mere token force at the
expense of leaving his ministerial post in England. Anyway,
Lady Shrewsbury, who had great power over him, "would
turn him from any design which would remove him from
her for too long a time." The command of the smaller corps

could be divided between Ossory and the Duke of Monmouth.[16]

At the same time, Ralph Montagu, Ambassador to France (an Arlington man), reported to King Charles the French feelings about Buckingham, skilfully coloring his report with the dye furnished by Arlington. The French, he declared, did not look upon Bucks "as a man well-affected to monarchy." They knew that the duke and his friends "desired to keep well with the Presbyterians and fanatic party, who never were well-affected to a French alliance" and would not join in "the destruction of Holland, which is a commonwealth." The French feared Buckingham as commander of the English troops; he was likely, they thought, "to play a thousand tricks when once he had such an authority in his hands." [17]

As a third device in their whispering campaign, the Arlington faction spread the rumor that Buckingham was becoming attached to the interests of Spain, which consistently ran counter to those of France. The rumor was so widespread that early in October Lady Shrewsbury summoned Ambassador Colbert to tell him that it was all a pack of lies. As Colbert wrote to King Louis, she protested vigorously "that the duke would remember all his life his obligations to Your Majesty, and would never fail to keep his word to you." She herself, she added, "would use all the influence she had over the duke's mind" to keep him faithful to the interests of France. Anna-Maria was still more French than English, and her pension of £800 a year (about $16,000) from King Louis was hardly a pittance.

Colbert, who feared and distrusted Bucks, was skeptical; however, a day or so later he met Bucks at Newmarket and received from him complete confirmation of everything Anna-Maria had said. The two gentlemen agreed to meet some evening soon at Lady Shrewsbury's house and discuss (as Colbert wrote) "everything which concerns Your Majesty's business." Since it was still necessary to keep Bucks well deceived, Colbert recommended that Lady Shrewsbury's pension be continued.[18]

A note to Colbert's letter touched briefly on still a fourth part of Arlington's plot against Buckingham. The duke's favor with King Charles, said Colbert, "seems to be much diminished since the affection which the King his master shows to Mademoiselle Keroualle has detached him from all those other pleasures in which the duke had formerly engaged him." Buckingham, absorbed in too many personal affairs, had been neglecting Louise de Keroualle. The injured beauty, who remembered only too well how long he had left her stranded at Dieppe, resented his cavalier attitude. When Arlington moved into the vacuum, offering his services, she accepted.

The two were well matched: both were cool, cunning, unscrupulous, and very genteel. Arlington told Colbert that he was glad to see King Charles attracted to Louise, "whose humor," he said, "is not mischievous, and who is a lady," rather than to "comediennes and the like [Nell Gwyn and Moll Davis], on whom no honest man could rely, by whose means the Duke of Buckingham was always trying to entice the King, in order to draw him away from all his Court and monopolize him." Under Arlington's careful tutelage, Louise had learned to keep always in the King's good graces, and to "let him find only pleasure and joy in her company." [19]

All pleasures and joys, that is, save one. For nearly a year the rampant King had pursued Louise, showered her with gifts and attentions, and received in return only elegant conversation. Colbert, distressed for the fame of France, had long urged her to give in. Now, needing her support in his intrigue against Buckingham, Arlington persuaded her to comply with the King's desires, and, as a good pimp should, he arranged the time and place. Early in October, shortly after King Charles had left London "on a progress," Ambassador and Madame Colbert escorted Louise to Euston Hall, where for three weeks they and "several lords and ladies" were Arlington's guests.

On October 4 the King visited Cambridge, where Buckingham received him in all his dignity as Chancellor and presented him with "a fair Bible." From there the King went on to Newmarket and thence to Euston Hall, where Arlington presented him with a fair maiden. It is doubtful that Charles took the Bible to bed with him, but the fact that he took the maiden to bed is attested by the gossips who saw him at Euston spending a long day of "fondness and toying" with Louise and witnessed a mock marriage preceding the bedding. The fact is attested also by the birth, nine months later, of Louise's son Charles, whom the King acknowledged and created Duke of Richmond.[20]

Bucks was not invited to the house party at Euston at which his fate was being decided. With Lady Shrewsbury and his band of fiddlers he was having a happy holiday at Newmarket. He and his friends formed a group of "jolly blades" who (said Evelyn) spent their time "racing, dancing, feasting, and reveling, more resembling a luxurious and abandoned rout than a Christian Court." Convinced that all was well, Bucks had no suspicion of Arlington's intrigues. It was not until his return to London in late October that he learned how he had been betrayed and outmanoeuvred. Since Arlington and the King could not bring themselves to face his anger, it fell to Colbert's lot to tell him that the two kings had agreed to reduce the English auxiliary force to 2,400 men, with Monmouth as their general and Ossory as second in command.[21]

Buckingham's passion was awful to behold. He wished to heaven that he had never signed the treaty and swore that he would refuse to sign any documents publicizing the alliance. It was utter nonsense, he shouted, to pretend that the King of England could not afford an army of 6,000 men—barely enough for a training force. It was all a trick "to dishonor him, and to give the command to Ossory." By God, to the campaign he would go, and as commander, no matter how small the English contingent!

For a week thereafter Bucks sulked like a child, refusing to attend Council meetings or to transact any business. Then King Charles summoned him, inquired about his obvious unhappiness, and declared that "he wished him well, and would gladly find means to heal his sorrow." The invitation was the cue for a passionate tirade. Unwittingly Bucks hit the nail on the head by accusing Arlington and Montagu of conspiring to cheat him of military fame and to bring about his disgrace. Solemnly, and with a great show of patriotism, he protested against the dishonor to his King and country in sending a smaller army than that stipulated in the treaty. All his accumulated bitterness poured out in a torrent of words.

When he had finished, the King reminded him coldly of

the "million" the duke had cost him in the last session of Parliament—a loss which made it impossible to support a large army. Should he burden the nation with unnecessary expense just to gratify Bucks with a military command? In such a situation, he declared angrily, he would consider Bucks "no more than he would his dog." He concluded by laying his express commands on the duke and the other signers of the Treaty of London that they should live in peace together. If one of them failed in his obedience he would be promptly disgraced and discharged.[22]

Sullenly Buckingham returned to his duties, silenced but not convinced. A few days later Lady Shrewsbury received word from Colbert that her annual "gratification" would soon be paid. She replied that she was deeply grieved at the breaking of King Louis' word to Buckingham; nevertheless, she wanted Colbert to tell her frankly what Louis wished the duke to do. Should he go abroad as commander of the little English corps, or should he remain in England? She was confident that she could make him do whatever His Most Christian Majesty desired!

Bucks stayed in England, of course. He was somewhat appeased by King Charles' grant of the offices of Master of the Game, Master Forester, and Ranger of Enfield Chace, Middlesex. In addition, King Louis offered him a lieutenant general's commission in the French army—a gaudy shadow of the substance he craved.[23]

As usual in his moments of defeat, Buckingham's sanguine temperament came to his rescue. Life was too full, too varied and interesting, for vain regrets. Anyway, if he could not be a general he could poke fun at the military ardor of his successful rivals. Perhaps he had the vain Duke of Monmouth in mind when he wrote, "The sound of a trumpet pleases him now more than 'twill fright him at the last day," and "He's like Orion, who is figured in the Heavenly constellations with a sword always about him, but never draws it." What with satire, music, hunting, conversation, chemistry, and Anna-Maria, the witty Duke of Bucks was soon his normal self again.

Shortly he had occasion to exercise his poetic skills in a serious vein. On November 12 his father-in-law, Lord Fairfax, died at Nun Appleton. Bucks had always liked and admired the sturdy old Parliamentary general, and the poem he produced as an epitaph shows the sincerity of his respect. It begins,

> *Under this stone does lie*
> *One born for victory,*
> *Fairfax, the valiant, and the only he*
> *Who e'er for that alone a conqueror would be.*
> *Both sexes' virtues were in him combined:*
> *He had the fierceness of the manliest mind,*
> *And yet the meekness, too, of womankind.*
> *He never knew what envy was, nor hate;*
> *His soul was filled with truth and honesty,*
> *And with another thing quite out of date,*
> *Called modesty.*[24]

Now that his hand was in, Bucks revived an old project, partly to vent his spleen and partly to show King Charles that he was still a master entertainer. Years before, in collaboration with Thomas Sprat and Martin Clifford, he had written a burlesque on the windy, pompous "heroic" plays that were just becoming popular on the Restoration stage. The hero of his farce, Bilboa, was a caricature of Sir Robert

Howard, the dramatist, who had perpetrated some of the worst examples of the type. The play had been ready for production by the summer of 1665, but the Lord Chamberlain's edict of June 5, closing the theatres because of the plague, had caused it to be laid aside. By the time the theatres reopened, more than a year later, Howard had become the duke's political ally and no longer a proper subject for Bucks to caricature. Now Buckingham decided to revise the play, bring it up to date, and use as its chief figure the popular playwright and Poet Laureate, John Dryden.

In earlier days Dryden and Bucks had been friendly, but the poet's use of rant and bombast in his plays had offended the duke's taste. Most of the Court wits shared that taste. However irregular their lives, they demanded classical order, regularity, and decorum in their dramatic fare. Like his friends, Buckingham never missed a chance to poke fun at the empty rhetoric so typical of the heroic play. When a character in Dryden's famous *Conquest of Granada* (December, 1670) declaimed these lines,

> *For as old Selin was not moved by thee,*
> *Neither will I by Selin's daughter be,*

Buckingham offered this as a commentary,

> *A pie a pudding, a pudding a pie,*
> *A pie for me, and a pudding for thee,*
> *A pudding for me, and a pie for thee,*
> *And a pudding-pie for thee and me!* [25]

In revising his farce, Buckingham had the help not only of his secretaries, Samuel Butler and Martin Clifford, and his chaplain, Dr. Sprat, but also of all his witty friends. The

London play-going public was so small that a play was rarely presented at either of the two theatres for more than three or four performances. Afterwards it was revived from time to time at intervals of six months or so. A popular play became as familiar as an old shoe, and parodies on it were instantly recognized. The task of Buckingham's friends, then, was simply to remember a particularly atrocious bit of rant in this play or that and suggest a parody of it. Bucks gathered in the suggestions and wove them all into his plot. *The Rehearsal* was indeed, as he said in the prologue, "a posy made of weeds instead of flowers." (It was also, as his enemies sneered, "twenty other men's farce.") It parodied seventeen popular plays—six of them by Dryden—with oblique references to a dozen more.

In addition to writing the play, Bucks oversaw its production. He rehearsed the actors in their rôles, making sure that they spoke with some exaggeration of the usual canting, or "toning," style that was considered proper for serious drama and slightly overdid the conventional stagey poses—hands half raised, head back, mouth open, to indicate admiration; head sunk on breast, arms folded, to show dejection, and so forth. He took particular pains with John Lacy, a veteran comedian who was to portray Dryden as Poet Bayes.

In the intimate little Restoration theatres, where apron stages jutted out into the pit, and tiers of boxes rose one above another around three walls, there were no footlights to separate actors and audience. Under the mellow glow of the chandeliers, the dainty, impudent actresses flirted with the wits seated on the backless benches of the pit and ogled the King in his side box adjoining the stage. Everybody knew everybody else. The gossip of the Court, the green-room, and the coffeehouses was brought together and traded in the theatres. The face, mannerisms, and personal affairs of a playwright were as well known as those of Thomas Betterton or Charles Hart, the leading actors of the Duke's and King's Theatres. Lacy must look like Dryden, wear clothes modeled on his, and speak with his hesitant delivery. Moreover, since the poet's affair with a little actress, Anne Reeves, was well known, there must be a reference to her in the play, no matter how obviously it was dragged in.

The plot of the farce defies narration. Two gentlemen, Smith and Johnson, are invited by Bayes to witness the rehearsal of his new play. What follows is a *ragout* of riotous nonsense and broad horseplay, doubly delicious to an audience that knew every passage parodied. Let one example suffice. An epic simile in *The Conquest of Granada* describes two loving turtledoves who see a storm gathering, call anxiously to each other, leave, "in murmurs, their unfinished loves," and take shelter in a grove where they "coo, and hearken to each other's moan." Buckingham parodied the simile thus:

> *So boar and sow, when any storm is nigh,*
> *Snuff up, and smell it gathering in the sky;*
> *Boar beckons sow to trot in chestnut groves,*
> *And there consummate their unfinished loves.*
> *Pensive, in mud they wallow all alone,*
> *And snore and gruntle to each other's moan.*[26]

The Rehearsal was presented at the King's Theatre on the afternoon of December 7, 1671. Tradition has it that

Bucks and his friends took Dryden to the theatre as their
guest, and sat with him in a side box to enjoy his squirming.
The farce was a tremendous success. Its fame spread even
to France, where King Louis asked Colbert (the Ambassador's brother, Minister of Finance) "when he would
write him a play?" When Colbert apologized for his lack
of talent, Louis warned him that "he would be out of
fashion, for the chief minister of state in England had got-
ten a great deal of honor by writing a farce." He was quite
serious.[27]

CONFLICT AND CRISIS
1672–1673

H AD THE DESTINY that shapes our ends been kinder, Buckingham might have left to posterity a name famous in the annals of literature. But, urged on by a complex of motives, he had chosen to control events rather than words and ideas. Now, in the winter of 1672 and for many months to come, he was to find events controlling him. Struggle as he might, the forces he and his fellow ministers had set in motion swept on through crisis after crisis to their relentless end.

The new note was first struck by Sir Thomas Clifford at a meeting of the Cabal on January 2. The last session of Parliament had refused to vote for a bill of supplies, and there was no use calling the fractious Members together again. What with secret treaties and an imminent war, none of the ministers dared face the House of Commons and ask for money. Clifford proposed that payments from the Exchequer to bankers who had made loans to the government

[203]

be stopped for one year, and the money thus saved (more than a million pounds) be used for fitting out the Fleet. Clifford asserted that "he knew no other way but this" to raise money, and "desired none would speak against it without proposing a better and easier way." His colleagues were dumb, "and the thing was passed. . . . Being immediately public, it was too late for any man to call in his money" on deposit with the bankers. A brief but severe panic shook the credit structure of the nation. However, the King had his money, and the Fleet was duly readied.[1]

Destiny was in the saddle, and Buckingham found himself running to keep up. A new treaty, a duplicate of the Treaty of London, was drawn up in February, to be published with the declaration of war against Holland. Caught in the web of circumstance, Bucks signed it with no enthusiasm. Then Clifford proposed a declaration of indulgence—a suspension of the laws against Nonconformists and Catholics—supposedly to keep the "fanatics" quiet while the country was at war, but actually to prepare the way for the Grand Design. Always a man for liberty of conscience, Bucks heartily seconded the plan. When the declaration appeared, it was said "to have been shot out of our Grand Minister's mouth," but it was not his idea; he was only a follower. Again, he was not even present at a meeting of the Cabal on March 11 when the pigheaded Earl of Lauderdale persuaded the King to attack the Dutch Smyrna Fleet in the Channel before declaring war. Yet he shared the blame for that evil decision and the subsequent failure of the action.[2]

The Declaration of Indulgence was published on March 15 and the declaration of war two days later. There was a brief, nationwide burst of enthusiasm for both. The terms of the treaty, with their promise of profit to England, appealed to the nation of shopkeepers. The Nonconformists were delighted by the suspension of the penal laws, and hundreds of clergymen hurried to take out licenses to preach. Encouraged by the general mood, the King rewarded his ministers. In April, Sir Thomas Clifford became Baron Clifford of Chudleigh, Lord Ashley became Earl of Shaftesbury, Lord Arlington became Earl of Arlington, and the Earl of Lauderdale became Duke of Lauderdale in the peerage of Scotland. While signs of greatness fell like stars upon his colleagues, Buckingham got nothing. He could go no higher in the peerage.

In May, when the English and French fleets had joined and were almost ready to set forth, the King and his Court junketed down to Portsmouth to see the combined armada. At the sight of the great ships, Buckingham's martial ardor revived. Again and again he had been cheated of his chance for glory. Even now the little English corps that he should have commanded was marching bravely with the vast French army (100,000 men) against the Netherlands. This time Bucks would join the English fleet and stay with it until—like his father, Lord High Admiral under two kings—he had won renown upon the seas.

His enthusiasm so infected Clifford and Arlington that it took the King's command to get them back to London. Bucks announced his intention of sailing with the Duke of York aboard his flagship, the *Prince*. When the news of his decision reached London, Lady Shrewsbury, unable to bear the thought of separation, hurried off to intercept her lover at Dover. She had no reason to fret. York refused to have Buckingham aboard his ship and ordered him to leave the Fleet. Defiantly, Bucks hired a small vessel for himself and went along when the Fleet sailed up the Channel to Southwold Bay, searching for the Dutch. York wrote to the King, who sent orders for Bucks to stop his foolishness and come home. By May 24, the crestfallen minister was back in London, where he badgered the King until he was given a regiment of fifteen hundred men to command —for home defense only. There seemed to be no end to Buckingham's frustrations. For years he had worked and plotted to get an alliance with France. Now that alliance was in force, and other men were reaping the profit.[3]

Perhaps it was well for London that the duke returned when he did. On the night of May 25 a fire started in the house of a Quaker tobacconist in St. Katherine's, on the riverbank east of the Tower. At first it spread with a speed reminiscent of the Great Fire of September, 1666. The Lieutenant of the Tower, concerned only for the safety of his charge, fought it by blowing up houses on both sides of the Iron Gate, near the Tower. Between three and four in the morning, Buckingham, Lord Clifford, and several other courtiers appeared on the scene. Bucks took command at once, requisitioning engines and gunpowder and setting men to blowing up houses in the path of the flames.

The main thing was to stop the fire from spreading east along the waterside. Bucks commandeered a lighter, brought it to the King's Stairs on Tower Wharf, and took aboard a fire engine with its crew. Then he "stood away eastwards where the fire was most raging," and, at great risk to himself and his men, brought the lighter close to shore so that the engine could play its streams on the blazing houses.

By eight o'clock in the morning the fire was under control, but the whole day was spent keeping it down with engines and bucket brigades. Tireless Buckingham kept at it until eight-thirty that night, "encouraging the men and giving them money." The magnitude of the fire may be judged by the casualties: eighty houses were burned, thirty blown up, and thirty badly damaged. Three people were killed and many injured. For once Buckingham was a hero.[4]

His heroism was quickly forgotten in the rising storm of reaction against the Declaration of Indulgence and the war with Holland. The Nonconformists were quick to realize that the Declaration gave liberty to Catholics as well as to radical Protestants. In their bigotry they were willing to give up their own liberty of conscience to see it denied the hated papists. Members of the House of Commons protested that the King had no right to dispense with the penal laws in religious matters and threatened what they would do at the next meeting of Parliament. Then the Battle of Southwold Bay on May 28, a bloody but indecisive struggle between the Dutch and English fleets (the French ships did very little fighting) disheartened all but the most belligerent Englishmen, and even those had qualms as they watched the swift progress of King Louis' armies. By mid-June, over the feeble opposition of only 13,000 ill-trained men under William of Orange, Louis had conquered three of the seven Dutch provinces and had set up his headquarters at Utrecht. English Protestants saw their coreligionists being devoured by the grim wolf of France.

The outcries against France and popery grew louder and

more menacing. There were strong suspicions that the Duke of York was a Catholic. His wife, Anne Hyde, daughter of ex-Chancellor Clarendon, had died on May 31, 1671, with all the sacraments of the Roman Church. Since that time, James had refused to take the Anglican communion with his brother. If Charles died, what would happen to England under a Catholic king?

To make matters worse, someone had leaked about the Grand Design. Early in June, Arlington showed Ambassador Colbert a libelous pamphlet which (wrote Colbert) "gives a perfectly true account of the designs of the King of England, and tries to unite Protestants . . . against the common enemy, who, it says, are the Pope, the King of England, and his ministers." Buckingham refused to believe any such nonsense. He had read every word of the Treaty of London, and he knew perfectly well that there was nothing in it of what Colbert called "the Roman Catholic question." Colbert and King Charles saw to it that he remained in happy ignorance of the Treaty of Dover.[5]

It was probably at this time that Bucks wrote and published his *Letter to Sir Thomas Osborne* in an attempt to justify the war. Osborne had sent him a pro-Dutch pamphlet, *The Present Interest of England Stated*. The anonymous author had argued that the English should love the Dutch because they too were traders. But, said Buckingham, as traders the Dutch are the rivals of the English. "Had the author been a lover instead of a politician, he would have known that rivals are the things in this world which men commonly do, and ought most, to hate." We must destroy the Dutch, he insisted, lest they destroy England. "We are . . . in a perpetual danger of being conquered. For though the Dutch alone cannot do it, yet by joining with France they may, and it is that which a considerable party amongst them has been laboring for these many years." For "the present interest of England," then, Holland must be destroyed.

All this was for public consumption. Privately Bucks and his colleagues were deeply concerned. If Louis conquered Holland by land while the English were thwarted at sea, would he turn over to his ally the towns, islands, and rights stipulated in the treaty? In June the Dutch sent emissaries to both kings pleading for peace. Gloomily Buckingham told the envoys to England that the business had passed out of the control of the Cabal ministry. Hostilities lagged while the two piratical monarchs thought things over, warily eyeing each other across the Channel.[6]

To make sure that England got her fair share of the loot, Bucks proposed to tear himself away from Lady Shrewsbury for a while, go to Holland, and arrange a peace. The King agreed, chiefly to shut him up, and sent Arlington along to keep the excitable duke in hand. The two ambassadors reached Holland on June 23 to find that a sudden revolution had placed King Charles's nephew, William of Orange, in power as Stadtholder of the United Provinces. The enthusiasm with which the Dutch populace welcomed the English envoys threw Bucks into transports of delight. Surely all would go well now. At The Hague he greeted the dry old Dowager Princess of Orange effusively. He and his colleague were good Dutchmen, he said.

"It will be enough if you are good Englishmen," she replied.

"Indeed, we do not use Holland like a mistress," said Bucks. "We love her like a wife."

"Truly," said the Princess, "I believe you love us as you love your own wife." [7]

At Newerbrugge the young Prince of Orange was as stiff as his grandmother. In character he was almost precisely Buckingham's opposite—a man of "good, plain sense," with no vices and very little humor, "besides being sleepy always by ten o'clock at night, and loving hunting as much as he hated swearing, and preferring cock-ale before any wine." Stubbornly he refused the English demands and brushed aside a tempting offer to make him King of Holland. On the other hand, his picture of the horrible results for England if Holland should be "totally over-run with the French" was so moving that Buckingham was all for signing a peace treaty then and there, upon reasonable terms. Arlington was not impressed.

The next day the envoys set out for Utrecht, Buckingham, to the last moment of their stay, urging the Prince to come to terms.

"You are not to think any more of your country," he said, "for it is lost. Do you not see it is lost?"

"I see it is indeed in great danger," the Prince replied, "but there is a sure way never to see it lost, and that is to die in the last dyke." [8]

The ambassadors were royally received at Utrecht. Now reinforced by the Duke of Monmouth and Viscount Halifax, they were flattered and caressed by King Louis, who renewed all his old promises. Bucks blossomed in the sunshine of royal favor, forgot his fears, and became very high against the Dutch. Just to be businesslike, the English and

French ministers drew up and signed the Treaty of Heeswick, by which the two kings repeated their original
pledges not to conclude anything with the Dutch without
mutual agreement. Louis gave his usual magnificent gifts:
jewels worth £3,700 to Arlington and £2,100 to Bucks,
a ring worth £1,200 to Monmouth, and a jeweled box
worth £800 to Halifax. The value of each gift showed
Louis' estimate of the envoy's importance.[9]

The ruinous allied demands were sent to Prince William,
along with a copy of the Treaty of Heeswick to show that
the allies meant business. To gain time, William pretended
indecision. (Eventually he refused the demands and the
war went on.) On July 21, the ambassadors returned to
London, still hopeful of peace with profit. Buckingham's
faith in the wisdom of the war was renewed. "The French
are honest people," he said. "One can do business with
them." He had always admired King Louis.[10]

Although they obeyed King Charles's command and
acted with some harmony as ministers, Bucks and Arlington
still carried on their running battle behind the scenes. In
this, too, Bucks was hamstrung by forces beyond his control. It had given him no pleasure to watch Arlington receive the blue ribbon of the Garter on June 15, but protest
was useless; the honor was inevitable for a minister who
had served his master so long and so faithfully. When the
time came that summer for the marriage of Arlington's
daughter, Isabella, to the King's natural son by the Duchess
of Cleveland, Henry, Earl of Euston, Bucks proposed to
King Charles that if the marriage were broken off he would
get a great heiress, the six-year-old Lady Elizabeth Percy,
as a wife for the royal bastard. But it was too late; every-

thing was "concluded," and on August 1 the nine-year-old boy and the four-year-old girl were duly married. Consummation was devoutly postponed until the young wife was twelve—the age of consent.[11]

In his futility, Bucks was reduced to writing a satiric description of his enemy: "Advice to a Painter to draw my Lord Arlington, Grand Minister of State."

> *First draw an arrant fop, from top to toe,*
> *Whose very looks at first dash show him so.*
> *Give him a mean, proud garb, a dapper face,*
> *A pert, dull grin, a black patch 'cross his face;*
> *Two goggle eyes, so clear, though very dead,*
> *That one may see, through them, quite through his*
> *   head.*
> *Let every nod of his and subtle wink*
> *Declare the fool would talk, but cannot think.*
> *Let him all other fools so far surpass*
> *That fools themselves point at him for an ass.*[12]

There was more in the same vein, but Henry Bennet, the proud Earl of Arlington, was proof against satire. As Bucks wrote on another occasion, "He lives as if the world were made only for him, and truly the world is so foolish a thing that I think it was so." Even the Duke of Ormonde once said of Arlington (his good friend), "That lord expects to be treated as if he had been born with a blue ribbon, and forgets Harry Bennet, that was but a very little gentleman."

In the autumn of 1672, Arlington met with a severe defeat. He had long coveted the post of Lord Treasurer (last held by the Earl of Southampton, in 1667), partly for the prestige of the office but more for the salary of £4,000 a year, with all kinds of perquisites. He hoped also that his valued services and close alliance with the King would bring him a dukedom. In November King Charles dismissed Sir Orlando Bridgman as Keeper of the Seals, took Shaftesbury from the Treasury Commission, and gave him the Seals with the higher title of Lord Chancellor. Then, on the Duke of York's advice, he dismissed the Treasury Commission and made Clifford Lord Treasurer. Charles knew that Arlington "was not fit for that office, and that should he give it to him, it would be his ruin and expose him to the malice of his enemies." The Secretary, still only an earl, was hurt and humiliated, and his enemies rejoiced. But Buckingham could not claim the credit for his defeat; at the time it all happened he was playing with bricks and mortar at Cliveden.[18]

Bucks had long ago lost control over his finances, and now they went rapidly from bad to worse as he poured money into his miniature Versailles at Cliveden. His only gain of any consequence was a grant from the King (in September) of £2,400 a year to repay him for the £20,000 he had given Albemarle for the Mastership of the Horse. Had this pension been paid for its full term of twenty years, Bucks would have realized a huge return upon his investment, but it was charged against the Irish revenues, notoriously unreliable and ill paid. The chief effect upon Buckingham was to make him more dependent than ever on the King's favor.

However, he found another source of income at the expense of his prestige. When Clifford became Lord Treasurer and needed a large official residence, Bucks rented him Wallingford House and moved into the Cockpit apartments at Whitehall that by custom belonged to the Master of the Horse. These were all very well for one of the King's servants, but they were cramped and small for the magnificent Duke of Buckingham. Meanwhile he pushed the work on his country house as fast as possible. If, as Pope put it, Cliveden was "the bow'r of wanton Shrewsbury and love," it was a bower of raw bricks and rough beams at this time. The house was years in the building.[14]

As his debts mounted, Buckingham's creditors became more pressing. A member of Parliament enjoyed immunity from suit or arrest for debt during sessions, but Parliament had not been summoned for more than a year. In an attempt to keep some of his more vulnerable property from the clutches of his creditors, Bucks signed, on August 24, 1672, a deed of gift to Lady Shrewsbury of his "glass works and all the stock at Vauxhall." He still retained control of the factory; a year later he was offering it for sale for £4,000.[15]

One of the witnesses to the deed of gift was a new friend, handsome Will Wycherley, a young dramatist whose first play, *Love in a Wood* (March, 1671), had brought him to the attention of the insatiable Duchess of Cleveland. With Churchill temporarily banished from Court, she took on Wycherley as an interim lover. The story is that when Buckingham, who had so recently exposed his cousin's affair with Churchill, heard of the new amour, he was very angry with Wycherley, whom he had never met. Lord Rochester and Sir Charles Sedley brought the two together at supper, promising that Bucks would be delighted by Wycherley's wit. "After supper, Mr. Wycherley, who was then in the height of his vigor both of mind and body, thought himself obliged to exert himself, and the duke was charmed to that degree that he cried out in a transport, 'By God, my cousin was in the right of it.' " From that moment, Wycherley became the duke's protégé. When Bucks took command of his regiment in June, 1672, he gave Wycherley a commission as lieutenant—not because of his military prowess but because even playwrights must eat.[16]

Buckingham's most difficult problem during the troubled winter of 1672–73 was that of reconciling his principles and his party with his conduct as a member of the Cabal ministry. He had convinced himself that the Declaration of Indulgence was a wise, liberal measure (as, indeed, it was), that the war with Holland was "for the good of England," that Louis XIV was a great king and an honest man, and that there was no design to Catholicize England. Yet he saw the Country Party, of which he was still a titular leader, disagreeing with him at every point. His position was so difficult that he absented himself from Council meetings on every pretext.

Even had he wished to go along with his party, financial considerations would have made him hesitate. To work against the King's established policy would have meant risking all his posts and pensions. Willy-nilly, he found himself on the unpopular side of the issues of the day, forced to agree with his enemies, Arlington, Clifford, York, and Louise de Keroualle, now the King's reigning mistress and soon to become a duchess.

His friends, with the exception of Shaftesbury and the uncouth Lauderdale, were all on the popular side. Shaftesbury found himself in a parallel situation, but his convictions were more elastic, and he was an old hand at changing sides. He knew precisely when to jump on the band wagon of a winning cause. Moreover, he was a first-rate business-man, and his estate was in a flourishing condition.

The war dragged on. The Dutch opened their water gates and drowned their land, resolved "to die in the last dyke." But King Louis' foot soldiers were poor swimmers. There were rumors of peace, and offers were made and re-jected by both sides. In December, the Cabal (with Bucks absent) debated long and anxiously over the question of summoning Parliament. The King needed money again, but what would the House of Commons do if the war was still going on when it convened? The ministers had all read the pamphlets complaining about the stopping of pay-ments from the Exchequer and accusing them of being in the pay of France. They knew how many libels were printed and sold, attacking them as traitors, papists, and Heaven knows what. One little squib summed up the pop-ular attitude toward the Cabal:

> *How can this nation ever thrive,*
> *Whilst 'tis governed by these five:*
> *The Formal Ass, the Mastiff Dog,*
> *The Mole, the Devil, and the Hog?* [17]

Nevertheless, the King had to have money to set out the Fleet again in the spring. Therefore Parliament was sum-moned to meet on February 4, 1673.

At the first session, Shaftesbury, as Lord Chancellor, made an aggressive speech to the two Houses, thundering that Holland must be destroyed as Carthage had been by Rome. Unimpressed, the House of Commons returned to its chamber and set to work on a bill of supplies. Then, holding tightly to its completed bill, it addressed a strongly worded petition to the King, asking him to withdraw the Declaration of Indulgence. The petitioners made it quite clear that until he did so he would get no money.

Clifford ("the Mastiff Dog") and the three Protestant ministers—Buckingham ("the Devil"), Lauderdale ("the Hog"), and Shaftesbury ("the Mole")—urged Charles to maintain the Declaration, dissolve Parliament, and call for a new election. Arlington ("the Formal Ass") urged him to give in to Commons so that he could get his money and carry on the war. So did King Louis, and his was the deciding voice. On March 7 the Declaration was formally withdrawn.[18]

Meanwhile Commons had worked out a bill destined to become famous as the Test Act. According to its provisions, holders of public office must not only take the usual oath of Allegiance and Supremacy but must also receive the sacrament according to the Anglican rites and swear to a new oath. No Roman Catholic could subscribe to a statement which ran thus, "I, A. B., do declare that I do believe there is not any transubstantiation in the Sacrament of the Lord's Supper, or in the elements of bread and wine, at or after the consecration thereof by any person whatsoever." All officeholders were required to take this new loyalty oath and the sacrament before August 1, 1673.[19]

When the bill was debated in the House of Lords, someone argued that Roman Catholics were too subversive to be enlisted in the armed forces. Buckingham, who thought the bill a very foolish thing, said with a smile that "all the sailors, when taken by the press gangs, would declare themselves Catholics to obtain their release, and that a preaching minister with a basket of sacramental bread ought to follow the drummer to offer it to the recruits" for the army. But the Test Act was not to be laughed off. Lord Clifford spoke against it with such passion that he unwittingly revealed his own religious conviction. Lord Shaftesbury, suddenly deserting to the opposition, spoke just as strongly for the bill. The cunning mole was not too blind to see the handwriting on the wall.[20]

The Test Act passed both Houses, and the King was obliged to assent. With its passage, the Grand Design to Catholicize England came to an inglorious death. But the King got his money—£1,238,750—and on March 29 the members of Parliament were sent home, still muttering about popery and arbitrary power. The war dragged on.

A great effort must be made to win it. England prepared to set forth its mightiest fleet, to sweep the Dutch from the seas, and to land an army on the coasts of Holland. The Duke of York was named as supreme commander on land and sea, and Bucks wangled a commission as lieutenant general under him. On May 16 he set out happily for Yorkshire to raise 5,000 recruits.

He was rudely received. Once so popular in Yorkshire that every town and village turned out to welcome him, he was now greeted with sullen suspicion. Because of his connection with Catholic policies (and a Catholic mistress), the honest Yorkshiremen thought him to be tarred with the brush of popery. To prove their Protestantism, he and his officers had to take the sacrament at York. Even after that, the volunteers failed to come in.

Everywhere the duke went he found the forces of Anglican reaction in power, and the vicious laws against Nonconformists and Catholics rigidly enforced. His old liberal-ism reasserted itself. At Halifax he inquired "if there were any Nonconformists about." "Yes, many," was the answer. Bucks insisted that "it was the King's pleasure they should have their liberty." Told that the rector of Halifax Church had been preaching against Nonconformists, charging that they murdered King Charles I, "and so forth," Bucks was very angry. It is reported that he was "heartily sorry the doctor was not at home, for his grace would have given him a rebuke." A clergyman at Leeds complained to him about "fanatics' meetings." Bucks "broke into a passion," swore at the preacher, and bade him begone. He was there, he said, "only to get soldiers for His Majesty." He was sarcastic with the pompous churchmen of York and of-fended them by walking out in the middle of a long service. His conduct did nothing to encourage volunteers.

Finally he fell back on his powers as Lord Lieutenant and drew his levies from the county militia. Thereafter he made frequent trips to Yorkshire and drilled his men re-ligiously, taking "great pains to teach the meanest soldier." The God-fearing Yorkshiremen admitted that Bucks was a great general, but they looked upon his officers as "de-bauched, profane persons, and atheists," and swore that the duke himself "believed neither Heaven nor Hell." [21]

Meanwhile in London there were strange discoveries and important changes. The Test Act forced the Catholic Lord Clifford to give up his post as Lord Treasurer and retire to the country. He was the first of the Cabal to go; three months later he was dead, suspected of suicide. Passing over the hapless Arlington again, the King named as Lord Treasurer Buckingham's protégé, Sir Thomas Osborne, who promptly moved into Wallingford House. Then the resignation of the Duke of York as Captain General and Lord High Admiral confirmed the long-held suspicion that the heir presumptive was a Catholic. Protestant England seethed with rumors and fears. On June 22 the Admiralty was put in commission, with Buckingham as one of the twelve commissioners. Prince Rupert became Lord High Admiral, and Bucks labored mightily to become supreme commander of the army.[22]

But his days as a King's favorite were over; Louise de Keroualle (created Duchess of Portsmouth on July 25) had completely displaced him. It was contrary to the French interests for Bucks to lead an army on the continent. At Arlington's suggestion a famous French Huguenot soldier, Frederick, Count Schomberg, was appointed to the command. In a passion, Bucks resigned his commission as lieutenant general.[23]

He was frustrated at every turn, out of sorts, moody, and quick to lose his temper. Early in July two "gentlemen of the Horse Guards" engaged in a violent quarrel near the Court Gate. For some unknown reason Lady Shrewsbury's coachman intervened and slashed one of them over the face with his whip. The Guardsman (a Mr. Ayne) "was so far provoked as with one thrust to run the fellow through the body, and broke his sword in him, with which he presently died." The killer was seized and "brought to be examined by the Duke of Buckingham," who flew into a passion, "beat the man very much and broke his head," and promised to see him hanged. The Court of the King's Bench (headed by the Duke of Ormonde as Lord Steward of the Household) was more reasonable. After all, the coachman, a mere commoner, had dared to raise his hand against a gentleman. On July 29 Mr. Ayne was honorably acquitted of the charge of manslaughter.[24]

Destiny had not finished with Buckingham. All that summer there was a spate of gossip about him: that he was "much discontented," that the old grudge between him and Arlington had "broken out into a declared enmity," and that at the next meeting of Parliament (October 27) he would labor to impeach the Secretary. Although he was often seen with the King, the gossips declared that he was "utterly out of favor" and was about to give up his post as Master of the Horse to the Duke of Monmouth, "the rising sun." As a playful courtier wrote, Bucks was angry at all the talk about a new Master of the Horse, "and he has cause, if he considers what he will be reduced to if ever he parts with that. . . . His grace is a little out of humor at present, but as he comes in grace again, the good humor will return to his grace."[25]

At least His Grace could say, "I told you so." Violent quarrels between Schomberg and Rupert disrupted the plans for a descent on Holland. Then in August Rupert ruined everything by a bullheaded attempt to destroy a Dutch Fleet that had every advantage of numbers and wind. Rupert blamed his defeat on the cowardice of a French squadron, which stood off and on and took no part in the action. No matter whose fault it was, there could be no attack on Holland that year. In England, the anti-French-and-Catholic sentiment deepened to passionate hate.

Disillusioned and bitter, Buckingham made one valiant effort to get free of the trap he himself had built. Suddenly turning against the French alliance, he began to negotiate with the popular party. Shaftesbury had already made his peace with the Country members and was standing with a foot in each camp. To propitiate Bucks, the King gave him the post of Lord President of the North (a purely honorary title) which he had sought so many years before. But, said Alberti, secretary to the Venetian Ambassador, "he is not satisfied with this, and Ormonde exclaims that it is too much for the King to purchase obedience of his subjects."

In Council, Bucks asserted that the only way for the King to "regain credit with the country and reputation with the world" was to repudiate the French alliance and "accept the good terms offered by Holland." Then he would get money bills passed with ease, "since there was not an Englishman in the country who would fail, after such a change, willingly to open his purse to him." Even though he was seconded by Osborne, Lauderdale, and Shaftesbury, his words fell on deaf ears; Charles was too deeply committed to France. When Bucks was summoned to a second meeting of the Council, he sent word that he would never attend it again, declaring that it was "hateful for him to act in concert with Arlington and to help others in ruining the country, as he is opposed to this most pernicious alliance with France." There was some speculation that Charles might send the duke to the Tower.

For three weeks Buckingham stayed in the country, hunting, and posing as a popular favorite. But the Country Party was too suspicious of its lost leader and his friends in it too few for him to be acceptable. By the middle of September, Osborne had brought about a reconciliation between Bucks and the King, and the lost sheep was back in the fold, tortured by doubts and fears. Still convinced that he had always acted for the best interests of England, he was resolved that not he but Arlington should be made to pay for all the diplomatic and military failures of the past two years. However, aware that mobs and Parliaments are fickle, he followed the example set by his fellow ministers, took out a pardon under the Great Seal "for all treasons, insurrections, murders, misprisions, manslaughters, &c," and prepared for the worst.[26]

CATASTROPHE
1673–1674

WHEN PARLIAMENT MET on October 20, 1673, the
House of Commons showed its temper by voting
an address against the Duke of York's marriage
with a Catholic princess, Mary of Modena, his second wife.
(Buckingham had urged the Duke to marry a Protestant,
at all costs.) Commons was too late with its protest; the
marriage had already been celebrated by proxy. Before the
rampant members could stir up any more trouble, the King
called a short recess.

A week later Lord Shaftesbury made his last speech to
Parliament as a member of the Cabal, urging support for
the war with Holland. "If you permit the sea, our British
wife, to be ravished," he intoned solemnly, "an eternal
mark of infamy will stick upon us." But Commons was not
interested in its watery bride. Faced with a request for
£1,400,000 to set out the Fleet in the spring of 1674, the
members refused even to consider a bill of supplies until

all grievances were redressed and the nation secured against popery. On November 4 they fell to discussing "evil counselors"—Lauderdale, Bucks, and Arlington—and were about to attack the hated Duke of Lauderdale when their proceedings were cut short by another recess, this time to January 7, 1674.[1]

The appearance that autumn of a small but closely reasoned pamphlet, *England's Appeal from the Private Cabal at Whitehall,* had brought home to everyone the imperialism of perfidious France. The author, a very knowing fellow (perhaps Sir William Coventry), pointed out carefully the dangers to England if France should conquer Holland and gain control of the Dutch fleet, accused the members of the Cabal of being in the pay of France, and urged a return to the principle of maintaining the balance of power on the continent. He concluded by calling on his readers to note "How faithfully our ministers have discharged their trust in these great emergencies! How free they have been from dependence upon foreign Courts! . . . Their industrious endeavors and various stratagems to engage His Majesty in this war, their engrossing all business of concernment and concealing the most important debates and resolutions from His Majesty's Privy Council! Nay, their keeping it unseasonably from his Great Council [Parliament], and putting off their sessions lest they might cross their designs!" The King could do no wrong; his ministers must be to blame. In its anti-papist hysteria, the nation was convinced that the French alliance had been made solely to set up popery and arbitrary power in England.

Beat upon by the winds of hatred, Ambassador Colbert found himself alone, avoided by the ministers and suspected by everybody. He begged to be recalled. Instead, King Louis sent over a Calvinist, the Marquis de Ruvigny, to help him. To quiet the Protestant clamor, King Charles forbade papists or suspected papists to enter Whitehall or St. James's, to walk in the Park, or to appear before him wherever he might be, and ordered all judges to execute severely the penal laws against Catholics.[2]

The ministry was in a hopeless mess, leaderless and confused. On November 9, Lord Shaftesbury, whose sympathies with the opposition were all too plain, was dismissed as Lord Chancellor, the second member of the Cabal to go. He doffed his lawyer's gown and smiled as he buckled on his sword, doubly symbolic of his new status as a private gentleman and leader of the militant opposition, the Country Party. The Duke of Ormonde replaced him in the Committee for Foreign Affairs and aligned himself with Arlington against Osborne and Buckingham. Now it was Arlington and Ormonde who wanted peace without victory, and Osborne and Bucks who wanted to continue the alliance and the war. The bickering and confusion were so great that, as Secretary Alberti reported, "The King calls a cabinet council for the purpose of not listening to it, and the ministers hold forth in it so as not to be understood." [3]

Buckingham's friends in Commons warned him that he had been cited as "a pernicious minister" and would be "called to an account concerning his negotiations when in France" in 1670. Although he was heartily sick of politics and talked of selling out and "retiring to Venice or some other place," he could not bring himself to leave the arena. To save himself he planned to reveal "great matters" to the House of Commons, willing to risk impeachment if he could bring about Arlington's fall. "Like the envious man," wrote a courtier, Bucks was "contented to lose an eye himself to leave his enemy none." To make sure of Arlington's destruction, Bucks planned to revive the old affair of the astrologer Heydon, setting his agents to collecting evidence again. It was probably at this time that Mrs. Frances Damport made the deposition in which she accused Arlington of "foul practice" against Buckingham, and called upon "my Lord Treasurer [Osborne] and Lord Buckhurst" to bear out her testimony.[4]

Meanwhile the King, who had no plan of his own but felt obliged to keep his word to France, lived in a clamor of contrary counsels. The Duchess of Portsmouth and Ambassadors Colbert and Ruvigny preached the virtues of a continued alliance with France. Timid Lord Arlington counseled his master to appease Commons by every possible means. Lord Shaftesbury, as leader of the Country Party, offered the King peace with Holland, an alliance with Spain, and money to pay his debts. All he asked in return was that Charles divorce his queen and marry again, "So as to exclude by his own offspring the suspected Catholic progeny of the Duke of York"—Princesses Mary and Anne.[5]

Rejected by the Country Party, Bucks had no choice but to stake everything on maintaining the French alliance and prosecuting the war to a victorious end. His bold advice suited the King's mood and brought him into high favor again. As he rose, his enemies fell. When Bucks came hastily into the withdrawing room at Whitehall one day he found the King closely surrounded by a circle of courtiers. Bucks had no time for amenities; he seized the nearest man by the shoulder, pulled him rudely aside, and found himself staring into the furious face of his old enemy, Ralph Montagu. There was a sharp quarrel, followed by a challenge from Montagu. But two of the King's grooms saw what was going on and tattled. Montagu went to the Tower to cool off, and Buckingham was not even scolded.[6]

Bucks had a plan to maintain the French alliance. He offered King Louis his own and his friends' support and promised, if Louis would foot the bill, to buy enough votes in Commons to assure continuance of the war effort. But Louis' ambassadors decided against throwing good money after bad. The duke had too few friends in Commons—perhaps ten out of five hundred members, they estimated. "There is no use hoping," said Colbert sadly, "that with two hundred thousand crowns [£15,000] one could gain a sufficient number of voices." [7]

With his optimism again at high tide, Buckingham refused to be discouraged. He set out on his own to win friends and influence legislators, drinking with the "debauchees" among them, discoursing gravely with the sober, and taking the sacrament at Westminster Abbey to prove his Protestantism. While he sought to demonstrate his own sterling worth he constantly described Arlington as "the most pernicious person in His Majesty's counsels."

When it came to drinking with the debauchees, Lady Shrewsbury was a great help to her lover. On November 29, an Irish politician wrote to the Lord Lieutenant of Ireland, "Last night my Lord Treasurer [Osborne] carried me to my Lady Shrewsbury's, where there was Nell Gwyn, the Duke of Buckingham, and Mr. Speaker [Seymour]. About three o'clock in the morning we went to supper, were very merry, and drank smartly. I wish I knew how to write your Excellency all our good discourse." What with gravity, piety, good wine, and beautiful ladies of pleasure, the witty duke came in time to believe that he had gained "a strong party of friends."

He was never more mistaken. All the enemies he had brushed aside in his drive for power and everyone he had ever offended—the Clarendon, Ormonde, and Coventry adherents, the Talbots and their allies—and even the Nonconformists whose cause he had championed, all sharpened their teeth and waited gleefully for "the great baiting." Arlington, too, had his friends in Parliament who put their heads together to scheme up some little surprises for Buckingham. As the crucial January session drew near, they polished up their plots, certain that they would "spoil his design" against Arlington.[8]

Convinced of his popularity, the duke plunged on. He had hit on a plan to win over the House of Commons. Still ignorant of the Treaty of Dover (although he may have had his suspicions), he proposed to show Parliament the Treaty of London, of December 21, 1670, as proof that the alliance with France was purely political and not a plot against the religion and liberties of England. Acting on his own, he got King Louis' authorization, and just a week before the session he and Osborne persuaded King Charles to agree. Both ministers were confident (said Colbert) "that if the King their master speaks to the assembly in the manner which they propose, he will have satisfaction from it." King Charles agreed to take their advice, and Bucks rode off happily to spend a few days at York, with "masques, plays, interludes, dancing," and other forms of merriment.

On January 7, 1674, King Charles again asked the two Houses for a bill of supplies. The alliance with France, he said, "hath been very strangely misrepresented to you, as if there were certain secret articles of dangerous consequence." To prove the contrary, he offered to show all the treaties to a small committee of both Houses, and, with barely a quiver at the lie, he declared, "there is no other treaty with France, either before or since, not already printed, which shall not be made known." The skeptical House of Commons trooped back to its own chamber, scowling darkly.[9]

As soon as the King had left the Lord's House, Buckingham's enemies struck their first blow. Lady Shrewsbury's brother-in-law, Charles, Earl of Westmoreland, rose to present a petition from the kinsmen and trustees of the young Earl of Shrewsbury. This was something new, and the Lords came to attention. The Clerk of the House cleared his throat and began to read.

At some length the petition set forth the pitiable state of the thirteen-year-old earl, who, as he grew in years and understanding, became "every day more and more sensible of the deplorable death of his unfortunate father, Francis, late Earl of Shrewsbury, not only by the occasion thereof, but even more by the continuance of that wicked and scandalous life led by George, Duke of Buckingham, with Anna-Maria, relict of the said Earl Francis, multiplying every day new provocations to two noble families [the Brudenells and Talbots] by that insolent and shameless manner of their cohabiting together since the death of the said earl."

The lords squirmed uneasily. Everyone knew about

Bucks and his mistress, but it was positively indecent to have the amour aired thus. The Clerk continued. The petitioners would not have complained, they said, had the two sinners "employed the usual care of such offenders to cover actions of guilt and shame," or given any "outward show of remorse or amendment." Instead, "they seem resolved, as it were, in defiance of the laws of God and man, to persist in their shameless course of life in the face of the sun with ostentation, having buried a base son of theirs in the Abbey Church at Westminster by the title of Earl of Coventry, with all the solemnities, rites, and formalities of such an interment." Therefore the petitioners did "most humbly pray" that their lordships, "the supreme court of honor as well as of justice," would do something drastic about the matter. When the Clerk finished reading, there was a great silence in the House.[10]

Buckingham was stunned. This was a blow under the belt, something he had never dreamed of. Adultery was not a crime. At most it was a breach of the peace, and all a magistrate could do to known adulterers was to require them to give sureties for good behavior. But what an ignominious situation for the great Duke of Buckingham! Suddenly he found himself like any common man caught with a draggle-tailed whore and carried by a constable before the nearest justice of the peace! What would the House do—require him to give sureties for good behavior?

Some reply must be made, and Bucks thought fast as the Lord Keeper called in the petitioners: three of the young earl's uncles, Bruno, Thomas, and Sir Gilbert Talbot, a cousin, William Talbot, and an uncle-in-law, Mervin Touchet. (One of the petitioners, Anna-Maria's brother,

Lord Brudenell, was absent.) At the bar of the House these
five acknowledged the petition as theirs and offered to
prove its contents. Proof was hardly needed.

Now it was Buckingham's turn to speak. He stood up in
his place and stammered that he was "astonished that these
gentlemen would place such a blemish upon their house by
dishonoring their kinswoman." He tried to protest his innocence—it was all very unfortunate—"he had done his best
to root out of his soul the passion he had for her." Then,
with quick inspiration, came a statement which could be
made into truth overnight, "she had left England, and he
would never see her again." [11]

It was no use; the plot was too well laid. The Arlington-
Ormonde faction supported the petition hotly and called
for action. Accordingly it was ordered that copies of the
petition be delivered to Bucks and his mistress, who were
required to give their answers in writing by the morning of
January 15. When the messengers came to Lady Shrewsbury's house with a copy and a summons, they found that
the frightened bird had flown—perhaps to Cliveden, more
probably to her father's house at Deene. The Talbots
wanted her "proceeded against as to banishment and loss
of her jointure," but Buckingham's political enemies were
less vindictive. They were interested in her only as a
weapon against the duke. [12]

Buckingham's situation was decidedly uncomfortable.
The House of Lords had full power to punish an errant
member. It could fine him heavily or send him to the Tower
for an indefinite stay, and no lesser court would honor a
writ of habeas corpus. If the House listened to the vindictive bishops and applied the old ecclesiastical laws against

adultery, Bucks might find himself sentenced to a degrading penance or, worst of all, excommunication. By the recent Test Act, if he could not take communion according to the Anglican rites he could not hold public office.

His greatest danger, however, lay in what the House of Commons planned to do. His friends warned him of a forthcoming accusation, "which contains fourteen articles, of which three are capital." Recessed for a long week end, Commons was due to sit again on Monday, January 12. Bucks had less than a week in which to meet attacks from both Houses at once.[13]

In this critical period the Duchess of Buckingham showed how truly she loved her husband. The courtiers were astounded to see her "crying and tearing herself," and going about from one grandee to another, soliciting "with the greatest passion, both for the Duke of Buckingham and my Lady Shrewsbury, that can be in the world." There were others working for Bucks in less spectacular ways: his political friends, Howard, Seymour, and Waller, for example; the Court wits, Sedley, Buckhurst, and Rochester; and via the back stairs, his protégée, Nell Gwyn, and all the gay rout who had so often helped him entertain the King. Bucks could even count on the support of a liberal bishop or two. But in the main he must rely on his own wit and eloquence.[14]

His answer to the Talbot petition in the Lords' House was written in the third person, as if he were looking with critical detachment at that strange creature, George Villiers. He began with a humble preamble, admitting "that his life has not been so regular nor so far from blame as that he should be willing that this most honorable House were

[233]

troubled with a relation of all the faults that he has committed against temperance and the strict rules of morality." At the same time he was not so hardened in sin as the "horrid and black representations" of the petitioners made him appear. He would deal "frankly and openly" with the honorable House, omitting "many arguments and excuses which he might in strict justice have alleged." In short, he would throw himself upon the mercy of the court.

He contended "upon his honor" (no small oath) "that as for any open and odious living together before the death of the late Earl of Shrewsbury as is objected in the petition, there was no such thing, and he believes that if the earl had been left to the goodness of his natural disposition, and had not been exasperated by others, he had not resented a thing so much for which there was so little ground."

He contended also, "That it is generally known that the Countess of Shrewsbury parted from her husband because she thought her honor was not vindicated upon one who had done her a public and barbarous affront [Harry Killigrew]; that she went to Paris and afterwards into a monastery; that the earl, upon a groundless jealousy of the duke's having been the cause of her going away, was much incensed against him.

"He further answers that after the death of the said earl (for which he professes to have had as sensible a grief as any of those gentlemen that subscribed the petition), the countess returning into England, being disowned by her friends and relations, and the greatest part of her jointure injuriously kept from her, sent to the said duke to desire his assistance, which he humbly conceived no man of honor could have denied a lady in her condition."

However softened in the relation, this was the truth as Buckingham saw it. But he could not soften or extenuate his "shameless course of life" with Anna-Maria after her return to England. "Some things in the petition are unjustly aggravated," he wrote, "and others falsely alleged," but he was careful not to particularize. It was safer to plead guilty and trust to the charity of his fellow sinners in the House of Lords. (If every noble adulterer were suddenly called to account, what a clamor would rise!) "Omitting all further justification of himself," he wrote, "he humbly asks God forgiveness and your Lordships for anything in this or his whole life that may have given occasion of scandal, and seriously professes he will take care to avoid any reproach of the same nature for the future." [15]

Whether or not Bucks was sincere in his promises he was certainly frightened and angry. In the depths of his bitterness he talked wildly about throwing up everything and fleeing to France. Hatred of Arlington sustained him. He would not wait for the House of Commons to impeach him. Following his own maxim that "in probability of a war, 'tis best to begin," he would appear before the House, trust to his eloquence for his own defense, and do everything possible to ruin Arlington. Osborne did his best to dissuade him and for a while thought he had succeeded. But the duke discovered that even King Charles had lent his weight to the party opposing him. He was convinced that he would be "absolutely lost" if he failed to strike the first blow. [16]

The House of Commons spent Monday, January 12, discussing grievances, "evil counselors," and "ill ministers about the King." On Tuesday the House chamber, the little Chapel of St. Stephen, was packed to the ceiling with angry, red-faced members. An address for the removal of the Duke of Lauderdale was being debated when a letter from Buckingham was handed to Speaker Seymour. Before he could read it aloud, Mr. William Stockdale, Member for Scarborough, Yorkshire, jumped up and insisted on first presenting a list of charges against Bucks. Reduced to the laconic language of the Clerk, these were: "that he had been an encourager of Popery, that he confined a man by martial law, that he hath raised money, that he was a party concerned in breaking the Triple Alliance, that he said the King was an arrant knave and not fit to govern, that he hath defrauded his Majesty's menial servants, that he hath attempted the sin of buggery [sodomy]." Stockdale concluded by moving "that a person so dangerous to the government, and of so ill a life and conversation, may be removed from the King's presence and from all his employments." He asked also for an act of banishment against Buckingham.

He had hardly finished when a dozen members clamored to add their bits. Bucks, they said, had taken presents from King Louis XIV and had sent his servants to treat with the ministers of France; he had given "night and lanthorn counsels." By taking the bridle from the King's horse, when he wanted His Majesty to stay longer at Windsor ["at a drinking bout"] he had endangered the King's life. In Scotland, years ago, did he not correspond with rebels "and ransack the King's close-stool for papers?"—improper behavior, even for a Privy Councilor. At Knaresborough, last Whitsuntide, he beat the overseer of the poor for not providing for the family of a pressed man. "He has not common bowels of mercy; he beat an old gentleman for desiring [him] not to ride over his corn, till the blood ran down his hoary head. At Barnet he beat a poor soldier in bonds about the unfortunate killing Lady Shrewsbury's coachman."

No one had anything more to say about the ridiculous charge of sodomy—"a horrid sin, not to be named; not to be named at Rome where their other practices are horrid!" Stockdale had cried. But of course the petition in the Lords' House was discussed. "Is it no crime to kill the husband and prostitute the wife?" cried a member. "For us to countenance such things will bring God's judgment upon us!" Bucks was not popular.

Nevertheless, cooler heads prevailed and his letter was read:

"*Mr. Speaker, I desire you to do me the favor to get leave of the honorable House of Commons that I may inform them in person of some truths relating to the public, by which you will much oblige, sir,*
Your most humble and faithful servant,
Buckingham."

Curiosity proved stronger than hate, and the House invited him to speak.[17]

A chair was set for him on the left of the bar, the Serjeant of the House standing beside it with his mace in his hand. Ushered to the chair, Bucks "saluted the House round" and sat down. Speaker Seymour asked him "whether he owned the letter he sent him, and what he had to communicate to the House of concernment." Bucks stood up to speak, holding "a paper in his hand."

Whoever led the duke in must have given him a quick summary of Stockdale's accusations. Bucks had intended to discuss the breaking of the Triple Alliance, which, he had been told, was to be the chief charge against him. Now, surprised at the tone of the House and horrified by the vicious charges against him (especially "buggery"), he was indignant and upset, hardly knowing what to say. As his enemies saw it, "he betrayed great guilt by his consternation, fear, and distracted discourse." [18]

His discourse was distracted indeed. He fumbled for a moment with his prepared speech and then ignored it, trusting, as he said, to his "present thoughts." He started to speak to the charge of breaking the Triple Alliance and protested his innocence, abruptly shifted to his advice on the conduct of the war—advice which was never followed, declared his respect for the House and summarized his sufferings "for favoring bills from this House," asserted that he could "hunt the hare with a pack of hounds, but not with a pack of lobsters" (presumably Arlington, Ormonde, *et al.*), offered to "remove from the King and go beyond seas," complained that he had "spent an estate in the King's service, when others have got thousands," and concluded by submitting himself "to the good construction of the honorable House"—all, practically, in a breath. After that he withdrew.[19]

The debate which followed his departure went on till the House recessed for the day at noon and was resumed the next morning. The loudest speakers wanted to take Bucks at his word and "let him go beyond seas." They repeated their charges, harping constantly on one theme, that Bucks was a most immoral man. "Here is a crime in the face of the sun," cried a member, unconsciously echoing the words of the Talbot petition, "a murder, and his living with that miserable woman in adultery." The purely political charges were forgotten as the members rose to denounce the wicked Duke of Buckingham. He was not only an adulterer but the leader of "a knot of persons . . . who have neither morality nor Christianity, who turn our Savior and Parliaments into ridicule." These persons were wits, and wit, said another member, "is little less than fanaticism, one degree below madness. . . . This kind of wit's best ornament is most horrid blasphemy, oaths, and imprecations."

Buckingham's friends spoke up for him and urged that he be heard again. Others wanted to hear the "truths relating to the public" which he had promised. Accordingly, on the morning of the fourteenth, the House made up a list of questions and again invited the duke to appear.

This time he was composed, dignified, and dressed with "great splendor." After apologizing for his incoherent speech of the day before, he gave the House a concise summary of the events leading up to the Treaty of London, giving himself and Shaftesbury credit for all good advice and blaming the ill on Arlington. It was always "Lord Shaftesbury and I were of opinion," and "Lord Arlington was of a contrary opinion." It was Arlington, he said, who worked always for the interest of France. "Consider who it was locked up with the French Ambassador, my spirit moves me to tell you. When we are to consider what to do, we must advise with the French Ambassador!" He protested his own honesty and touched again on his financial losses; he had not taken a penny for himself. "If I am a grievance, I am the cheapest grievance that ever this House had!"

To some of the prepared questions he gave straightforward and reasonably honest answers. Some he evaded by hiding behind the dead Lord Clifford. Asked whether anyone had ever proposed anything against the liberties of England, he replied, "This reflects upon one now not living, and I would have pardon for not naming him, and fear it will be thought a malicious invention of mine. I have said nothing yet but what I can justify, but this not."

He denied responsibility for shutting up the Exchequer, making war without advice of Parliament, and attacking the Smyrna fleet, and in each case blamed Arlington. When he was asked "who made the first treaty with France, by which the Triple League was broken?" he replied with unconscious truth, "I made no treaty." He was honest about the Declaration of Indulgence: "I do not disown that I advised it, but no farther only than what might be done by the Declaration by law." He was honest also about the Treaty of Heeswick: "I think it a wise article that France should not make peace without us." On the general subject of the war he stuck to his guns, contending that it was "for the good of England." Finally he laid himself "at the feet of the House as an English gentleman," and again withdrew.[20]

Had it not been for "common fame," the chances are that Buckingham would have escaped scot-free. Nothing more was heard of what Ambassador Ruvigny called "the infamous and ridiculous accusations" first leveled at him. His friends claimed that nothing had been proved against him, and even some of his enemies thought he was probably "less guilty as to state affairs" than they had surmised. His frankness had stopped all thoughts of impeachment, but the majority of the House, inspired by the Talbot petition, held him guilty of "public scandal." One member called for a vote against this wicked man who had "made bold with his own King in contempt, and with the King of Kings!" Another quoted piously, "Neither fornicator nor adulterer, etc., shall enter into the Kingdom of Heaven," and urged his fellows to cast out this adulterer from the pure Kingdom of England. The question was put, and it was duly voted "That an address be presented to his Majesty to remove the Duke of Buckingham from all his employments that are held during his Majesty's pleasure, and from his presence and councils for ever." [21]

Well aware of his enemies' power, Bucks went directly from the House of Commons to the home of his chaplain, Dr. Sprat, where he lay close until he could see which way the wind was blowing. Meanwhile his friends, on January 15, struck back at Arlington with articles accusing him of being popishly affected, of breaking the Triple Alliance, embezzling the revenue, betraying the King's councils to the enemy, and "suborning false witnesses to take away the life of a peer"—Buckingham, in 1667. Several of their accusations were true.

With the permission of the King and the House of Lords (permission which Bucks had not bothered to get), Arlington, too, appeared before Commons, cleverly hid behind the cloak of collective ministerial responsibility, and managed to make it appear that Buckingham was to blame for all the failures of the Cabal. For five days the House debated what to do about the Secretary, while his brother-in-law, Lord Ossory, stood in the lobby, soliciting the members in his behalf. The Buckingham faction made the mistake of trying to prove their charges, and failed. Finally, by a close vote, Arlington was given a clean bill of health. Unlike Buckingham, he had always lived "with prudence, decency, and sobriety"; no one could accuse him of murder and adultery.[22]

On January 14, while Bucks was being baited by Commons, his answer to the Talbot petition was being read in the House of Lords. Afterward the petitioners were ordered to present their case at the bar of the House on January 21. There was nothing for Buckingham to do but wait out the slow grinding of the legal gears. He came out of hiding when word of Commons' decision reached him but wisely stayed away from Court. It was still a question how King Charles would respond to the address of the House of Commons. Ambassador Ruvigny heard that Lady Shrewsbury was going to Dunkirk to take refuge in a nunnery, that Buckingham "would see her no more," and that he had promised his friends "to lead a more regular life in the future."[23]

Surely there must have been a final meeting between the two lovers and some discussion of their plight. It is quite possible that both of them had been living in a fool's paradise of love and had been jarred back to reality by the Talbot petition. It was always hard for Buckingham to remember that he was not, like his boyhood companion, King Charles, superior to law and morality. As for Anna-Maria, she had been brought up according to the teachings of the Catholic Church; her life with Buckingham had violated those precepts; her first, frightened reaction could only be to flee from him back to the widespread wings of the Mother Church.

Separation was inevitable, of course. No matter what the House of Lords decided, the lovers were marked forever with the brand of adultery. There could be no future for them together so long as Bucks remained a married man. Flight to a foreign land or to one of the colonies would have meant the loss of property as well as reputation, and they were no hotblooded youngsters to dare death and poverty for love. Bucks was forty-six and Anna-Maria almost thirty-two—both middle-aged by Restoration standards. That they had loved each other there can be no doubt, but after nearly eight years even the hottest fires may burn a bit lower. Now there was nothing for them but tears and vain regrets.

While awaiting action by the House of Lords, Bucks worked desperately to save something from the wreckage of his career. As if unable to realize how completely the House of Commons had turned against him, he tried various expedients to get the members to withdraw or modify their address to the King, all without success. He tried also to see the King, but, even though Lord Treasurer Osborne spoke for him—or said he did—Charles refused to grant him an audience. Charles was angry at Bucks for revealing the secrets of the Privy Council and for appearing before Commons without permission. Anyway, the Grand Design was dead; the King no longer needed his Protestant ministers as stalking-horses. In spite of petitions and addresses, he would keep the brutal Lauderdale as High Commissioner of Scotland; but he had already dismissed Shaftesbury, and now it was Buckingham's turn to go. Osborne, a strong man who had prospered mightily under the duke's patronage, had formed an alliance with the Duchess of Portsmouth and was now emerging as chief minister. Professing to be Bucks' friend, he was actually superseding him. The King had no further use for the dashing Duke of Buckingham and at last sent him word that he was dismissed from all his places.

The decision was hardly a surprise. By now Bucks was aware that he had backed the wrong horse. He had staked everything on winning the war with Holland. Had that war succeeded—as it might well have with his vigorous boldness directing the campaign—he would have been a national hero. Now, as Secretary Alberti saw it, he was "left with a broken head, having misused it, and an empty purse."

Bucks realized, too, that his amour with Lady Shrewsbury had given his enemies the lever to topple him from power. But for "common fame" he might have won the sympathy and favor of the House of Commons. Now he was out of office, discredited, and, as he had told Commons, "in danger to pass for a vicious person and a betrayer of my country, all the world over." He was not exaggerating. Already the little poets and ballad-makers—the editorial writers of the age—had gone to work against him. One jingle quickly became popular,

> *When great men fall, great griefs arise*
> *In one, two, three, four families.*
> *When this man fell, there rose great sorrow*
> *In Rome, Geneva, Sodom, and Gomorrah.*[24]

Out of office, Bucks was out of lodgings, too, and, with
Wallingford House rented to Osborne, he was dependent
upon friends for a bed. Of course the mob of courtly syco-
phants deserted him at once, to his ironic amusement. "Men
ruined by their Prince and in disgrace are like places struck
with lightning," he said, "it's counted unlawful to approach
'em." As always, his sanguine temperament and ready wit
came to his rescue. He had lost all his posts of honor and
dignity? No matter. "Use honors as men do their mistresses," he said, "take 'em at first and leave 'em at last with
a great deal of joy."

But his honors also involved money, and it was no longer
easy for the duke to dismiss gold, "the corruptible god of
all the world" (as he called it), with an airy wave of the
hand. According to custom, a Household post was private
property, and even the House of Commons had suggested
that Bucks be compensated for the loss of his places. Yet
the King had dismissed him as brusquely as he might a footman, without cash or character.[25]

With the aid of his faithful friend and kinsman, Brian
Fairfax, Bucks wrote the King a long letter that must have
cost him a considerable measure of his pride. It was not
his wont to beg—even from a King—yet he knew he must.
He once told Bishop Burnet that "Princes thought their
favors were no ordinary things. They expected great sub-
missions in return; otherwise they thought they were de-
spised." Submissively, then, but with the creaking of his
stiffnecked pride as an undertone to his eloquence, Bucks
wrote to beg the King's permission to sell his place as
Master of the Horse.[26]

His preamble was a complaint at the "hardness" of his

lot. "I wonder very much," he wrote reproachfully, "that you can find [it] in your heart to use me with so much cruelty who have ever loved you better than myself, and preferred the following you abroad in the worst of your misfortunes before staying at home to enjoy a plentiful estate."

Then his anger and pain came out in a burst. "Pray, sir, what is it I have done that should make you thus angry with me? Was it my fault that other men did really prejudice your Majesty's affairs upon the hopes of doing me a mischief? Did I say anything in my defense which could possibly be wrested to a reflection upon your Majesty? Or, if I was forced to reflect upon others, was it any more than what you yourself gave me leave to do in case I should be first attacked?"

More calmly now he turned to the question at issue. "Your Majesty may please to remember that by your gracious permission I bought the place of Master of the Horse, which I hold by patent under the Great Seal during my life, with power of nominating my deputy. It is therefore my most humble request to your Majesty [that] I may be allowed to name such a deputy as your Majesty shall approve. If so I may not wholly lose my right to an office which I purchased by your Majesty's favor, and which the House of Commons were so far from desiring should be taken from me that upon the mention of it in the House it was universally agreed that no man's freehold ought to be invaded . . ."

There were more appeals to the King's kindness. "I hope at least you will not be harder to me than the House of Commons were." Then Bucks went into a lengthy summary of his career and his sacrifices for the Stuart cause. "Consider, I beseech you," he began, and then, evidently thinking the phrase too submissive, he ordered his amanuensis, Fairfax, to strike it out and begin again. "I hope you remember that I had the honor to be bred up with your Majesty from a child." Step by step, he went over the great events of the days of exile before the Restoration, without vanity or boasting, pointing out how many opportunities he had had to live a life of ease upon his estates —"worth near thirty thousand pounds a year." Instead, he had chosen with the hazard of his life to wait upon King Charles in all his poverty and danger overseas. Since the Restoration, of course, "I have been so far from getting that I have wasted the best part of my estate in following and waiting upon your Majesty." Bucks badly needed the £20,000 the Mastership of the Horse had cost him.

"All these things being considered, I conceive it will appear but just that if your Majesty have a desire to make me quit my place, I may be allowed to receive for it the full of what it is worth. Were I now as well in my affairs as when I first came into your Majesty's service, I should never have thought of making this request . . . But my whole estate being at present mortgaged, and I having lived to this age without being acquainted with any one way of making money, I hope Your Majesty will not be offended if, being forced to part with my freehold, I desire at least to sell it for the payment of my debts."

Buckingham signed the letter and sent it off. Now there remained only the House of Lords to be dealt with. Here, too, submission was his only hope. The cynical courtiers thought he was carrying submission too far when they saw him on Sunday, January 25, going "with his own lady to St. Martins to church." They jeered at him as "a great convert" who had to give a public testimony of his conversion. But Bucks did everything by extremes. For years he had been a sinner; now, for a while at least, he would be a saint.

On January 31, when the Talbot petition came up for debate after several postponements, the duke "acknowledged his fault and asked pardon of God and the House." Lord Cardigan, Anna-Maria's father, spoke for his daughter. He had received from her "a letter of submission," he said, and begged "that she might not be made desperate." On February 5 the debate was resumed. This time Buckingham "touched the assembly so strongly by his discourse that," said Ruvigny, "he was let off with a caution." [27]

It was a most extraordinary "caution." Formally, and with what dignity it could muster, the House of Lords ordered that George, Duke of Buckingham, should not "converse nor cohabit with the said Anna-Maria, Countess of Shrewsbury, for the future," and to make certain of obedience it required both the duke and the countess to "enter into security to the King's Majesty in the sum of £10,000 apiece for that purpose." In short, like any pair of casual fornicators caught in the slums of Covent Garden or Whetstone's Park, Bucks and Anna-Maria were required to give sureties for good behavior!

On February 11, King Charles announced the completion of a separate treaty of peace with Holland. Bucks' long-cherished plan to make England supreme upon the seas was defeated as thoroughly as his other dream: liberty of conscience. The wreckage of his political career was now complete. However, there was some comfort for him; the King finally gave him permission to sell his places.[28]

XII

EPILOGUE

1674–1687

PERHAPS THE KING's conscience bothered him. After all, he had used Buckingham shamefully in the matter of the Treaty of Dover. At any rate, now that everything was over, he treated the duke generously.

Bucks had to give up without compensation his posts as Lord Lieutenant of the West Riding (to Osborne) and Chancellor of Cambridge (to the Duke of Monmouth) and suffered dismissal from the Privy Council, the Council for Trade and Plantations, and the Admiralty Commission. But he was permitted to sell his place as Gentleman of the Bedchamber to the Earl of Lindsey for £6,000. The King himself bought the Mastership of the Horse for his son Monmouth, giving Bucks £2,400 a year for twenty-one years (on surrender of his Irish grant), plus a pension of £1,500 a year for life. This pension Bucks turned over to Richard, Viscount Ranelagh, in return for an unspecified lump sum to pay off some of his debts. In addition, the kindly King, touched by Anna-Maria's wretchedness, gave her a pension, too— £ 1,600 a year for life.[1]

In the autumn of 1674, Buckingham left London with the avowed intention of making his home in Yorkshire. At about the same time, Lady Shrewsbury journeyed across the Channel to take up residence in her old retreat, the convent of Benedictine nuns at Pontoise, near Paris. A friend who visited her there in December wrote that she was making "strong resolutions," and that her confessor had "great faith."

A year later, her sick soul was pronounced out of danger. Growing restive, she sought permission to return to England and take up her life again. Sir John Talbot, the autocrat of the family, opposed her wishes, but her older son, the young earl, took her part, and eventually she had her way. She was back in England early in 1676, living with her father at Cardigan House in Lincolns Inn Fields. In December, 1676, both the Queen and the Duchess of York admitted the penitent to their Courts.

Early in 1677 she married secretly George Rodney Bridges, an undistinguished man-about-town, second son of a Somersetshire baronet, and hardly a match for a Brudenell, even one with a tarnished reputation. When the marriage was acknowledged in June, Lady Shrewsbury (she kept her title, of course) left Cardigan House in a storm of reproaches. To everyone's surprise she proved a good wife to her George the Second, buying him a post as Groom of the Bedchamber to the King, and, in July, 1678, presenting him with a George the Third.[2]

In Yorkshire, Buckingham soon tired of fox-hunting, solitude, self-pity, and country ale. He seems to have cher-

ished a tender resentment against Anna-Maria, as if he had
urged her to defy the world with him and she had refused.
At least there is among his works a poem entitled "The
Lost Mistress, a Complaint against the Countess of ——."
In this the duke described himself as "forsaken Strephon"
bemoaning the loss of a cruel mistress who had left him
"forsaken and forlorn." He admitted that Fate was as much
to blame as she, because " 'twas a destiny she could not
shun." He summarized his plight thus:

> *In love the blessing of my life I closed,*
> *And in her custody that love disposed.*
> *In one dear freight all's lost! Of her bereft,*
> *I have no hope, no second comfort left.*
> *If such another beauty I could find,*
> *A beauty too that bore a constant mind,*
> *Even that could bring [no] med'cine for my pain;*
> *I loved not at a rate to love again.*

Although Baroness D'Aulnoy (a late seventeenth-century writer of fairy tales) told a marvellous story about
Buckingham's intrigue with Jane, Countess of Norwich,
in 1675, and Captain Alexander Smith (an eighteenth-cen-
tury romancer) spun a yarn about his hopeless love for a
certain Madam Cosens, the chances are that Bucks lived
discreetly, if not always continently, for the rest of his life.
At least, contemporary gossips had nothing to say about
any amours. Perhaps Baroness D'Aulnoy was not romanc-
ing when she described Bucks (some time in 1675) sighing
at a reference to Lady Shrewsbury. " 'If you wish,' he said,
'to see me in the profoundest melancholy, you have but to
recall to me that happy time when I was so tenderly loved

by one of the most beautiful people in the universe!' " Perhaps it was true that Bucks had "loved not at a rate to love again." [3]

In the spring of 1675 Bucks was back in London for a new session of Parliament. He found some changes. His old *bête noir*, Harry Killigrew, was happily installed as a Groom of the Bedchamber to the King, sponsored by Buckingham's enemies, Arlington and Ormonde. Ormonde was in high favor, and slated to go to Ireland again as Lord Lieutenant. Arlington, worn out by years of politics and gout, had sold his secretaryship and bought the post of Lord Chamberlain of the Household. His influence was rapidly waning. Osborne, now Earl of Danby, was chief minister, and, as Bucks was to find, a dangerous enemy. King Charles received the duke formally, but with a touch of his old kindness, and in 1676 appointed him to the Privy Council again. [4]

Shaftesbury and the Country Party (the Whigs) accepted Bucks with some reservations at first. The odor of the French alliance still hung about him, and his restless energy made him an unpredictable colleague. However, the first chance he got (in November, 1675) he made a speech in the House of Lords, asking leave to bring in "a bill of indulgence to all dissenting Protestants." "It is certainly a very uneasy kind of life to any man that has either Christian charity, humanity, or good nature," he declared, "to see his fellow subjects daily abused, divested of their liberty and birth-rights, and miserably thrown out of their possessions and freeholds, only because they cannot agree with others in some niceties of religion, which their consciences will not give them leave to consent to; and which, even by the confession of those who would impose upon them, are no ways necessary to salvation." Even though his bill would have meant no relief for Catholics, the Anglican-Tory majority in the Lords would have none of it. To the Nonconformists, however, Bucks was once more a hero.[5]

Buckingham was born for opposition, not responsibility, and the principles of the Whigs were not far from his own. For the next six years he took a leading part in the Whigs' attempt to disinherit the Catholic Duke of York and substitute as heir to the throne either James, Duke of Monmouth, an empty-headed wastrel, or William, the sour Prince of Orange. Buckingham's hatred of York moved him to join with a will in any plot against the heir presumptive, but his dislike for the two Protestant claimants made him a lukewarm partisan. After all, he was a Plantagenet on his mother's side and a better candidate for kingship—so he thought—than a bastard duke or a foggy Dutchman.

Out of power, Bucks was still powerful, and in some ways happier, too. He had his friends, music, chemistry, hunting, and a cause to fight for—liberty of conscience and constitutional government. Publicly he was linked with Shaftesbury as a joint chief of the Whig party. To protect themselves against Danby, the two politicians took houses within the liberties of the City—a Whig stronghold. (In derision, the King called Bucks "Alderman George.") They courted the London masses, built up their following in the House of Commons, and awaited their chance to overthrow Danby's ministry.

Privately, with the return of his normal ebullience, Bucks came to believe that he could intrigue his way into power again. Still a blind admirer of Louis XIV, he suggested a thousand wild schemes to France. With his friends at Court he played backstairs politics and even flattered and feasted the Duchess of Portsmouth. In 1677, when he and three other Whig lords were sent to the Tower for stubbornly insisting that Parliament was legally dissolved, his friends of the "merry gang"—Rochester, Buckhurst, Nell Gwyn, and others—secured his release and brought him to a convivial meeting with the King. It was rumored that he was to replace Ormonde as Lord Steward of the Household. But Danby, York, and the all-powerful Duchess of Portsmouth blocked the appointment, and Bucks was forced to remain where he belonged, with the opposition.

The Whigs' chance came in 1678 when the Popish Plot —the insane invention of Titus Oates, thief, perjurer, unfrocked clergyman, and sodomite—set off a shock wave of national hysteria. Capitalizing on the still unexplained murder of a London magistrate, Sir Edmond Bury Godfrey, and upon the "disclosures" of Oates and his fellow informers, the Whigs whipped the country into a frenzy against Catholics in general and the Duke of York in particular. While Oates sent his innocent victims to the scaffold in a steady procession, Bucks and Shaftesbury, as heads of an investigating committee, bullied and browbeat suspects and witnesses, and published amazing stories about the Plot— all in the name of antipopery. (It may be that by this time they knew the truth about the real Popish Plot—the secret Treaty of Dover.) In 1679 the Whigs brought about Danby's dismissal and sent him to the Tower. But for all their threats and promises they could never persuade King Charles to agree to the exclusion of his brother from the throne.

Late in 1679, remembering one of Commons' foulest accusations against Bucks at the time of the "great baiting," some of his enemies hired a gang of informers to accuse him of "buggery" again. It was charged that he had misused one Sarah Harwood and afterward sent her overseas and ordered her killed. Buckingham had no difficulty proving his innocence. Later the principal witnesses against him were found guilty of perjury, and the ringleader of the gang, accused of *scandalum magnatum*, was fined £30,000.[6]

In 1681 the tide of public opinion turned in the King's favor, and the Whigs found themselves on the defensive. Shaftesbury, accused of high treason, was freed by a London grand jury; soon afterward he fled to Holland, where he died on January 21, 1683, a broken and embittered man. Buckingham, who had never quite approved of his colleague's fiery extremism, was left unharmed but shorn of all his power.

It was at the height of the battle for exclusion that John Dryden finally got even for Bucks' caricature of him in *The Rehearsal*. In his great poem, *Absalom and Achitophel*, he described the duke as

> *A man so various that he seemed to be*
> *Not one, but all mankind's epitome.*
> *Stiff in opinions, always in the wrong,*
> *Was everything by starts, and nothing long;*
> *But in the course of one revolving moon,*
> *Was chemist, fiddler, statesman, and buffoon;*
> *Then all for women, painting, rhyming, drinking,*
> *Besides ten thousand freaks that died in thinking.*
> *Blest mad-man, who could every hour employ*
> *With something new to wish or to enjoy!*

To judge from a short poem, "To Dryden," in Bucks' Commonplace Book, the duke was hurt by the poetic "witchcraft" which had wounded his name. He had reason. His name is remembered more for Dryden's satire than for any achievement of his own—even his long, steady fight for liberty of conscience.

Early in 1685, King Charles died. James, Duke of York, ascended the throne and did his best to become as absolute a monarch as his cousin of France. Only Monmouth and a rabble of fanatic peasants opposed him in open rebellion. Monmouth's forces were crushed at Sedgemoor by the Duchess of Cleveland's former lover, Jack Churchill, and on July 15, 1685, the gay young duke came to a bloody end on Tower Hill. A few days later another actor in the great drama, Lord Arlington, died peacefully in bed. With his usual caution, he waited until he knew there was no hope of recovery before sending for a priest and admitting his faith. Since Lauderdale had died in August, 1682, Buckingham was now the last survivor of the famous Cabal.[7]

With the exception of one member, Lady Shrewsbury's family prospered during the short reign of King James. In 1686, John Talbot, Anna-Maria's second son by her first husband, followed his father's example, fought a duel with Henry, Duke of Grafton (the former Earl of Euston), and lost his life. But Charles, the young Earl of Shrewsbury, was a promising and hopeful gentleman. In 1681 he turned Protestant and entered politics. In his maturity he became a duke and held a number of important offices of state.

After the Revolution of 1688, which dethroned King James and set up William and Mary, Lady Shrewsbury remained loyal to the exiled Stuarts and figured in several

Jacobite plots. She died on April 20, 1702, and was buried in the Church of St. Giles in the Fields, London. Her second husband and her sons Charles and George survived her; both sons died childless, and her line came to an end.[8]

When the Whigs finally admitted defeat in 1683, Buckingham withdrew from politics and turned again to literature. In the next three years he turned out a number of fugitive pieces, among them two dramatic sketches, *The Militant Couple*, and *Sedgemoor Fight Rehearsed at Whitehall*; a revision of Beaumont and Fletcher's *Philaster*; a satire on transubstantiation, *The Duke of Buckingham's Conference with a Priest*; and one serious pamphlet, *A Short Discourse Upon the Reasonableness of Men's Having a Religion*. This eloquent little essay, essentially an argument for liberty of conscience and against religious persecution, drew fire from several dogmatic and intolerant writers. The great Quaker, William Penn, defended it ardently as "the undertaking of a person over whom a great reason and the love of his country does predominate." [9]

By 1686 Bucks was down to his last shilling. One by one he had sold off nearly all his properties in town and country. All he had left was an estate at Helmesley, Yorkshire, and even that was plastered with mortgages. After his death, the Duchess of Buckingham—who survived until 1705—was left with nothing but a life interest in her father's property, Nun Appleton.

Bucks went to Helmesley to live. In his rustic retreat he spent his time hunting, looking after the pitiful remnants of his property, and drinking with his friends. He was fifty-eight years old, but he still hoped some day to return to politics and do something about "securing to every man in

England his religion and liberty and estate." Ebullient and witty as ever, he continued to extract a good deal of pleasure out of life. His pack of hounds became famous, and his exploits at the chase are still remembered in the folklore of Yorkshire. Always friendly with his social inferiors, he became very popular in the countryside. The story is told that once when he dropped into a rustic inn and called lustily for a pot of ale, the loutish inn-keeper grumbled, "Your grace is in a plaguey hurry. I'll come as soon as I've served my hogs." Bucks promptly improvised a quatrain,

"Some ale, some ale," the impetuous Villiers cried;
To whom the surly landlord thus replied,
"Plague on your grace, you treat me as your dog;
I'll serve your lordship when I've served my hog."

In April, 1687, after a fox hunt, Bucks caught a chill from sitting on the damp ground. He was put to bed in a tenant farmhouse at Kirkby-Moorside—not, as Pope wrote viciously, "in the worst inn's worst room," but in the best bedroom of a substantial farmer. When a high fever developed, a physician was called in, but the duke grew rapidly worse. On April 17 his friends, warned that the end was near, summoned a clergyman to administer the last rites. When the parson asked the duke about his religious affiliation, Bucks replied, "It is an insignificant question, for I have been a shame and a disgrace to all religions. If you can do me any good, do." As the grim shadows darkened about him, he received the sacrament "with all the decency imaginable, and in an hour afterward he lost his speech, and so continued till eleven that night, when he died." Two months later he was buried in Westminster Abbey with full rites and ceremonies.

The Muse of History has not been kind to George Villiers, second Duke of Buckingham. She has preferred to listen to the prejudiced accounts of Clarendon, Echard, Burnet, Carte (biographer of the Duke of Ormonde), and Macaulay. Because of his love for Anna-Maria, Countess of Shrewsbury, and his duel with that lady's unfortunate husband, Bucks has been stigmatized as "the wicked duke," rather than accepted for what he truly was, a witty duke, in the Restoration sense of wit—a man of intelligent and speculative mind. Brought up with princes and overshadowed always by his famous father, he was ambitious to be great in politics, but he was too versatile, too easily distracted into fascinating byways, to press forward along the narrow path to fame. He was born a century too soon to see his dream of England's supremacy upon the seas come true. He was born a millennium too soon for the realization of his greatest dream, "a true and perfect liberty of conscience."

NOTES

A great deal of material about Buckingham appears in the usual printed histories, diaries, memoirs, and collections of letters and records from the Restoration period. Much remains in manuscript, particularly in the despatches of the French ambassadors preserved in Les Archives des Affaires Etrangères, Paris; in the Carte and Clarendon collections of letters and documents in the Bodleian Library, Oxford; in the Harleian, Additional, and other collections of the British Museum, and, of course, in the papers preserved in the Public Record Office, London.

In the following notes, some abbreviations and short titles are used to save space:

Barbour: Violet Barbour, *Henry Bennet, Earl of Arlington*, 1914.

Burghclere: Winifred Gardner, Lady Burghclere, *George Villiers, Second Duke of Buckingham*, 1903.

C.A.: Correspondence Angleterre, Archives des Affaires Etrangères, Paris.

Clarendon: *The Life of Edward, Earl of Clarendon. Written by Himself*, 1827.

CSPD: Calendars of State Papers Domestic.

CSP Venetian: Calendars of State Papers Venetian.

Evelyn: *Diary of John Evelyn*, ed. H. B. Wheatley, 1906.

Grammont: Anthony Hamilton, *Memoirs of Count Grammont*, ed. Gordon Goodwin, 1903.

HMC: Reports of the Royal Historical Manuscripts Commission.

Mignet: M. Mignet, *Négociations relatives à la Succession d'Espagne*, 1835–42.

Pepys: *The Diary of Samuel Pepys*, ed. H. B. Wheatley, 1893.

POSA: Poems on State Affairs, 1705.

S.P.: State Papers, Public Record Office, London.

I. THE HERO

1. For Buckingham's estates, debts, and income, see Brian Fairfax's MS account of his life in Harleian MS 6862, and see also Additional MS 5821, f. 218. For other items see H. B. Wheatley, *London Past and Present*, 1891; Burghclere, *Buckingham; Memoirs of Thomas, Earl of Ailesbury*, 1890, I, 13; Commonplace Book, f. 1, 14.

2. Robert Bell, *Memorials of the Civil War*, 1849, ii, 253; Fairfax, *Life of Buckingham* (Arber Reprints); Laurence Echard, *History of England*, 1718, III, 252; Clarendon, III, 133.

3. Grammont, I, 136–39; Pepys, Nov. 6, 1663.

4. Commonplace Book, f. 53; Harleian MS 6947, f. 194; Evelyn, Aug. 15, 1662; Echard, *History*, III, 191.

5. Grammont, II, 37; I, 119; II, 105; Commonplace Book, f. 78.

6. Fairfax, Harleian MS 6862; Julia Cartwright, *Madame*, 1900, pp. 74–84.

7. Commonplace Book, ff. 100, 117.

8. Grammont, I, 97, 103, 137.

9. Pepys, Dec. 20, 1665; Thomas Brown, *Miscellanea Aulica*, 1702, Jan. 9, 1666.

10. John Aubrey, *Brief Lives*, 1898, I, 189; A. H. Nethercot, *Abraham Cowley*, 1938, pp. 244 ff.

11. Albertus Warren, *An Apology for the Discourse of Human Reason*, 1680; Fairfax, Harleian MS 6862; Evelyn, a letter to Pepys on Aug. 12, 1689.

12. Fairfax, Harleian MS 6862; Thomas Sprat, *History of the Royal Society*, 1668, p. 37; Clarendon, III, 280.

13. Fairfax, Harleian MS 6862; *CSPD*, 1661–62, October; 1662–

63, June 30; Evelyn, Sept. 12, 1677; *CSP Venetian*, 1671–72, Sept. 27/Oct. 7, 1672.

14. Thomas Birch, *History of the Royal Society*, 1756, I, 26, 35.

15. H. C. Foxcroft, *Life of Halifax*, 1897, I, 51; *CSPD*, 1663–1664, Aug. 4, 1663; John Heydon, Preface to *El Havareuna*, 1665; S.P. 29/187/160.

16. Pepys, Jan. 6, 1668; John Hayward, *Letters of St. Evremonde*, 1930, p. 95.

17. M. Des Maizeaux, *Oeuvres de M. de Saint-Evremonde*, 1739, II, 203–69.

18. Fairfax, Harleian MS 6862; White Kennet, *A Register and Chronicle*, 1728, p. 891; Burghclere, pp. 130–32.

19. White Kennet, *A History of England*, 1706, p. 271; John Oldmixon, *History of England in the Reigns of the Stuarts*, 1730, p. 543; Clarendon, III, 134.

II. ENTER ANNA-MARIA

1. HMC *Fifth Report*, p. 145; Collins' *Peerage*, III, 28.

2. See Sloane MS 1684, f. 8, for Anna-Maria's horoscope; *CSPD*, 1657–58, Aug. 3, 1658; HMC *Seventh Report*, Sept. 24, 1658.

3. *Acts and Ordinances of the Interregnum*, II, 715-16.

4. G.E.C., *Complete Peerage*, Shrewsbury; *Biographical Dictionary of the English Catholics; House of Lords Journals*.

5. Grammont, I, 109; II, 3, 24.

6. Grammont, I, 110; Pepys, Aug. 19, 1662.

7. HMC *Seventh Report*, Aug. 21, 1662; *CSP Venetian*, 1661–64, April 30/March 10, Aug. 29/Sept. 8, 1662; Grammont, II, 3.

8. HMC *Le Fleming*, p. 30; *Correspondence of the Family of Hatton* (Camden Society, 1878), I, 42; A. H. Browning, *Thomas Osborne, Earl of Danby*, 1944, II, 10.

9. Grammont, II, 135; HMC *Third Report*, July 21, 1660; Bevil Higgons, *Historical and Critical Remarks on Burnet's History*, 1725, p. 450.

10. Grammont, II, 136; Commonplace Book, ff. 45, 65.

11. *CSP Venetian*, 1664–65, March 17/27, 1665; HMC *Hastings MS*, April 5, 1665; *Journal of the Earl of Sandwich*, 1929, April 10, 12, 17, 20, May 6, 13, 14, 1665; *CSPD*, 1665–66, April 16, 1665. Historians have long accused Buckingham of cowardice because

of a story of this time first told by Burghclere (p. 145). This story actually relates to a battle two years later and to John Sheffield, Duke of Buckinghamshire. See the latter's *Works*, 1740, II, 6.

12. Anthony Wood, *Life and Times*, 1891, II, 42.

13. Commonplace Book, ff. 3, 12, 31, 65.

14. HMC *Somerset MS*, p. 174; *CSPD*, 1665–66, Dec. 20, 1665.

15. Commonplace Book, ff. 13, 31, 66.

16. Burghclere, pp. 147-49; *CSPD*, 1665–66, July 14, 1666.

17. *Memoirs of Sir John Reresby*, 1936, pp. 58-59; Commonplace Book, ff. 13, 66, 79; C. J. Smith, *Historical and Literary Curiosities*, 1840, pp. 42-43.

III. Persons of Quality

1. *House of Lords Journals*; Commonplace Book, f. 12; Pepys, Jan. 17, 1668.

2. George Etherege, *The Man of Mode*, III, 2.

3. Grammont, II, 136; Pepys, Oct. 21, 1666.

4. Commonplace Book, ff. 49, 94.

5. "To Mr. Clifford on His *Human Reason*," Buckingham, *Works*, 1705, II, 65.

6. Burnet, *History*, I, 158; Commonplace Book, f. 30.

7. Clarendon, III, 133.

8. E. Chamberlayne, *Angliae Notitia*, 1673, p. 179; Ailesbury, *Memoirs*, pp. 86-87.

9. Burghclere, pp. 141-42; Burnet, *History*, I, 180.

10. Pepys, Oct. 5, 15, 1666; *CSPD*, 1666–67, Oct. 6, 1666.

11. *House of Lords Journals*; Pepys, Oct. 27, 1666. For full accounts of this affair, see Clarendon, III, 145-150; Thomas Carte, *Life of James, Duke of Ormonde*, 1851, II, 332-36; and Arlington's letters in *Miscellanea Aulica*, p. 424. It should be remembered that these stories are all by Ossory's apologists.

12. Pepys, Nov. 19, 1666; *House of Lords Journals*.

13. Browning, *Danby*, II, 31; Pepys, Nov. 15, 1666.

14. *House of Lords Journals*; Clarendon, III, 178.

15. Pepys, Dec. 19, 1666; Clarendon, III, 153-54; Oldmixon, *History*, p. 533.

16. *House of Lords Journals*; Echard, *History*, III, 171; Carte MS 217, f. 433, Jan. 4, 1667.

17. Clarendon, III, 178.

NOTES

IV. Episode in Villainy

1. John Lilbourne, *A Defensive Declaration*, 1653; Clarendon, *Life*, III, 270.
2. *CSPD*, 1663–64, April 23, 1664.
3. S.P. 29/181/136.
4. Additional MS 27,872, f. 15.
5. Carte MS 35, f. 302, Leving to Sir George Lane.
6. HMC *Le Fleming*, p. 44; *CSPD*, 1668, March 16, 18.
7. Clarendon, III, 272–77; Carte, *Ormonde*, II, 347; S.P. 29/187/160.
8. S.P. 29/187/184.
9. S.P. 29/191/91.
10. Carte MS 46, f. 456; *CSPD*, 1666–67, Feb. 26, 1667.
11. Clarendon MS 85, f. 96.
12. Echard, *History*, III, 171; Carte MS 35, f. 329.
13. *Orrery State Letters*, 1742, p. 224; Carte MS 35, f. 238.
14. Additional MS 27,872, ff. 6, 8; HMC *Le Fleming*, March 18, 1667.
15. *Diary of Sir Henry Slingsby*, 1836, p. 375.
16. Clarendon, III, 276; Pepys, June 28, 1667.
17. *Poems and Letters of Andrew Marvell*, 1927, II, 297; Carte MS 215, f. 183.
18. Additional MS 27,872, ff. 10, 11.
19. *CSPD*, 1667, May 18, 22; June 10, 26; July 4, 11, 13.
20. Clarendon, III, 276–78.
21. *CSPD*, 1667, July 9, 10; Clarendon, III, 278.
22. Carte MS 35, ff. 502–3; *CSPD*, 1667, June 28; Pepys, June 28, 1667.
23. Additional MS 27,872, f. 13.
24. Carte MS 35, f. 520; Pepys, July 12, 1667.
25. Pepys, July 12, 17, 1667; Clarendon, III, 280.
26. Anchitell Grey, *Debates of the House of Commons*, 1769, II, 250.
27. *CSPD*, 1667, July 14, 20, 25, 30, 31; Aug. 5; Sept. 28; Oct. 1; *CSPD*, 1668, April 14; Aug. 20; James Granger, *A Biographical History of England*, 1775, IV, 110.

V. Exit the Husband

1. HMC *Le Fleming*, pp. 51–52; HMC *Seventh Report*, p. 486; Pepys, July 23, 1667; Carl Neimeyer, "Henry Killigrew and the

Duke of Buckingham," *Review of English Studies*, XII (July, 1936), 326; S.P. 29/214/115; C. H. Hartmann, *Charles II and Madame*, 1934, p. 194.

2. Arthur Bryant, *The Letters of King Charles II*, 1935, p. 218; Commonplace Book, f. 22; Nethercot, *Cowley*, pp. 275-77.

3. Clarendon, III, 296-98: *POSA*, p. 59; *Savile Correspondence* (Camden Society, 1858), p. 20.

4. HMC *Tenth Report*, I, 267.

5. HMC *Le Fleming*, p. 53; *London Gazette*, Sept. 23, 1667; Commonplace Book, f. 65.

6. *Savile Correspondence*, p. 22; *Notes & Queries*, CLXV (July 15, 1933), 22.

7. S.P. 29/360/35; Commonplace Book, ff. 98-99.

8. HMC *Buckinghamshire MS*, p. 370; Barbour, pp. 119, 139.

9. Echard, *History*, III, 252; *Reresby*, p. 72.

10. *A Short Discourse upon the Reasonableness of Men's having a Religion*, 1685.

11. Kennet, *History*, p. 271; Carte MS 47, f. 176; Maurice Ashley, *John Wildman*, 1947, p. 184; Pepys, Dec. 12, 21, 1667; CSPD, 1667-68, Dec. 19, 1667.

12. *A Letter to Sir Thomas Osborne . . . Upon the reading of a Book called The Present Interest of England Stated*, 1672.

13. Mignet, II, 513, 525, 527.

14. Commonplace Book, f. 68; *House of Lords Journals*.

15. Pepys, Nov. 16, 1667; Clarendon, III, 309.

16. Clarendon, III, 308-9; *House of Lords Journals*.

17. Echard, *History*, III, 204.

18. Commonplace Book, f. 7.

19. Pepys, Nov. 17, 27, 1667.

20. Buckingham, *Works*, 1705, II, 201.

21. Ailesbury, *Memoirs*, p. 104.

22. Commonplace Book, ff. 29, 60, 67, 72.

23. Burnet, *History*, I, 457; J. H. Wilson, *Nell Gwyn*, 1952, pp. 83-85.

24. Sir William Temple, *Works*, 1754, III, 252.

25. Grammont, II, 138; Richard Baxter, *Autobiography*, 1931, p. 200; S.P. 29/360/35; Pepys, Jan. 17, 1668.

26. *The Bulstrode Papers*, 1897, Jan. 16, 1668; HMC *Seventh Report*, Jan. 23, 1668; *Notes & Queries*, CLXV (July 15, 1933),

22; J. H. Wilson, *The Court Wits of the Restoration*, 1948, pp. 43-44.

VI. RIVALS AND RIBALDRY

1. *Notes & Queries*, CLXV (July 15, 1933), 22; *CSPD*, 1668, Jan. 27, 28; Pepys, Feb. 6, 1668; Bryant, *Letters of Charles II*, p. 220; *London Gazette*, Feb. 14, 1668.

2. *Bulstrode*, March 16, 18, 1668; HMC *Le Fleming*, p. 55. An eminent pathologist, Dr. Emmerich von Haam, suggests that Shrewsbury's death might have been caused by a traumatic aneurism.

3. Commonplace Book, f. 36; Grey, *Debates*, I, 118; Carte MS 48, f. 254; *CSPD*, 1667-68, Feb. 18, 1668; Pepys, Nov. 4, 1668.

4. Pepys, Feb. 14, 1668; Barbour, p. 139.

5. Carte, *Ormonde*, II, 362; Buckingham, *Works*, I (Pt. 2), 12. His speech is incorrectly dated 1675.

6. S.P. 29/360/35; Pepys, May 15, 1668.

7. Grammont, II, 138; A. E. Dasent, *The Private Life of Charles II*, 1927, p. 231; Harleian MS 1579, f. 145.

8. The Commonplace Book of Sir Francis Fane, f. 346.

9. Commonplace Book, f. 12; *Harleian Miscellany*, III, 93.

10. Pepys, May 22, July 18, 1668; Clarendon, III, 360; Harleian MS 7312, ff. 113-17; Commonplace Book, f. 73.

11. Commonplace Book, f. 91.

12. Peter Cunningham, *Nell Gwyn*, 1927, p. 107; Wilson, *Court Wits*, pp. 49-51. An MS list of annuities and pensions (checked by Clarendon) in the Pierpont Morgan Library lists the amount paid to the Master of the Horse as £66. 13s. 4d.

13. *Bulstrode*, May 28, June 4, 1668; HMC *Le Fleming*, p. 56; Pepys, Sept. 9, 1668.

14. Barbour, pp. 149-53; HMC *Le Fleming*, p. 57; C. E. Ward, "An Unpublished Letter of Sir Robert Howard," *Modern Language Notes*, LX (1945), 119; "The Duel of the Crabs," *POSA*, p. 150.

15. HMC *Le Fleming*, p. 57; Pepys, Oct. 29, 1668; Burnet, *History*, I, 438; Bernard Falk, *The Way of the Montagus*, 1947, pp. 77-78.

16. Pepys, Oct. 23, 1668; Jan. 16, 1669; Burnet, *History*, I, 457-58; Pepys, May 5, 1668; H. Forneron, *Louise de Keroualle*, 1887, p. 26.

17. Pepys, Oct. 23, 1668; *CSPD*, 1668–69, Oct. 8, 1668.
18. Pepys, Sept. 28, Nov. 13, 23, 1668.
19. Commonplace Book, ff. 29, 33.
20. Mignet, III, 57, 63; Sir John Dalrymple, *Memoirs of Great Britain and Ireland*, 1773, II, 9.
21. Forneron, *Keroualle*, pp. 32-35.

VII. The Plot Within the Plot

1. Hartmann, *Charles II and Madame*, pp. 231-33, 260; Barbour, pp. 154-57.
2. Carte, *Ormonde*, II, 362; *Bulstrode*, Feb. 11, 1669.
3. Carte, *Ormonde*, II, 377; Burnet, *History*, I, 288.
4. Pepys, March 1, 4, 6, 1669; Burghclere, p. 207; Cartwright, *Madame*, p. 283.
5. Pepys, March 10, 1669; Carte MS 48, f. 340.
6. Pepys, March 29, 1669; James Macpherson, *Original Papers*, 1775, I, 51; *CSPD*, 1669, April 8.
7. *POSA*, p. 406; J. S. Clarke, *Life of James II*, 1816, I, 440.
8. Pepys, March 21, 1669; Buckingham, *Works*, II, 89.
9. Bryant, *Letters*, pp. 232, 234, 237.
10. Mignet, III, 74-76; Bryant, *Letters*, p. 232.
11. HMC *Seventh Report*, p. 486; Pepys, July 30, 1668.
12. Pepys, May 19, 1669; *Bulstrode*, pp. 100-101; HMC *Le Fleming*, p. 64; HMC *MS in Various Collections*, II, 127; Forneron, *Keroualle*, p. 50.
13. Lorenzo Magliotti, *Travels of Cosmo III*, 1821, p. 349.
14. HMC *Sixth Report*, June 8, 1669.
15. John Sheffield, Earl of Mulgrave, "Essay on Satire," *POSA*, p. 136.
16. Wilson, *Court Wits*, pp. 6, 177-80; Roger North, *Life of Sir Dudley North*, 1742, p. 21.
17. Dryden's *Miscellany Poems*, 1702, III, 88.
18. HMC *Le Fleming*, p. 66; G. Thorn-Drury, *Poems of Waller*, 1893, I, lxvi; Commonplace Book, f. 93.
19. HMC *Buccleuch MS*, Sept. 28, Oct. 19, 1669; HMC *Seventh Report*, Sept. 20, 22, Oct. 13, Nov. 10, 16, 1669; F. R. Harris, *Life of the Earl of Sandwich*, 1912, II, 315.
20. Harris, *Sandwich*, II, 316; Mignet, III, 151-52, 134-35.

NOTES

VIII. Intrigues and Farce

1. *House of Lords Journals;* C.A. 95, f. 222; Marvell, *Poems,* II, 302-3.

2. Harris, *Sandwich,* II, 328; Helen Darbishire, *The Early Lives of Milton,* 1932, p. 41.

3. Burnet, *History,* I, 456; Higgons, *Historical Remarks,* pp. 233-34, 247; *Herald and Genealogist,* II, 118.

4. Arthur Bryant, *King Charles II,* 1931; pp. 209-11; Hartmann, *Charles II and Madame,* pp. 307-16; HMC *Sixth Report,* June 21, 1670.

5. Hartmann, *Charles II and Madame,* pp. 330-31; Mignet, III, 209; C.A. 98, f. 31; Commonplace Book, f. 21.

6. A. H. Browning, *Thomas Osborne, Earl of Danby,* 1913 (Vol. I), p. 68.

7. Ruth Clark, *Anthony Hamilton,* 1921, pp. 37-38; Burghclere, pp. 219-21.

8. HMC *Fifth Report,* p. 652; HMC *Sixth Report,* p. 367; V. de S. Pinto, *Sir Charles Sedley,* 1927, pp. 114-15; CSPD, 1670, July 28.

9. CSP *Venetian,* 1669-70, Aug. 3/13, 1670; HMC *Buccleuch MS,* Aug. 3/13, 1670; Echard, *History,* III, 252; Buckingham, *Works,* II, 67, 68.

10. CSP *Venetian,* 1669-70, Aug. 10/20, 1670; C.A. 98, f. 117, Aug. 15/25, 1670.

11. Robert Bell, *Memorials of the Civil War,* 1849, II, 223; CSPD, 1670, Aug. 2, 27; C.A. 98, f. 117. Lady Salisbury is listed in CSPD as the duchess's companion, an obvious error for Shrewsbury.

12. *Despatches of William Perwich,* 1903, Aug. 17/27, Sept. 3/13, 1670; Burghclere, p. 225.

13. Burnet, *History,* I, 585; *Perwich,* Sept. 7/17, 1670; CSPD, 1670, Sept. 10; Burghclere, pp. 226-27; HMC *Buccleuch MS,* Sept. 14/24, 1670.

14. *Calendar of Treasury Books,* 1671, Jan. 9; Harleian MS 6862, f. 20.

15. C.A. 98, f. 347, Aug. 18/28, 1670; C.A. 100, f. 15, Jan. 7/17, 1671.

16. *Bulstrode,* p. 202; Macpherson, *Original Papers,* I, 58.

17. Barbour, pp. 170-74; Mignet, II, 230, 236, 247-54.

18. Wilson, *Nell Gwyn*, pp. 110-11.

19. Commonplace Book, f. 91; Forneron, *Keroualle*, pp. 56, 61.

20. Burnet, *History*, I, 458; Winston Churchill, *Marlborough, his Life and Times*, 1933, I, 61.

21. Clarke, *Hamilton*, p. 200; for other versions see Mary Manley, *The New Atalantis*, 1709; Grammont, II, 151-53; and *The Life of Francelia*, 1734. An English translation of *Hattigé* appeared in 1680.

22. *CSPD*, 1670, June 1; *Journals of Sir Thomas Allin*, 1940, pp. 171, 174. Winston Churchill argues that Churchill was out of England from 1668 to 1671, but he marched in the Duke of Albemarle's funeral procession on May 2, 1670. See E. F. Ward, *Christopher Monck, Duke of Albemarle*, 1915, p. 36.

23. See Mrs. Anna Jameson, *The Beauties of the Court of Charles the Second*, 1851, p. 101.

24. Burghclere, pp. 238-244.

IX. The Gaudy Stage

1. HMC *Portland MS*, March 11, 1671; *Westminster Abbey Registers*, p. 173; C.A. 100, f. 133, March 23/April 2, 1671; Commonplace Book, f. 96.

2. Commonplace Book, ff. 8, 14, 33, 60, 91, 96.

3. Barbour, p. 176; C. H. Hartmann, *Clifford of the Cabal*, 1937, p. 211.

4. Carte, *Ormonde*, IV, 484.

5. Harris, *Sandwich*, II, 223-31, 335; Barbour, pp. 178-79.

6. *CSPD*, 1671, May 9, 11; Burghclere, pp. 247-48.

7. Evelyn, May 2, 26, 1671; *CSPD*, 1671, May 30; *Bulstrode*, May 11, 17, 1671.

8. Additional MS 5852, ff. 423-25; *CSPD*, 1671, June 8.

9. *Conway Letters*, ed. Marjorie Nicolson, 1930, p. 336; Burghclere, pp. 250-51.

10. Additional MS 5821, ff. 217-18; *CSPD*, 1671, Jan. 7.

11. Commonplace Book, f. 1.

12. Wheatley, *London*, III, 539.

13. HMC *Seventh Report*, Sept. 24, 1674; Evelyn, Oct. 16, 1671.

14. HMC *Sixth Report*, Aug. 20, 1671.

15. J. H. Jesse, *Memoirs of the Court of England*, 1840, III, 494; Evelyn, July 23, 1679.

NOTES

16. Aubrey, *Brief Lives*, I, 137; C. A. 101, f. 8, Aug. 28/Sept. 7, 1671.

17. HMC *Buccleuch MS*, I, Sept. 13/23, 1671.

18. C.A. 101, ff. 225-29, Oct. 12/22, 1671.

19. Barbour, p. 181.

20. Wilson, *Nell Gwyn*, pp. 129-30; Evelyn, Oct. 9-16, 1671; Echard, *History*, III, 281.

21. Evelyn, Oct. 21, 1671; Burghclere, p. 254.

22. Burghclere, pp. 255-56; Barbour, p. 180; C.A. 101, f. 317, Oct. 30/Nov. 9, 1671.

23. C.A. 101, f. 399, Nov. 9/19, 1671; *CSPD*, 1671, Nov. 29.

24. Commonplace Book, f. 76; Buckingham, *Works*, I, 1.

25. Buckingham, *Works*, II, 89.

26. *POSA*, p. 407. For a detailed account of the play see Montague Summers, *The Rehearsal*, 1914.

27. HMC *Sixth Report*, Dec. 16, 1671.

X. CONFLICT AND CRISIS

1. Barbour, p. 184; Temple, *Works*, III, 506.

2. HMC *Le Fleming*, p. 90; Barbour, p. 183.

3. *CSPD*, 1671-72, May 7, 11, 22, June 19, 1672; *Letters of Rachel, Lady Russell*, 1854, May 16, 1672; C.A. 103, f. 571, May 9/19, 1672.

4. *CSPD*, 1672, May 28.

5. See W. D. Christie, *Life of Shaftesbury*, 1871, II, 85, Appendix II.

6. Foxcroft, *Halifax*, I, 78, 79.

7. Mignet, IV, 46; Temple, *Works*, I, 180.

8. Kennet, *History*, p. 279; Barbour, pp. 194-95; Burghclere, p. 271.

9. Foxcroft, *Halifax*, I, 89, 95, 96.

10. Barbour, p. 196.

11. Macpherson, *Original Papers*, I, 67; Evelyn, Aug. 1, 1672.

12. Buckingham, *Works*, II, 80.

13. Commonplace Book, f. 60; Barbour, p. 187; Clarke, *James II*, I, 482; Christie, *Shaftesbury*, II, 98.

14. *CSPD*, 1672, Sept. 15; Hartmann, *Clifford*, p. 255; Pope, *Moral Essays*, Epistle III.

15. Eleanore Boswell, "Footnotes to Seventeenth Century Biog-

raphies," *Modern Language Review*, XXVI (July, 1931), 345; *CSP Venetian*, 1673–75, Sept. 5/15, 1673.

16. Wilson, *Nell Gwyn*, p. 122; John Dennis, *Original Letters*, 1721, I, 218-19.

17. Additional MS 23,722, f. 15.

18. *House of Lords Journals*; Foxcroft, *Halifax*, I, 103-05; Barbour, pp. 207, 209.

19. Kennet, *History*, p. 294.

20. *CSP Venetian*, 1673–75, March 7/17, 1673; Christie, *Shaftesbury*, II, 134-40.

21. *CSPD*, 1673, May 13, 19; *Letters to Sir Joseph Williamson* (Camden Society, 1874), June 6, 26, 1673; *Autobiography of the Rev. Oliver Heywood*, 1882, I, 348-49.

22. Hartmann, *Clifford*, p. 276; *CSPD*, 1673; June 22.

23. *Williamson*, July 11, 14, 1673; *CSPD*, 1673, July 4, 11.

24. *Williamson*, July 4, 1673; HMC *Le Fleming*, July 30, 1673.

25. *Williamson*, July 18, Aug. 1, Sept. 23, 1673; *CSPD*, 1673, Aug. 1.

26. *CSP Venetian*, 1673–75, July 25/Aug. 4, Aug. 22/Sept. 1, Aug. 29/Sept. 8, Sept. 3/13, Sept. 19/29, 1673.

XI. CATASTROPHE

1. Macpherson, *Original Papers*, I, 67; *House of Lords Journals*; Grey, *Debates*, II, 222.

2. Mignet, IV, 233, 237, 251.

3. Barbour, pp. 220-22; *CSP Venetian*, 1673–75, Dec. 12/22, 1673.

4. *Williamson*, Oct. 3, Nov. 5, Dec. 11, 1673, Jan. 2, 1674; Additional MS 27,872, f. 11.

5. Mignet, IV, 245, 252; *CSP Venetian*, 1673–75, Nov. 28/Dec. 8, 1673.

6. Browning, *Danby*, II, 50; *Williamson*, Dec. 8, 1673.

7. Mignet, IV, 238-41.

8. *Williamson*, Jan. 2, 1674; *Conway Letters*, p. 377.

9. Mignet, IV, 253-55; C.A. 111, f. 100, Dec. 25, 1673/Jan. 4, 1674; Heywood, *Autobiography*, III, 209; *House of Lords Journals*.

10. Harleian MS 1579, f. 145.

11. *House of Lords Journals*; C.A. 111, f. 241, Jan. 8/18, 1674.

12. Williamson, Jan. 16, 1674; *House of Lords Journals*.

13. C.A. 111, f. 243, Jan. 8/18, 1674.

14. *Essex Papers* (Camden Society, 1890), Jan. 10, 1674.

15. S.P. 29/360/35.

16. C.A. 111, ff. 243, 288, 298, Jan. 8/18, 15/25, 19/29, 1674.

17. Grey, *Debates*, II, 245-46; S.P. 29/360/37; Additional MS 33,051, f. 192.

18. *Williamson*, Jan. 16, 1674.

19. Grey, *Debates*, II, 250-51.

20. Echard, *History*, III, 346; Grey, *Debates*, II, 251-65. See also William Cobbett, *State Trials*, 1810, Vol. IV.

21. Grey, *Debates*, II, 270.

22. Grey, *Debates*, II, 270-311; *Williamson*, Jan. 23, 1674.

23. *House of Lords Journals; Williamson*, Jan. 23, 1674; C.A. 111, f. 303, Jan. 19/29, 1674.

24. *Reresby*, p. 93; *CSP Venetian*, Feb. 20/March 2, 1674; Dryden, *Miscellany Poems*, II, 230.

25. Commonplace Book, ff. 60, 67, 75; Grey, *Debates*, II, 270.

26. Burnet, *History*, II, 29; for Buckingham's letter to the King see Additional MS 18,979, f. 285.

27. *Essex Papers*, Jan. 27, 1674; HMC *Ninth Report*, p. 36; C.A. 111, f. 517, Feb. 9/19, 1674.

28. S.P. 29/360/129; *CSP Venetian*, 1673–75, Feb. 13/23, 1674.

XII. Epilogue

1. *Calendar of Treasury Books*, 1672–75, March 16, April 1, July 29, 1674; HMC *Seventh Report*, March 20, 1674; *CSPD*, 1687, April 21.

2. *Bulstrode*, Sept. 28, 1674; HMC *Fitzherbert MS*, p. 51; HMC *Montague House MS*, I, 19-20; HMC *Rutland Papers*, II, 33, 52; *Savile Correspondence*, p. 62.

3. Buckingham, *Works*, I, 110; Alexander Smith, *The School of Venus*, 1716, pp. 97-108; Baroness D'Aulnoy, *Memoirs of the Court of England* (ed. Mrs. W. H. Arthur), 1913, p. 144.

4. C.A. 111, f. 303, Jan. 19/29, 1674; Chamberlayne, *Angliae Notitia*, 1676. For most of the details about Buckingham's life after 1674, see Burghclere, *Buckingham*. Hester W. Chapman's *Great Villiers*, 1948, is riddled with errors.

5. Buckingham, *Works*, I (Pt. 2), 10.

6. *A Letter to a Friend concerning Buckingham,* 1679; *A True Narration of the Design Lately Laid by Philip Le Mar,* etc., 1680; Julia Cartwright, *Sacharissa,* 1901, p. 268.

7. Barbour, p. 261.

8. G. Steinman Steinman, *Althorpe Memoirs,* 1869, pp. 25-34.

9. William Penn, *A Defense of the Duke of Buckingham,* 1685.

INDEX

Albemarle, George Monck, Duke of, 42, 56, 66, 102, 114, 117, 129, 145, 159.

Alberti, Girolamo, Venetian Secretary, 222, 226.

Allin, Sir Thomas, 177.

Anglesey, Arthur Annesley, Earl of, 132.

Arlington, Henry Bennet, Earl of, and Mrs. Stuart, 13; his character, 59; plots against Bucks (1667), 67; hires informers, 71; examines Heydon, 75; questions Montague, 81; deeply worried, 87; examines Bucks, 88; flatters Bucks, 98; his foreign policy, 112; gets his friends in office, 133; joins plot against Coventry, 134; quarrels with Bucks (1669), 156; signs Treaty of Dover, 163; pretends to oppose sham treaty, 173; a leader of the Court Party, 184; his houses and income, 190; plots to displace Bucks (1671), 192; manages De Keroualle, 194; created an earl, 205; embassy to Holland, 209; a proud man, 212; wants to be Lord Treasurer, 212; appears before Commons (1674), 241; Lord Chamberlain, 253; dies, 257. See also, 56, 58, 67, 73, 77, 85, 90, 121, 129, 139, 183, 184, 217, 239.

Arran, Mary Stuart Butler, Countess of, 58.

Arran, Richard Butler, Earl of, 58, 80, 86.

Arundell of Wardour, Henry, Lord, 139, 140, 163.

Aubigny, Louis Stuart, Sieur de, 25.

Aulnoy, Marie Catherine, Baroness d', 252.

Ayne, Mr., 220, 221.

Barcroft, Serjeant John, 77, 78.

Belasyse, Sir Henry, 79, 84.

Bellings, Sir Richard, 140, 163.

Bennet, Isabella, 211.

Betterton, Thomas, 201.

Bradshaw, Peter, 32.

Brémond, Sebastien, 177.

Bridges, George Rodney, 251, 258.

Bridgman, Sir Orlando, 102, 213.

Brudenell, Francis, Lord, 31, 33, 47, 232.

Brudenell, Mary, 30.

Buckhurst, Charles Sackville, Lord, 20, 55, 82, 84, 87, 113, 117, 132, 134, 153, 166, 227, 233, 255.

Buckingham, George Villiers, 1st Duke of, 106, 187.

Buckingham, George Villiers, 2nd Duke of, born, 4; at the Restoration, 6; loves Princess Henrietta, 16; a wencher, 17; his friends, 18; buys a house for Cowley, 19; his chemistry, 20; his glass works, 21; joins Royal Society, 22; meets Heydon, 22; attacked by Goodman, 23; his music, 24; *Sir Politick Would-Be*, 25; as